SHROPSHIRE RECORD SERIES • VOLUME 5

CENTRE FOR LOCAL HISTORY • UNIVERSITY OF KEELE

The Glebe Terriers of Shropshire
Part 1 (Abdon to Llanfair Waterdine)

edited by
SYLVIA WATTS

SHROPSHIRE RECORD SERIES • VOLUME 5

Published by the Centre for Local History, University of Keele,
Keele, Staffordshire, ST5 5BG

ISBN 0 9536020 2 8

British Library Cataloguing in Publication Data
A catalogue record for this book is available from the British Library

Printed in Great Britain by Herald Printers (Whitchurch) Ltd

Contents

Introduction

The purpose of drawing up glebe terriers was primarily to prevent alienation of church property, particularly land. The episcopate by the late 16th century was increasingly alarmed by the realization of the losses suffered by the church in the earlier years of the century. They were concerned that the consequent poverty of many of the parish clergy made it very difficult to recruit men into what was intended to be a graduate profession. With the aim of lessening the danger of permanent alienation, an Act of 1571 forbade the parish clergy to lease glebe land for more than 21 years. The Act was accompanied by a Canon of Convocation in the same year that directed the bishops to ask for terriers describing the glebe land in all their parishes, but few bishops appear to have responded. The earliest surviving terriers are for the diocese of Rochester (from 1575), Lincoln (from 1577) and Worcester (from 1585). Canon 87 of 1604 repeated the request for terriers and expanded on the information to be given by asking also for details about tithes, and more dioceses responded—Salisbury in 1608, York in 1613, Ely in 1615 and Winchester in 1616. Archbishop Laud was particularly concerned to protect the revenues of the clergy, and Dr D. M. Barratt has stated that every diocese of the southern province has some terriers for 1634–7, the period of his visitations.[1] The second period during which most dioceses requested terriers was during the reign of Queen Anne when there was renewed concern about the revenues of the church.[2] By the mid 19th century terriers began to seem less relevant as tithes were commuted and open fields enclosed, and in the later 19th century inventories of church furnishings and equipment gradually became usual.

Shropshire from the 12th century until 1920 was divided between three dioceses—Lichfield, Hereford and St Asaph's. Most of the present boundary between Lichfield and Hereford dioceses follows the River Severn, but before major changes in 1846 and 1905 the boundary was considerably more

[1] *Ecclesiastical terriers of Warwickshire parishes*, ed. D. M. Barratt, i (Dugdale Soc. xxii, 1955), p. xiii.
[2] Ibid. p. xiv.

complicated; for example Badger and Beckbury, north of the Severn, were in Hereford diocese, while Berrington, Cound, Kenley and Sheinton, south of the Severn, were in Lichfield. In Henry II's reign part of north-west Shropshire around Oswestry was annexed to St Asaph's diocese, in which nine ancient parishes remained until 1920 when they were transferred to Lichfield on the disestablishment of the Welsh church.[1] This division into three dioceses is of great significance in the production of glebe terriers and the information which they were required to include. Shropshire's division between the three dioceses was reflected in differences of timing and content in the terriers. Although the *raison d'être* for terriers was the same for the whole of England and Wales, and though the Canons requiring the compilation of terriers seem to have been applicable to all bishops, the terriers for the three dioceses vary greatly.

Of the three bishops, Hereford's was the first to respond to the 1571 Canon and about three-quarters of the Shropshire parishes within the diocese returned a terrier in 1589.[2] The questions sent out by the bishop have not survived, and may have been asked orally at visitations, but the information was presented in such a uniform manner that it must have corresponded to specific questions. After 1589 about half the Hereford churches returned a terrier in the first decade of the 17th century, mostly in 1607, and a few, about 15 per cent, in the 1630s. Thereafter there was no consistent pattern, some returned a terrier in the later 17th century and a few in the early 19th. Nearly a third of Shropshire parishes in Hereford diocese are represented by a single terrier, only Aston on Clun had as many as seven, and only Little Wenlock six. Either the bishops of Hereford neglected to ask for terriers, or terriers have not survived. No terriers appear to have survived for the parishes of Ashford Carbonel, Chirbury and Ford. There may have been purely local reasons for these omissions. Ford was appropriated by Battlefield College and was said to have had no parsonage house and no glebe land and the tithes were all in lay hands; there was, therefore, very little information to record in a terrier. Even the surplice fees must have been very small as part of the township of Ford lay in Alberbury parish and burials had to take place there.[3] In the Shropshire archdeaconry of the Hereford diocese there appear to have been many chapelries which were to a varying degree subject

---

[1] *A History of Shropshire*, ii, ed. A. T. Gaydon (*The Victoria history of the counties of England*, 1973), 1.

[2] In editorial matter the terms 'church' and 'parish' are applied interchangeably to any place returning a terrier, but the edited terriers preserve the terminology of the originals.

[3] Introduction to the printed parish register (Shropshire Parish Register Soc.).

Introduction

to a mother church such as Much Wenlock and which achieved independence at different times and to different degrees. The survival of terriers for these chapelries varies greatly; there are terriers for Astley Abbots, Benthall and Shipton, but not for the chapelries of Acton Round, Barrow, Church Preen, Hopton Cangeford, Linley and Monkhopton.

The earliest surviving Lichfield terriers (except one of 1603 for Ruyton XI Towns) are usually those of 1612, when nearly 60 per cent of churches are known to have returned one. Thereafter they were returned sporadically in the 17th century, though 27 per cent of parishes compiled terriers in the 1630s. About 32 per cent of parishes returned none before the end of the 17th century or even the early 18th. Nevertheless from the late 17th century until the mid 19th century many returned a terrier every three or five years, and from such places as many as forty may survive. Dr Barratt has said that in many dioceses few terriers were demanded in the later 18th century and that Lichfield and York were exceptional.[1] From about the second quarter of the 18th century until 1841, however, the terriers became very repetitive; the names of those whose lands were adjacent to the glebe or of those who paid compositions for tithe hay might be updated, but the terriers were often stated to be copies. That was regarded as a virtue, for a long series of documents was seen to be more effective in legal disputes, particularly over tithe where local custom was paramount; the frequent copying apparent in the Lichfield series was valued for that reason.[2] In 1841 up-to-date information was required by specific questions, and many churches returned two terriers for that year, one in traditional form, often restating tithing customs when tithes had been commuted, and one stating the questions and their answers. During the middle of the 19th century the production of terriers became more variable from parish to parish, but in 1884 printed forms were sent out, and the replies survive for most parishes. The only Shropshire places in the Lichfield diocese without early terriers are the peculiars of St Mary, Shrewsbury (though terriers survive for St Julian's, Shrewsbury, also a peculiar), Prees and the group of parishes in the peculiar of Bridgnorth—Alveley, Claverley, Quatford and St Mary Magdalene's and St Leonard's, Bridgnorth.

The earliest terriers from St Asaph's diocese date from the 1630s, and six of the nine parishes have surviving terriers from this date. All nine returned

---

[1] *Ecclesiastical terriers*, ed. Barratt, i, p. xv.

[2] E. J. Evans, 'Tithing customs and disputes: the evidence of glebe terriers 1698-1850, *Agricultural History Review*, xviii (1970), 29.

a terrier in the 1680s when William Lloyd was bishop, but thereafter most produced one only at long intervals—in 1749, 1774, 1791 and 1856.

There is no known letter from any of the bishops of the three dioceses specifying what information to include. Dr Barratt assumed that oral instruction was given at the visitations, but that the terrier's precise form was left to the discretion of the parish.[1] It was the minister who had most to gain from the compilation of an accurate terrier, and E. J. Evans said that it was usual in the Lichfield diocese for the incumbent to compile it and for the churchwardens to countersign.[2] Some terriers, however, said that the testimony of the more substantial inhabitants of the parish was sought. The 1589 terrier for Stoke St Milbrough is most unusual in stating that the terrier had been drawn up by 'by anciente reporte of dyvers substantiall men and *women*'. In the Lichfield diocese the absence of the signature of the incumbent was usually associated with a dispute with the churchwardens, but the majority of the Hereford terriers were signed only by the churchwardens.

The terriers echo the organisation of the medieval church with its division of livings into rectories, vicarages and curacies. Rectors in theory were entitled to all the profits of the parish, the glebe land, the tithes and the fees for conducting churching, marriage and burial. In the Middle Ages many churches were given to monasteries by their local lord and then, with the consent of the bishop of the diocese, the monastery appropriated the great tithes of corn and hay and presented a vicar, usually endowed with the glebe land and the small tithes. Such arrangements were echoed in many terriers, but Lilleshall's of 1698 unusually quoted the whole deed of 1285 whereby the vicarage was ordained. Dr Barratt estimated that in about half of English parishes tithes were appropriated before the Reformation, usually by a monastery.[3] In the Lichfield diocese about 44 per cent of the ancient Shropshire livings were rectories, 30 per cent vicarages and 20 per cent curacies. In the Hereford diocese the proportions were about 52 per cent rectories, 28 per cent vicarages and 20 per cent curacies.

In rather fewer instances the entire profits of a parish were appropriated and a curate installed; he might only have a stipend, or, as at Uffington, sometimes money and sometimes a small proportion of the tithes. After the Dissolution when rights to tithes and patronage passed into lay hands, curacies were particularly vulnerable, both to inadequate support from the patron and to reliance on a money stipend in a time of inflation. The curate

---

[1] *Ecclesiastical terriers*, ed. Barratt, i, p. xxiii.
[2] Evans, 'Tithing customs', 19.
[3] *Ecclesiastical terriers*, ed. Barratt, i, p. xxvii.

of Broughton, for example, said in 1693 that everything was in the hands of the impropriator, Richard Lyster, who paid him only £4 6s 8d a year. The curate of Leebotwood complained in 1783 that the patron paid him £8 10s which had once represented half the value of the small tithes, whereas £50 would have been a fairer value. The curate of Shrewsbury St Julian was allowed a stipend of £4 in 1612 and the Earl of Tankerville still paid £4 in 1841. The poorest curacies of all were the incumbents of donative chapelries which were outside episcopal jurisdiction. Patrons could appoint clergy to these chapels without reference to the bishop of the diocese.[1] There were a few donative chapels in both the Lichfield and the Hereford dioceses— Astley Abbots and Shipton in Hereford, and Buildwas, Childs Ercall, Dawley, Kenley, Longnor and Welshampton in Lichfield.

The poverty of many Shropshire livings, particularly curacies is revealed in the many references in the 18th and 19th-century terriers to grants from Queen Anne's Bounty. The Bounty was established in 1704 for the augmentation of the maintenance of poor clergy using the First Fruits and Tenths of the annual profits of livings originally paid to the papal exchequer but appropriated by Henry VIII.[2] Awareness of the possibility of grants from the governors of the Bounty Board is evident very soon after the scheme was initiated. In 1718 the curate of Dudleston, a chapel of ease in Ellesmere parish, said that he was dependent on 'precarious subscriptions' and that he had nothing to make a terrier of, 'till the late Queen's Bounty with other Gentlemens Charity be laid upon lands or Tythes which I hope in short time will be happily perfected'. As early as 1705 the curate of Childs Ercall wrote that he hoped the impropriator, Lady Poole, would 'be pleas'd to order me an augmentation'. In fact, the earliest grant recorded there was in 1788. Most beneficiaries gained from a system whereby the Bounty matched an endowment given by a benefactor. Fewer received money 'by lot', a system that was used less widely than first envisaged because it required the patron's cooperation; the patron of a donative was expected to put it under the usual supervision of the diocese and to settle a permanent income on the curate, which many were reluctant to do. This may have been the reason for the long delay in Childs Ercall. The Bounty Board tended to respond first to applications for augmentation that were met by gifts of money or land and to attend to the allocation of money by lot only if any funds for the year re-

---

[1] R. Burn, *The Ecclesiastical law*, ed. S. Fraser (1809), ii. 222.
[2] G. F. Best, *Temporal pillars: Queen Anne's Bounty, the Ecclesiastical Commissioners, and the Church of England* (1964), 31.

mained.[1] Welshampton, however, had received money by lot by 1742. In Battlefield, where the curate said in 1718 that the impropriator had for some years past given him £12, but only 'at his pleasure', the living was twice augmented by lot by the 1740s, and in 1745 the Bounty granted £400 to match a benefaction from the patron and others. Terriers of the 19th century also frequently mentioned grants from the Ecclesiastical Commissioners, who were created by an Act of 1836 and whose powers were extended by later acts.[2] Much property was vested in them and the profits were primarily used to augment the incomes of poor clergy, particularly of new parishes carved out of ancient ones in the mid 19th century such as Annscroft, Ash, and Astley.

THE CONTENT OF THE TERRIERS

The Canon of 1604 said that the bishops should require 'a true note and terrier of all glebes, lands, meadows, gardens, orchards, houses, stocks, implements, tenements and portions of tithes lying out of their parishes which belong to any parsonage or vicarage or rural prebend . . . for the perpetual memory thereof'.[3] However, the content of the Shropshire terriers varies with the date and the diocese. The 17th-century Lichfield terriers briefly described the parsonage house,[4] and the glebe land in more detail. In 1693 the rights to particular tithes were included and in 1698 the customs for levying them. Surplice fees were also usually included in the terriers of the 1690s. In the early 18th century the clerk's fees and wages were frequently mentioned and extra information about tithable products or the methods of tithing was often added. Although the terriers followed a broadly similar format, there is no evidence of an interrogatory until 1841. Church inventories are rare in the Lichfield terriers, but from 1841 the communion plate was usually described. Before 1841 benefactions and bequests were rarely included unless the benefaction was particularly noteworthy.

The first terriers of the Hereford diocese, those of 1589, consistently record the name of the patron of the living, information rarely included in those of Lichfield or St Asaph's. Most of the Hereford churches have very few terriers, one for 1589 and another early in the 17th century, usually

[1] Best, *Temporal pillars*, 29.
[2] Ibid. 298.
[3] *Ecclesiastical terriers*, ed. Barratt, p.xiv.
[4] In editorial matter the term 'parsonage house' is used for both rectory and vicarage houses, but the edited terriers preserve the terminology of the originals.

1604 or 1607, and record only the parsonage house and the glebe land; tithes and tithing customs were rarely described.

For most of the parishes in St Asaph diocese there is a terrier of the 1630s which gives details of the house and land. The next terrier for most parishes was in the 1680s, called for by Bishop William Lloyd who was particularly concerned to maximise clergy incomes. The 18th-century terriers and those of 1856 differ from those of Lichfield and Hereford in describing the parsonage house in great detail and also in including a full inventory of the furnishings and equipment of the church.

The house. The parsonage house was usually the first item to be described in the terriers of all three dioceses. A house was appreciated as significant in securing worthy clergy for the parish and preventing pluralism. Rectories and vicarages were almost always supplied with a house, though the rector of the small parish of Tasley reported in 1589 that he had none. Some parsonage houses suffered from events quite outside the vagaries of ecclesiastical organisation; the Oswestry terrier of February 1685/6 reported that the vicarage house had been burned in 1644 when the town was a garrison and under siege, and not until 1748 did the vicar appear to have been provided with another. According to the Moreton Corbet terrier of 1679 the rectory house was pulled down when the nearby castle was a garrison. There, however, the house was soon rebuilt, the patron made an allowance of timber and a new house was erected on the old foundations, but higher and larger and 'lookeing towards the noon sunne'.

The detail given varied greatly, but even where there was little, incidental phrases give clues as to the nature of the medieval houses in use at the time of the early terriers. Some of the larger houses, as at Adderley and Whitchurch, were still moated in the early 17th century, and some, as at Chetton, Cleobury North, Kynnersley and Longford, appear to have still had their kitchens in separate buildings; Longford's kitchen, however, had been converted to a stable by the end of the 17th century. Some terriers show that medieval open halls had recently been floored over; in 1635 the Bolas Magna house had two bays 'floored over head', and that of Cheswardine in 1635 had three bays boarded with lofts throughout. Parsonage houses in the 17th century appear from the terriers to have been of the standard of a farm house rather than a gentry house; the terrier of West Felton in 1634 referred to glass in the windows as noteworthy. The medieval and 16th-century houses appear like most farmhouses to have been timber–framed and thatched. A few timber-framed houses survived into the 19th century; the

Berrington terrier of 1805 said the timber rectory house was so decayed that it would be best to take it down.

Most of the 18th-century terriers of St Asaph's diocese (except Knockin's) recorded the parsonage houses in great detail and consistently described the house in terms of the building materials. The Kinnerley terrier of 1749 for instance says that the house was of brick and timber with a thatched roof, the adjacent buttery was not ceiled or plastered, the brewing kitchen had an earthen floor and the parlour though not ceiled was whitewashed. The Selattyn terrier of 1774 said that the kitchen, pantry and cellar had earthen floors, the hall a stone floor and the parlour and upstairs rooms board floors. The Llanyblodwel terrier of 1791 even described the wallpaper; the best parlour had handsome printed paper, while the common sitting parlour had blue painted paper somewhat damaged.

Occasionally terriers include comments about the standard of accommodation as well as factual details about the number of rooms or materials of construction. At Llanyblodwel in 1791 the vicar said that his study was a pleasant room, whereas the rector of Llanymynech said in 1749 that while his house had a good brew house, the kitchen was indifferent. The vicar of High Ercall said in 1612 that he had a 'fair ancient dwelling house of Timber covered with Slate Shingle and Tyle', and the rector of Quatt in 1612 described his house as a fair dwelling very well repaired. On the other hand the vicar of Shawbury complained in 1701 that he had found the house and outbuildings most deficient and that, with a very small allowance for dilapidations, he had had to lay out considerable sums of money on them. With the rise in status of the clergy in the later 18th century, complaint about the standard of the parsonage houses was expressed more often than satisfaction. The vicar of Sutton Maddock said in 1845 that there was no house suitable for the vicar, and the old vicarage house had been converted into two cottages. Many old parsonage houses were rebuilt in the 18th century, and many more had been replaced by the mid 19th century. Many parishes, such as Berrington, Bolas Magna, Dawley, Hodnet, Smethcott and Ruyton XI Towns, took advantage of the provisions of Gilbert's Act of 1777 which authorised the governors of Queen Anne's Bounty to lend money on easy terms for the building or rebuilding of parsonage houses. The rector of Longford referred to an application for such a mortgage in 1784, an unusually early date as that aspect of the work of the Bounty Board was not a prominent until after 1811.[1] It can be seen from the terriers that many of the later parsonage houses were of considerable size. The rectory house of

[1] Best, *Temporal pillars*, 217.

Introduction

Stockton, rebuilt in the second half of the 18th century, was of four storeys and had 22 rooms, and even the nearby curate's house had 18 rooms. The Revd Robert Eyton said of his rectory house in Ryton in 1841 that it was an irregular building apparently erected at three different periods. In 1845 the house was replaced by one said to be very large with five sitting rooms and as many as fifteen bedrooms.

Curates had no parsonage house and accommodation if provided was very variable. A curate's house would usually be supplied by the patron or impropriator but could just as easily be taken away. The patron of Chirbury built a house in Hyssington on former priory lands and allowed the curate a room in this. The terrier of Grinshill in 1682 appears to be uncertain whether there was a parsonage house, and in 1685 states that it had been converted to a barn. The curate of Astley Abbots in 1589 was said to have no house, only a chamber at the end of a barn, and the curate of Broughton was said in 1748 to have had a house but it had been pulled down. Many curates still had no house in the 19th century. The curate of Tibberton said in 1845 that he had no house, only a cottage 'of the meanest description suitable for a labourer'.

The outbuildings of the house were also described—in Lichfield terriers often in more detail than the house. It is clear that clergy houses were accompanied by service rooms such as bakehouses and kilns and also by stables, cow houses and pigsties, the essential outbuildings of a working farm. The farm buildings were often still of timber and thatch in the 19th century after the dwelling had been replaced in brick. It appears that barns in particular were often of cruck construction; Moreton Corbet had a building on crucks, and the Baschurch terrier of 1693 referred to a barn 'sustayned by forkes'. In Little Ness in 1726 the framing of the barn was changed from cruck to sill construction, but in 1756 the other farm buildings were still cruck-built. Several parsonage houses had a turf house among their outbuildings as late as the 19th century, as for example at Cheswardine in 1845. It is uncertain whether these structures were named after the material from which they were built or for their function in storing turf. As all the references to turf houses were in places in north-east Shropshire (other than a single one in Selattyn) where turf was frequently used as fuel, perhaps it may be inferred that they were used for storage.

The glebe land. Preservation of the glebe land was the main motive for the encouragement of terriers, and those of all three dioceses described the glebe in full. Rectors and vicars were often well aware of the difficulties of preservation. The rector and churchwardens of Bolas Magna in 1635 put a curse on usurpers of the glebe, saying that it could not be taken away without sacrilege, and if any one tried to take it, 'the curse of god will pursue that man to the utter extirpation of him and his posterity for ever'. The terriers, however, show that glebe could be and was alienated. The Much Wenlock terrier of 1607 said that the parish had thirty acres of arable land in the fields of Benthall in the Middle Ages, and according to depositions in the Council in the Marches of Wales had still had them up to forty years previously, but they had since been sold to Lawrence Benthall of Benthall. Benthall parish had lost its own glebe of thirty acres, said to have been taken for the queen's use, 'by what title we know not'. Glebe land could be lost by negligence as well as rapacity; some incumbents showed a degree of vagueness about their glebe that cannot have helped to preserve its integrity. The rector of Hordley said in 1612 that the living had had land in each of the three open fields of the village, but the meres and bounds were unknown and no incumbent had possessed them for about forty years. Alienation must have been particularly liable to occur in parishes such as More where the churchwardens said *c.* 1589 that they did not know the bounds of the glebe. Although apprehension that glebe land might be alienated was behind restrictions on long-term leasing, the vicar of Shawbury in 1705 expressed willingness to lease his whole living for £50 a year. Agricultural change such as inclosure might lead to confusion about the location of the glebe, particularly where after amalgamation and enclosure the minister's land was surrounded by the land of others. The West Felton terrier of 1763 said that the fields had been inclosed and it was not easy to say where the glebe land was, and the 1767 terrier referred to exchanges of glebe land, 'by whom we cannot say'. It is clear that although the requirement for terriers arose from an awareness that glebe land was vulnerable, deliberate depredations continued, even in the Lichfield diocese where terriers were regularly returned. As Dr Barratt found in Warwickshire and Richard Potts in Cornwall, the offenders where named were usually the patrons, who were often lords of the manor.[1] The rector of Longford in 1810 complained that he had received less land in return for an exchange of glebe land with Ralph Leeke of Longford Hall. The Tong terrier of 1845 said that the glebe land had been alienated by the Durants of Tong Castle in about 1790 and had become part of the inheritance of the Tong estate, and the Lee Brockhurst terrier of 1836 said that the patron had sold the glebe many years earlier to the late Sir Richard Hill.

---

[1] *Ecclesiastical terriers*, ed. Barratt, i, p. xxx; *A Calendar of Cornish glebe terriers, 1673-1735*, ed. R. Potts (Devon and Cornwall Record Soc. N.S. xix, 1974), p. xiv.

Introduction

Dr Barratt has suggested that 25–75 acres of glebe was usual for a rural living,[1] but in Shropshire the acreage varied enormously. In the Lichfield diocese it ranged from a very large glebe in a few parishes such as Donington with 159 acres and Stockton with 184 acres, to a substantial minority with no glebe at all, mostly town parishes (such as Ellesmere, Newport and Market Drayton) and poor curacies. An average therefore has little meaning, but was about 27 acres. The largest glebe in the Hereford diocese by a wide margin was that of Munslow with 134 acres, the average being 26 acres. Selattyn with 64 acres and Whittington with 58 acres had the largest glebe land of the small number of St Asaph parishes. In fact, the precise extent of the glebe land is not always easy to determine in the earlier terriers and the averages given above are very approximate. Some terriers listed the names of parcels of land, but did not give areas, and where areas were given, they could appear to vary from one terrier to the next. Land might be measured by area using the apparently obvious term 'acre', though this did not necessarily mean a standard statute acre; the vicar and parishioners of Stanton Lacy in 1607 categorically stated that an acre is not the king's measure but 'such quantity of ground as we among our selves do hold and account for an acre'. In addition to the problem of local interpretation of an apparently standard measure, a wide range of other measures was used. Rather than by area, arable land might be quantified by the number of strips (known as ridges, selions, butts or flats) in the open fields, by the number of days' ploughing that it required (as in Stanton Long), or by the amount of seed needed, usually by reference to a number of strikes or hoops of 'seedness' or 'sowing'. Measures of 'seedness', however, also varied. The High Ercall terrier of 1612 referred to 'old Shrewsbury measure' and defined this as twelve gallons to a strike, but the strike was not thus defined elsewhere. In the early 17th century the churchwardens of Richards Castle said that they used the king's measure, but Ruyton XI Towns measured its glebe by seedness of 'Winchester measure', and West Felton in 1634 used 'Oswestry old measure', which was said to be the 'custom of this country', and Kinnerley in 1685 also referred to 'Oswestry old measure'. Even within the same parish measurement by strikes seedness was not consistent over time; Ruyton XI Towns described crofts in 1698 in Winchester measures, but in 1701 in Chester measures. Measurement in strikes was also inconsistent geographically within a parish; the Llanymynech terrier of 1637 described land in one township in Winchester measure and in Oswestry measure in another. Land was still described in strikes seedness in Meole Brace

---

[1] *Ecclesiastical terriers*, ed. Barratt, i, p. xxx.

as late as 1801. Pasture might be measured by beasts' grass, as at Neenton in 1604, and common land at Chetton was measured by the 'strake' of sheep. In 1612 St Alkmund's, Shrewsbury described a parcel of ground near the vicarage as two woollen yards long and two wide, a form of measurement not found elsewhere.

Only the early terriers of the Hereford diocese consistently stated whether any common rights formed part of the glebe. Pasture rights were particularly important for the parishes round the Brown Clee and Titterstone Clee, such as Caynham in 1589 which had feeding for sheep on the Clee, 'being Common without ratement'. The incumbent of Bucknell in the late 16th century unusually mentioned common of estover in the woods of the lord of the manor. Some ministers in north-east Shropshire had rights to gather turf from the heath; the Cheswardine terrier of 1635 recorded that the rector had the right to one day's delf of turves on Lipley Heath and pannage and estover in Haywood. The value of such privileges tended to decrease over time, not always as the result of inclosure; the Cheswardine terrier of 1705 restated the rector's right to turbary, but said that none was then to be found.

Most terriers describe the location of the parcels of glebe by describing the boundaries in considerable detail. The bounds are of great value for the historian of an individual place because they refer to the names of neighbouring plots or to prominent topographical features, particularly rivers and roads. The bounds are usually stated, whether the land was in closes or intermingled with the lands of others in the open fields, but some parish officers appear to have thought that when the land was in closes it was sufficiently well delineated not to need written boundaries; for instance, the Acton Burnell terrier of 1698 said, 'we do not butt or bound the Lands being all entire Inclosures, & well known', and Shawbury's in 1698 said that as the parish was all inclosed except for the heaths and commons, the pieces of glebe were easily distinguishable and well known.

The use of probate inventories to discern agricultural change has become widespread; the evidence of glebe terriers is much less familiar, although, as Dr Barratt has said, 'no other single source throws as much light on the agricultural pattern of large areas under Elizabeth and the Stuarts as diocesan collections of terriers'.[1] Descriptions of the glebe land can give valuable

---

[1] *Ecclesiastical terriers*, ed. Barratt, i, p. xlvi. Examples of the use of glebe terriers are M. W. Beresford, 'Glebe terriers and open-field Leicestershire', in *Studies in Leicestershire agrarian history*, ed. W. G. Hoskins (*Leics. Archaeol. Soc. Trans.* xxiv, 1949 for 1948), 77-126; idem, 'Glebe terriers and open-field Yorkshire', *Yorks. Archaeol. Jnl.* xxxvii (1950), 325-68.

evidence of land use, and in particular of the progress of inclosure of the open arable fields in the 17th century and of common land in the 19th. Shropshire is well known as an area where inclosure was 'silent' because for the most part it took place before the era of inclosures by Act of Parliament.[1] Sometimes terriers specifically mentioned inclosure, those of Waters Upton, for example, referred in 1718 to the recent inclosure of the arable fields and in 1841 to that of the moors. Inclosure was often piecemeal; the Leighton terrier of 1612 referred to a furlong recently inclosed, but it is clear that open-field land remained. The Highley terrier of 1626 was unusually explicit, saying that the parishioners, being all freeholders, had exchanged and inclosed the common field lands, 'for theyr more commodious use thereof, therefore the said Robert Barrett [vicar] like wyse for the good of the Church'. The Waters Upton terrier of 1718 said that the glebe land had been altered after inclosure. An early 17th-century terrier for Broseley referred to parcels of glebe land as being formerly in the open fields and gave the names of those responsible for hedging the enclosures, giving the impression that inclosure was very recent. The 1705 terrier for Cheswardine referred to recent inclosures and highlighted a situation that frequently occurred during inclosure, when the minister's glebe was surrounded with other men's lands, 'until they are exchanged, if ever'. In those circumstances the glebe was particularly liable to encroachment. More usually, where part of the glebe land had consisted of strips in the open fields it is possible to deduce that inclosure took place during the interval between terriers. One must remember, however, that if the glebe included no open-field land, it does not follow that the place had none. Shifnal, for instance, kept its open fields until the end of the 18th century, but the terriers are silent about it as the vicar's glebe consisted entirely of closes near the vicarage house and of more distant pastures that had always been inclosed.

Tithes and tithing customs. The 1604 Canon asked for the rights to tithes to be included, but only if they were due from outside the parish. Dr Barrett assumed that this would involve only a very few parishes,[2] but in all three dioceses there are instances in Shropshire of complex rights to tithes. The 1686 Oswestry terrier, for instance, stated that the Easter dues of Pentrebach in Oswestry parish went to Llansilin parish, but that, on the other hand, the vicar of Oswestry received a third of the tithes of Llynclys, which was in Llanyblodwel parish; a third of the tithe of Acton Burnell went to the rector

[1] C. G. A. Clay, *Economic expansion and social change: England 1500-1700* (1984), i. 73.

[2] *Ecclesiastical terriers*, ed. Barratt, i, p. xviii.

of Cound, and the rector of Leighton received a third of the tithes of Eaton Constantine parish; the vicar of Baschurch had the right to two-thirds of the tithes of Bagley township in Hordley parish and two-thirds of those of Noneley township in Loppington. The rights might relate to the tithes of whole townships as in these examples or just to the tithes of small patches of land, such as the vicar of Condover's right to tithes from two home closes in Stapleton parish.

Perhaps because the bishops did not initially ask specifically about tithe, many of the early terriers did not include rights to tithe or mentioned them only in very general terms. The first Lichfield terriers, of 1612, simply stated that tithes are due and only in 1693 during William Lloyd's episcopate did they define which produce was liable to tithe. Bishop Lloyd then apparently asked for further details, for most terriers of 1698 explained the customs by which particular tithes were levied. The Lichfield terriers of the early 18th century tended to add to the list of produce liable to small tithes and to elaborate further on the tithing customs. Most churches in the Hereford diocese had early terriers (from the late 16th century and early 17th) which stated merely that tithes were due. Only Diddlebury in 1637, Ludlow in 1636, Deuxhill in 1802, Little Wenlock in 1802 and Hughley in 1810 have extant terriers that describe tithing customs in the detail usual in the Lichfield terriers. That of 1696 for More is wholly exceptional in its full description of tithing customs and its repeated emphasis that the customs had the consent of the parishioners. The early terriers for the St Asaph's diocese referred only briefly to tithes, but most churches had a terrier for 1684, 1685 or 1686 that listed tithable products and the customs for their collection, which suggests that such information was required at the instigation of William Lloyd, bishop of St Asaph's from 1680 to 1692; he was particularly determined to preserve and recover the church's rights.[1].

Tithes had been levied since Anglo-Saxon times, and were important because, whereas the glebe land was supposed to be for subsistence, it was from tithes that the minister was intended to make a profit.[2] They were usually divided into 'great' and 'small'; great tithes consisted of grain and hay, and small tithes comprised all other agricultural produce. Tithes were also categorised as predial, mixed and personal tithes. Personal tithes, supposed to be levied on the profits of work, were in decay by the 17th century. Predial tithes were from agricultural produce arising directly from

---

[1] A. Tindal Hart, *William Lloyd 1627-1717: bishop, politician, author, and prophet* (1952), 62.

[2] *Ecclesiastical terriers*, ed. Barratt, i, p. xxvi.

the soil (such as corn, wood and hay) and mixed tithes were from livestock and products that owed more to the work of man. The essence of tithe was that it was levied on crops or stock which renewed themselves annually and could thus be tithed only once a year. The Quatt terrier of 1738 was most unusual in stating that a special custom prevailed in the parish of taking tithe twice in a year if two crops were grown.

The pattern of tithe rights was closely related to the three-fold division of livings into rectories, vicarages and chapelries. Rectors were usually entitled to all the tithes, great and small, but this was not always the case. The great tithes could sometimes be split between the rector and the patron; the rector of Kynnersley, for instance, took half the great tithe of corn and hay while the patron took the other half. Often certain parcels of land, usually the lord of the manor's demesne, did not owe rectorial tithe; for instance at Pitchford in 1698 the rector did not receive the great tithes of the demesne. The demesnes of abbeys and priories had often been tithe free,[1] and such land remained exempt after it had passed into lay hands. The lord of the manor might allow the rector a certain field in lieu of tithe, as in Hopton Wafers in 1683. but many examples could be given where the lord of the manor's demesne was completely exempt from tithe, as at Ightfield, or paid a fixed modus to the rector's increasing disadvantage: at Quatt a modus of £2 a year, due to the rector in 1679, remained payable until commutation in 1841.

When a religious house was given the advowson of a rectory in the Middle Ages, it often appropriated the rectory and, with the bishop's consent, presented a vicar to the living, to whom were assigned the small tithes and at least part of the glebe land. In those circumstances the division of tithes could give rise to complex situations like that in Sheriffhales, where the vicar had small tithes while Woodcote chapel which served a detached part of the parish, received rectorial tithes.

Curates, whether in donatives or perpetual curacies, only had the right to collect tithes if the patron (who was also the impropriator) specifically allowed it. The terrier for Astley Abbots (a donative) at the end of the 16th century stated that the patron, Francis Billingsley, allowed the curate part of the tithes of corn and hay and the small tithes. Such a situation was, however, precarious; the curate of Battlefield said in 1694 that he was allowed the small tithes and that his predecessor had, by gift of the patron, gathered the tithe of corn, but in 1699 the curate received only money.

---

[1] W. E. Tate, *The Parish chest: a study of the records of parochial administration in England* (1969), 141; also Burn, *Ecclesiastical law*, ed. Fraser, iii. 379.

Grain was always classified as one of the great tithes, but in a few places (Chelmarsh, Longnor, Meole Brace, Montford, Shawbury, Stapleton, Sutton Maddock, Wrockwardine and Wroxeter) the vicar was entitled to at least part of it. The vicar of High Ercall had the right to tithe corn and hay in Haughton and Isombridge townships, and the vicar of Diddlebury had corn tithes from Corfton and Sparchford townships and, in the rest of the parish, the tithe corn grown in the home closes (those immediately next to the houses). A vicar's right to tithe corn from home closes was relatively common in Shropshire, being recorded in Kinlet, Montford, Great Ness, Shawbury, Stanton Long, Sutton Maddock, Wrockwardine and Wroxeter. In such cases the terriers can be valuable for local and family historians for the closes were usually described in great detail and the changes in tenure recorded over a long period. For the vicar this privilege was of doubtful and decreasing value; the terriers of Atcham in 1705, Wroxeter in 1759 and Shawbury in 1792 recorded problems with home closes; in 1759 the vicar of Wroxeter said that the closes frequently changed hands and were difficult to determine, thus leading to great loss to the church. Grain was usually the most valuable tithe, but the Shelve terrier for 1589 said that the whole parish did not sow more than twenty bushels of rye and twenty of oats in a year.

Hay was usually considered to be a great tithe, but there was considerable variation in the way it was actually treated—as great or small, and payable in kind or by composition. By the 17th century the situation was often very complicated. The vicar of Great Ness, for instance, received tithe hay from the whole parish, but the vicar of Shawbury had hay in kind only in the township of Shawbury, while moduses were customary in the parish's other townships. Sometimes vicars were only entitled to hay produced in certain meadows, and in some places, such as Stanton Lacy in 1607 and Tibberton in 1705, the minister was allocated particular meadows in lieu of tithe hay. Under another arrangement, similar to that for corn and followed for instance at Stowe, the vicar was entitled to hay grown on home closes. A further complication was that whereas the tithe of corn was never commuted to a money payment, tithe hay often was, as in Eyton upon the Weald Moors, Leighton, Sheriffhales Sutton Maddock, Upton Magna, Whittington and Wroxeter. As a composition was often highly individual, varying from one landholding to another, the records of compositions can provide evidence for local and family historians of tenants and their land. The Kinlet terrier of 1621, for instance, named 49 parishioners from whom the vicar was entitled to tithe hay on their home closes. Commutation of tithe rights to hay caused considerable loss of income during periods of inflation and was the subject of many disputes.

Introduction

Relatively few terriers mention wood; that of Dowles in 1589 mentioned income from it, and the rector of Stockton was said in 1705 to have a stand of trees in lieu of the tithe. The tithing of wood was complicated as tithes were levied on crops or products that were renewed annually. This concept of annual renewal meant that tithe was usually expected on wood cut for coppicing and sale, as stated at Market Drayton in 1631, Wrockwardine in 1705, Donington in 1726 (where it was termed *sylva caedua*), Sutton Maddock in 1733 and Meole Brace in 1801. Timber more than 20 or 30 years old was usually exempt from tithe, but the custom of a particular parish was all-important, and in some parishes it was accepted that tithe was due if timber was felled and sold.[1]

Small tithes consisted of all agricultural produce other than corn, hay and wood. The list of items on which tithes were due can be useful in detecting when particular agricultural crops were introduced, such as rape and carrots mentioned in Shifnal in 1693 and turnips, noted at More in 1696. Stress on a particular product can be most revealing of its importance in the local economy; the Stoke on Tern terrier of 1722 stated that every fleece must be valued individually as every fleece was different, and that its value must then be divided into ten equal parts. In Worfield the tithes of sheep and lambs must have been particularly valuable as they were taken by the lay rector. Sometimes the demand for tithe explicitly refers to agricultural change; the rector of Kynnersley in 1730 said that all the parish's uplands (as distinct from the marsh of the Weald Moors) had formerly been open-field tillage so that few cattle were kept and the tithe of calves had been taken in money; now, however, those lands had been lately enclosed and there might 'be such Dairyes kept hereafter as may afford calves to be gathered in kind'. In some places the terriers included the tithe rights to herbage in some detail indicating that commercial grazing was important; in Bedstone in 1637 4d was due for every Welsh cow pastured in the summer and in Quatt and Sheriffhales tithe was due for sheep wintered in the parish.

The custom of the parish was all important in determining which products were tithed. Many terriers referred to tithes on stalls of bees falling due when the bees were killed; strictly speaking, however, bees themselves were not liable to tithe being considered *ferae naturae,* wild creatures.[2] Honey was liable to tithe but rarely mentioned, Abdon, Kinnerley, Llanfair Waterdine, More, Smethcott and Whittington being amongst the few places where it

---

[1] Burn, *Ecclesiastical law*, ed. Fraser, iii. 411-79.
[2] Ibid. 516.

was. According to Burn turkeys were also judged to be wild animals,[1] but terriers of Ludford, Moreton Corbet, Quatt and Stanton upon Hine Heath include them among the list of small tithes. Fish are rarely mentioned; the vicar of High Ercall said in 1612 that he was entitled to three strikes of eels from the River Tern, but apparently he did not receive them. Like the extent of the glebe, descriptions of small tithes sometimes used archaic measures: the Quatt terrier of 1755 referred to a 'bottle' of hemp and flax which in More, Ruyton XI Towns and Stanton upon Hine Heath was measured by the 'handful' and in Norton in Hales by the 'hattock'.

A tithe had been levied on wages in the Middle Ages, but an Act of 1548 exempted day labourers from this tithe, and Christopher Hill said that personal tithes had largely lapsed by the 17th century, partly because of the statute and partly because they were difficult to collect.[2] Nevertheless a nominal sum of 4d for artisans, and similar sums for the work of servants, were demanded in many Shropshire parishes until the middle of the 18th century. It is possible that some terriers maintained a theoretical right to those tithes, but that the money was not actually paid. In some places, such as Stanton upon Hine Heath in 1730, the payment due from artisans was known as 'groat the hand'. The Whitchurch terrier of 1701 was unusual in stating that 4d was due from both men and women in manual trades or in shopkeeping. S. J. Wright argued that by the early modern period personal tithes had usually been subsumed within or replaced by Easter offerings or oblations, and that their origin as a form of tithe was often obscured.[3] A payment of 4d was usual for a married couple, sometimes 2d for anyone over the age of 16, or of an age to receive communion. Payments for grown-up children were variable; sometimes 2d for a son or daughter over twenty-one living at home or for one over sixteen. The origin of the offering as a tithe was more apparent when payments were demanded for servants; it was always the master or mistress who paid, usually 4d for a manservant and 2d for a maidservant, though in Baschurch there was a scale—4d for a servant earning more than 40s a year, 3d if earning more than 30s and 2d if less.

The work of mills was also tithed (if they were not legally ancient—dating from before 1315).[4] There were, however, recurrent disputes about the type

[1] Ibid. 435.

[2] C. Hill, *Economic problems of the church from Archbishop Whitgift to the Long Parliament* (1956), 86.

[3] S. J. Wright, 'A guide to Easter books and related parish listings: part i', *Local Population Studies*, xlii (1989), 18-31.

[4] A. Tarver, *Church court records: an introduction for local and family historians* (1995), 100.

of tithe due; if it was predial a tenth was due, if personal only a tenth of the clear profit, but by the early 18th century it appears to have been accepted that mills should be subject to personal tithe. The legal rulings only concerned corn mills; other mills such as fulling mills were governed by local custom only.[1] A money payment was usually agreed because of the difficulty of determining a tenth of the year's work. Terriers thus provide extremely useful evidence of the existence of particular mills and sometimes of forges; for example, there was a forge in Chetwynd that can be dated to the 1690s, and the Pitchford terrier of 1726 referred to a forge which had formerly been a mill. In 1612 the Ruyton XI Towns terrier included a new claim for payment for additional corn mills. In Ryton in 1693 a new mill can be inferred from the inclusion of a payment due from land flooded by a new dam. The 18th century terriers for Worfield included particularly interesting references to mills; of the two fulling mills mentioned in 1708, one had three years later been converted to an oil mill and there was a new wash-leather mill at Rindleford. The 1732 terrier said that the remaining fulling mill on the River Worfe had become a paper mill, and by the end of the 18th century it was a corn mill.

From 1698 onwards the Lichfield terriers described the customs for levying tithes in great detail. Only a few Hereford terriers did so, such as Diddlebury in 1637 and Deuxhill and Hughley in 1802. Whereas the tithing of grain was relatively straightforward—the tenth sheaf of corn, for example, being paid in kind, the customs for small tithes were varied and complicated, and terriers were always particularly careful to state whether tithes were due to be paid in kind or by money in lieu. In the Middle Ages tithe was generally paid in kind, but by the 17th century commutation for money had become usual for a variety of products. The Adderley terrier of 1701 began its section on tithes by stating that 'all things in nature' were tithable in kind, but went on to list compositions of 1d for milk cows, 1d for colts, 4d for a stall of bees put down, 1d for a garden and 1d for a house and smoke. Lambs and wool, pigs and geese were usually tithed in kind, but milk, which was perishable, almost always in money (the Leebotwood terrier of 1730 referred to this payment as 'lactuals'). Where lambs were tithed in kind, a lamb was usually due when the number owned reached seven, but the arrangements for making up the difference to ten were complicated, and varied from place to place, leaving much scope for dispute. Standardised small money payments were due for items for which it was difficult to calculate a precise value, such as 1d for a garden in lieu of a tenth of garden

[1] Burn, *Ecclesiastical law*, ed. Fraser, iii. 436.

produce and 1d smoke in lieu of firewood consumed. It was frequently the custom for hemp and flax to be tithed in kind, but an Act of 1696 which said that they were of particular value of the economy, acknowledged that they were difficult to tithe and a money payment of 5s per acre could be substituted.[1] Money payments were classified as moduses or compositions; whereas moduses were customary, binding and permanent, compositions bound only the individuals—the minister and tithepayer—who agreed them, and they were therefore more usual. The rector of Dowles was careful to state that the compositions accepted by him were not to bind future rectors. Moduses were usually first mentioned in the Lichfield terriers of 1698, but were probably much older.

In the later 18th century demands for commutation of tithe increased, and after several unsuccessful attempts the Tithe Act of 1836 was passed allowing for commutation of tithe rights to a tithe rent charge.[2] Many of the later terriers refer to commutation and the value of the rent charge, while restating the tithable products and the tithing customs.

Tithe disputes. Given the all-embracing nature of tithe demands and the complexity of tithing customs, it is not surprising that disputes arose. Collection of tithes, especially of the small tithes which were levied at various times of the year, was difficult. The problems were sometimes purely practical; the Dowles terrier of 1698 said that although tithes should have been paid in kind, but 'in as much as there is noe Barn belonging to the Rectory and the parish lying on both sides Seaverne the gathering Tythes in kind would be very troublesome', and that there were therefore compositions. In Eyton upon the Weald Moors a tithe dispute reflected the unresolved issue of the boundary between Eyton and Wellington, which was further complicated by the divided lordship of the small manor of Eyton. Practical difficulties of collection presumably lay behind the rector of Rodington's statement in 1711 that he leased the small tithes because he and his wife had often quarrelled about them. Even where there was no dispute, ministers often revealed that a watchful attitude was necessary to preserve their rights, as when the rector of Cound said in 1705 that a parcel of land belonging to St Giles's, Shrewsbury was claimed to be free of tithe but that enquiry was needed. The rector of Llanymynech appears to have been anticipating disputes in 1686; he said that difficulties were 'ready to arise' concerning hemp, geese, orchards and eggs. It was in the interests of ministers to

[1] Burn, *Ecclesiastical law*, ed. Fraser, iii. 496.
[2] Tate, *Parish chest*, 140.

maintain their rights, but the 1696 terrier for More recognised that a clear statement of customs was also in the interests of the parishioners (26 of whom signed) when it said that '[we] annex . . . our particular customs to continue Peace and Prevent disputes'.

Many disputes centred round commutation and the important legal difference between modus (permanent) and composition (temporary). The problem was that parishioners would want compositions, while ministers would not, for compositions over time might become moduses and increasingly unrealistic. Under a statute of 1571, if a modus dated from before 1570 payment in kind could not be enforced. Moreover, if the lord of the manor (who was often the patron) claimed to owe a modus, the minister was in a weak position.[1] The precise status of money payments was therefore a frequent cause of dispute. The rector and churchwardens of Norton in Hales in 1698 were very conscious of this problem writing (of a payment for hay) that, 'when this custom commenced or whether it bee a modus soe ancient beyond hopes of being destroyed wee cannot positively declare'. It is clear that ministers could come under pressure to commute their rights to tithes in kind to money payments. A Moreton Corbet terrier of 1685, signed by the vicar alone, showed that he was resisting the pressure of the lords of the manor, the Corbets, for money payments—he said that the parishioners accepted the compositions from fear of the Corbets, and that may have been true, for there was another terrier for the same year signed only by the churchwardens, which recorded that tithes on corn and hay were due in kind except from the demesne lands, which paid money by custom 'time out of mind'. The vicar of Leighton was in dispute with his parishioners and would not sign the terriers of 1824, 1828, 1832, 1836 and 1841; he refused to accept their moduses and compositions on the grounds that he had no details of the premises involved. In a dispute in Hinstock the terrier of 1698 also revealed the rector's fear of the gentry. The regulations concerning the tithing of wood were complicated, but the terrier said that Sir John Corbet had had two falls of wood in Lockley Wood for which £10 was due in tithe but had not been paid. The rector said that he was terrified to sue Sir John as the vicar of Market Drayton had met with failure in a similar case.

Many of the terriers referred to lawsuits, mostly in the Exchequer, brought after ministers and parishioners had failed to resolve their differences. Terriers had value as evidence in disputes, and it was written on the dorse of the Lilleshall terriers from 1698 to 1782 that they had been produced in an Exchequer suit. The Donington terrier of 1693 referred to the rector's

[1] Evans, 'Tithing customs', 27.

success in the Exchequer in recovering the tithes of the 300-acre Cosford Grange lands. The Market Drayton terrier of 1816 listed the tithe rights and moduses determined in the Exchequer in 1781; the situation in the parish was particularly complicated as some townships were in Shropshire and some in Staffordshire, and there were granges that claimed to be tithe free. Many Lichfield and St Asaph terriers were signed by parishioners as well as the minister and churchwardens, sometimes in such numbers that in small rural parishes most of the inhabitants must be represented. Burn stressed that terriers were of greater legal authority in the temporal courts if they were signed not only by the minister and churchwardens but also by the more substantial inhabitants.[1].

Surplice fees. Fees payable to the incumbent for celebrating ceremonies such as marriage were often called surplice fees. They had been laid down in the reign of Edward VI at 4d to 11½d for churching, 1s to 4s for weddings by banns, 3s to 6s for weddings by licence, 2d to 1s 4d for burials in the churchyard and 6s 8d for burials inside the church.[2] Though not absolutely uniform, they were similar from place to place. In Shropshire, however, significant variations were recorded in later terriers. In many places the fees required were double for outsiders; the Dudleston terrier of 1845 said that the fees for churching mothers of illegitimate children were double; and that of Whitchurch in 1841 said that baptism, which was usually free, cost 4d for an illegitimate child. The Whitchurch terrier of 1701 was an early example of sensitivity about social differences and the ability of people to pay; 6d was required for churching or burials, but only 4d from the 'poorer sort'. Such distinctions became more common in the town parishes in the 19th century. St Julian's, Shrewsbury in 1853, for example, demanded 1s for a pauper burial but 5s for 'trades persons' and 10s for 'independents'. A few places, such as Smethcott in 1772, imposed punitive fees for parishioners marrying elsewhere without the vicar's consent. Some terriers referred to fees lost; by 1693 the rector of Donington had no burial fees from the papists at Boscobel and White Ladies who used their own burial ground. Fees for baptism were not usual (medieval canon law said that fines for sacraments were illegal),[3] but the vicar of Worfield in 1703 said that 'Enforcing a reasonable allowance for these [baptism and registration] . . . would be somthing beneficial to the Church', especially

[1] Burn, *Ecclesiastical law*, ed. Fraser, ii. 273.
[2] Hill, *Economic problems*, 168.
[3] *Ecclesiastical terriers*, ed. Barratt, i, p. xliii.

his church where 'the Indowment is so poor and small and the maintenance so insufficient'.

Fees were prescribed but attitudes to their collection could be pragmatic; the 1698 terrier for Shawbury stated the expected fees, adding that the vicar took what 'what they [the parishioners] please and wee can gett'. The 1701 terrier said that while no more than 4d was usually due for baptism and churching, more should be paid by 'persons of quality' and others who lived in remote parts of the parish where the vicar had to go to them.

Many terriers referred to mortuaries, but often seemed uncertain as to whether they were fees or tithes. A mortuary of a beast or (in towns) a gown had been demanded in the Middle Ages when a parishioner died on the assumption that it was in lieu of personal tithes unpaid during life. An Act of 1529 regulated mortuaries, exempting those dying with goods worth less than £6 13s 4d, and requiring 3s 4d from those with goods worth less than £30, 6s 8d on goods worth £30 to £40 and 10s on goods worth over £40. If the custom of paying mortuaries had lapsed, however, the minister could not recover it.[1] Many Shropshire ministers seemed uncertain as to the custom of their own church; the West Felton terrier of 1718 said that some people had paid mortuaries, while others disputed them, and did not seem to know what the true position should be. Most terriers which mention mortuaries state that they are due, but perhaps they did so for the form only; for many terriers recorded rights to mortuaries well into the 19th century when they were clearly not being paid.

The clerk's fees and wages. Dr Barratt assumed that in the Lichfield diocese there must have been special instructions in 1698 for terriers to include payments to the parish clerk whom many terriers first mentioned at this date; in fact he was frequently not included until 1722.[2] The Ellesmere terrier for 1726 recorded the clerk's fees on a separate sheet, and thereafter, though they were included in the main terrier, they were separately signed. The clerk's fees, like surplice fees, were often double for non-parishioners, as at Leebotwood in 1730. Some churches likewise had a pragmatic attitude to the clerk's actual fees (as distinct from his theoretical ones); the Cheswardine terrier of 1722, stipulated his fees for churchings and burials, but said that those for weddings were to be as much as he could get. In some places the fees were vague in the extreme; the Petton terrier of 1726 said that the clerk's wages were not customary but were more or less as the rector,

---

[1] Hill, *Economic problems*, 171.

[2] *Ecclesiastical terriers*, ed. Barratt, i, p. xx.

churchwardens and parishioners agreed. This vagueness may have lain behind the widespread perception that parish clerks were greedy for fees.

Although most of the 1698 Lichfield terriers referred to the clerk's fees, an annual wage or salary is usually not mentioned until the early 18th century, and only about half of all Lichfield terriers referred to his entitlement at all. The clerk's principal duties in the late 17th and early 18th centuries were to attend the services, lead the singing, act as verger, clean the communion plate, wash the surplices and altar linen and maintain the clock. The Wroxeter terrier of 1722 described the work of the clerk and its remuneration in unusual detail; he was to wash the surplices for 4s 6d a year and other linen for 6d, sweep the leads for 6d, clean the church walls for 6d, look to the clock for 3s and supply oil for it at 3d, and scour the plate for 2d. In the Lichfield and St Asaph's terriers a sexton was rarely mentioned and some explicitly stated that the clerk carried out his functions. The earliest references to the clerk's wages seem to suggest that the amount was uncertain; the Childs Ercall terrier of 1698 says that, other than a payment for looking after the clock, the clerk received only what the parish chose to give him. A common method of payment was by contributions from the parishioners, usually paid at Easter, 4d for a tenement with a plough and 2d for a cottager. The 1698 Leighton terrier listed the payments due from 28 parishioners, probably most of the parish's householders, and the Sheinton terrier of 1698 named 15 householders and their prescribed payments—from 4d to 1s—and stated that another 20 unnamed cottagers paid 2d each. Another common method of payment was by eggs at Easter as in High Ercall. In some places, mainly in St Asaph's diocese, the clerk was entitled to a proportion of the corn tithe. In Llanyblodwel a sheaf of each grain grown was due from everyone producing more than five sheaves, and in Kinnerley one sheaf of winter corn and one of spring corn was due from every parishioner sowing corn; in some places in that north-western area of Shropshire this payment was known as the 'bell sheaf'.

In the 18th century these customary payments tended to be replaced by a fixed wage paid by the churchwardens out of the church lewn or rate. The Melverley terrier of 1749 stated that contribution by sheaf had been commuted to a money payment of £2. The Rodington terrier of 1708 said that the clerk's wage from customary contributions had been small and not paid by all who were liable, so the method had been changed to a yearly wage of £1 15s 0d paid by the churchwardens. During the 18th century the annual wage was of the order of £1 to £1 10s 0d and in the 19th century of £2 to £2 10s 0d.

Introduction

Benefactions. Benefactions and bequests were not included in the Hereford terriers and only when particularly noteworthy in the 17th and 18th-century Lichfield ones. The Lichfield terriers of 1841 were the first to include benefactions systematically, the printed questions having asked for them. Town churches, such as those of Bridgnorth, Market Drayton, Shrewsbury and Whitchurch, were the recipients of most benefactions and bequests—to the churches themselves, to the poor and to schools. Bequests for sermons were also particularly favoured in the towns, especially in Shrewsbury, but also in Ellesmere in 1694, Market Drayton in 1701, Oswestry in 1791 (in English and Welsh), and in Whitchurch. In the countryside bequests specifically for sermons were concentrated in north-west Shropshire (for example at Baschurch, Dudleston and Kinnerley), Worfield being the only other rural church endowed in this way.

A terrier's list of benefactions can provide evidence for almshouses and schools. The High Ercall terrier of 1884 referred to a free grammar school founded in 1663 but closed in 1876, the building being judged to be incapable of repair. Eleanor Harris was recorded as founding a generously endowed school at Baschurch in 1720. The Oswestry terrier of 1791 was accompanied by a separate one describing a schoolhouse built about sixteen years previously with details of its endowment. Another terrier of the school lands, which is undated but appears to be of the late 18th century or early 19th, included small maps of the school lands in the margin of the terrier.

Inventory of the church. One of the Canons of 1604 stipulated that the churchwardens should provide at the cost of the parish a Book of Common Prayer, a large Bible and Book of Homilies, surplices and a cloth for the communion table. Nevertheless, as Dr Barrett has said, few terriers described the property of the church as well as they did the benefice.[1] The Hereford terriers never referred to church goods, and the Lichfield ones gave no information about communion plate until 1841, when there were specific questions about it; before then references to church goods were most unusual, though isolated examples can be found, as in the Sutton Maddock terrier of 1748 and the very full terrier of St Leonard's, Bridgnorth in 1803. The printed terrier forms of 1884 asked about communion vessels and some terriers included details of church furnishings, books and linen. The 18th and 19th-century St Asaph terriers by contrast gave a full inventory of all the church goods. An interesting feature of these terriers is the noticeable decline in Welsh Bibles and prayer books between the terriers of 1791 and

---

[1] *Ecclesiastical terriers*, ed. Barratt, i, p. xix.

those of 1856. Even the St Asaph terriers, however, did not mention all the items required by the 1604 Canon, such as a pulpit, font, alms chest and Commandment boards.

Other information. Although the terriers of each diocese have a relatively similar format and included roughly comparable information, some parishes recorded details which were not found elsewhere, but were presumably of local importance. Opinions about the clergy were not required, but the churchwardens of Leebotwood in 1698 expressed their approval of their curate: 'Our Curate is very well satisfyd with what he hath and Wee with Him'. The Market Drayton terrier of 1698 has a long description of their 'sober Chast Honest and peacable' vicar, and also says that the parishioners 'demeane themselves Reverently'. Churchwardens were entitled to report on the minister and his conduct, but very few did, and it is possible that these somewhat defensive remarks may have been motivated by the practice of the bishop of Lichfield of that date, William Lloyd, of keeping detailed notes on his clergy. When Lloyd left his previous diocese of St Asaph in 1692 he left his successor a commentary on the character of every clergyman, and on his translation to Lichfield he continued his policy of strictly disciplining the clergy and the laity.[1] An unknown letter writer referred to 'his despotical government in the diocese of Lichfield and Coventry' and in particular to his book, a sort of 'Church Domesday'. 'As to the colours of his clergy, some were painted in dismal colours, and drawn as ugly as it was possible'.[2] It is not known, however, why only Market Drayton and Leebotwood felt disposed to defend their clergy. While it is known from other sources that plurality and non-residence were common, the only explicit reference to a non-resident incumbent was in the Hinstock terrier of 1767 which was signed by the curate 'instead of Mr Roberts who is not come to reside'.

Repair of the chancel fell to the rector, whether clerical or lay, by common law, and that of the nave (which terriers usually termed the 'church') by custom and common law to the churchwardens and parishioners.[3] From the first half of the 18th century the Lichfield and St Asaph's terriers often stated who was responsible for the upkeep of the chancel, the body of the church and the churchyard wall, and sometimes commented on the state of repair, otherwise the church received only an occasional brief reference; Hordley's terrier of 1845 said that

[1] Hart, *William Lloyd*, 62.
[2] Ibid.139.
[3] Burn, *Ecclesiastical law*, ed. Fraser, i. 247.

the church was ancient, Lee Brockhurst's of 1801 recorded that a screen had been removed for the inhabitants' convenience, and Frodesley's of 1809 that the church had recently been rebuilt.

THE DOCUMENTS

Almost all the terriers are on parchment and they vary greatly in size. Their condition also varies. Many of the Hereford ones are in poor condition, being faded and worn; the St Asaph's terriers are mostly very large and have been stored in rolls, consequently being very worn at the edges; most of the Lichfield terriers, except some of those of 1612, have been stored folded and are in good condition, though extremely dirty.

Most of the terriers can be found in the relevant diocesan repositories. Those from the diocese of Lichfield are housed in the Lichfield Record Office as class B/V/6. Some terriers were sent to Lichfield on the same parchments as the bishop's transcripts of parish registers and are listed and shelved with them as class B/V/7/1; in this edition a footnote indicates where that is the case. Terriers for the Shropshire parishes that were transferred from St Asaph's to Lichfield diocese in 1920 on the disestablishment of the Welsh church are also in the Lichfield Record Office; they, too, are classed as B/V/6 but are listed separately. Terriers of Hereford diocese are in the Herefordshire Record Office, classed as HD 2/8–14. Some terriers can be found among the parish records deposited in the Shropshire Records and Research Centre. For the most part they duplicate those in the diocesan records, and if so the existence of a parish copy, where known, is indicated in this edition with an asterisk (*); but sometimes the parish's copy appears to be the only one known, and if so it is indicated by a dagger thus †. Dr Barratt said that she knew of no instance where parish copies had survived when diocesan returns had not, but seven of the fourteen terriers from the Hereford diocese found in parish records are the only extant copies as are three of the St Asaph's terriers found there. Even among the much more numerous and well preserved terriers of the Lichfield diocese eight survive only in the parish records. Some terriers have been printed with the parish registers and these are indicated in the footnotes; where the SRRC catalogue of unpublished registers notes that a terrier is included, this is also indicated in the footnotes. A few terriers have been printed in journals such as the *Transactions* of the Shropshire Archaeological Society; these are also indicated in the footnotes. Occasionally terriers are found in SRRC deposits of estate or solicitors' papers, and these are indicated in the footnotes, but discovery of isolated survivals can only be fortuitous.

Glebe terriers of Shropshire

EDITORIAL NOTE

Many of the terriers are very long, particularly the 18th and 19th-century Lichfield ones, and it would have been impractical to print them in extenso. The terriers are therefore printed in calendar form, with any material of unusual interest quoted in full. Even in that form the terriers fill two volumes of this Series. Bounds of open-field parcels, of home closes or compositions for hay are of great value for historians studying a locality, but are very lengthy; it has been practicable only to indicate where such bounds were given. Where a terrier had a great many signatories, that is noted, but they are not all named. The content of the terriers expanded over time; the house and land were described in the earliest ones, and later the tithes, tithing customs, clerk's fees and wages and benefactions were added; in this edition each such topic is calendared fully when first mentioned, but thereafter only where there is substantially new or changed information.

The terriers are printed in alphabetical order of parish irrespective of diocese, and with the following conventions. Original spelling is retained for field names, personal names, and direct quotations but modern spelling is used for parish names (in their ecclesiastical form) and for the names (according to the Ordnance Survey) of townships, villages and hamlets. Round brackets indicate interpolations in the original document, square brackets editorial ones. If a terrier called itself a copy or gave the date of the terrier from which it was copied, this edition describes it as a copy without using square brackets.

Acknowledgements. For permission to publish the terriers preserved in the Hereford Record Office thanks are due to the Bishop of Hereford and the Record Office Manager, and for those in the Lichfield Record Office to the Diocesan Registrar and the Archivist in Charge. Those terriers found only in the Shropshire Records and Research Centre are published by permission of the Head of Records and Research.

Glossary

Definitions unless otherwise stated are taken from the *O.E.D.* This glossary includes words which are used in various terriers; words which are only used in one particular terrier are defined in a footnote to that terrier.

ADVOWSON. Right of patronage to a benefice or living.

BING. Literally a heap but transferred to the place in which the heap is contained; in context it appears to mean a place where food for cattle is stored.

COMPOSITION. Temporary money payment in lieu of tithe in kind.

DELF. Digging; in Shropshire usually referring to turf for fuel.

ESTOVER. The right to wood for the repair of houses, hedges and farm implements.

MATH. Mowing or crop mowed.

PLECK. A small piece of land.

MODUS. Permanent money payment in lieu of tithe in kind.

MUNCORN. A mixed grain, often wheat and rye.

OBLATION. Offerings made in church for the use of the church.

OBVENTION. Money income for the clergy.

OLLER. Alder.

PREDIAL. Relating to the land or farming.

SHORE (also SHERE or sometimes SHIRE). Literally a prop or strut of timber against the end of a building, but in Shropshire terriers usually a lean-to building.

Abbreviations

a.	acre(s)
C	curate
CW	churchwarden
Eccl. Com.	Ecclesiastical Commissioners
F.	Field
Fur.	Furlong
L.	Leasow
LRO	Lichfield Record Office
M.	Meadow
QAB	Queen Anne's Bounty
R	rector
SRRC	Shropshire Records and Research Centre
V	vicar

The Glebe Terriers of Shropshire

Part 1 (Abdon to Llanfair Waterdine)

Abdon

n.d. [?1589]. [CWs' signatures illegible].
Richard Cresset of Upton is reputed patron.
Land: 3 a. in Church F., 13 a. in . . . [details illegible].

2 Jan. 1604/5. Abraham Deuce, parson; Edward Millinchope, Thomas
Trump, Francis Wever, William Millinchope.
Land: Nether L. 6 a., another leasow 2 a., Lynen L. 3 a., close of 1 a., parcels
of 5 a. and 1 a. arable in Mill F., ½ a. in Wollersley, 2 separate acres
in . . . [further details torn].

26 Oct. 1692*. John Barker and Abraham Benet, CWs.
House with gardens to N. and S., hemp yard and kitchen garden adjoining
and Lower Yard.
Land: 2 parcels called Furlong with Coblers Lane on S., New Tinding with
Brown Clee on E., Hill F. butting on Long Ridge Lane, Well F., Langnet,
Lower L. with Furnace Lane on E. [bounds].
Tithes are due in kind on hay, corn, oats, fruits like apples and pears, tow,
hemp, flax, pigs, lambs, geese, eggs, honey; 1s is due per colt, 4d per calf,
½d per sheep sold, 1d for milk, 1d for garden herbs.
Easter offerings: 2d per communicant.

22 June 1801. Richard Fleming, C; Richard Tasker and Thomas Bradley,
CWs.
Land: Broad M., Furlong in 2 parcels on Abdon Lane, Langnet M., leasow of
arable on Furnace Lane 11 a., 3 a. arable in Mill F., 1 a. arable in Nell F.,
New Tinding with Brown Clee on SE. 2 a. [bounds]; also 20 a. of arable,
pasture and meadow at Clee Stanton purchased by Edward Baldwyn, the
present rector, with money for augmenting poor livings.
Great and small tithes are due.
The parson has 2 pews in the chancel.

Acton Burnell[1]

20 Oct. 1612*.[2] John Mullard, R; Simon Dunn and William Tayllor, CWs. [6
other signatories].

---

[1] Acton Burnell was transferred from Lichfield to Hereford diocese in 1905: *Victoria
history of Shropshire*, ii. 1.
[2] The terrier for 1612 is transcribed in *Shropshire Notes & Queries*, i–ii (1886 for 1884–6), 102.

1

Parsonage house with 2 little gardens between it and the street, barn, cow house, ox house, yard and 2 little closes.

Land at Acton Burnell: enclosed pastures called Becknollshatch, Old Mills or Radnor Bridge, 6 lands and 6 butts arable in a field towards Frodesley W. of the town, 1 furlong, 3 butts arable and a dole of meadow in Shootfield, 2 furlongs and 4 butts in a field towards Acton Pigott.

Land at Acton Pigott: house with barn, orchard and backside, pasture called Brode L., little piece of land with a warden tree,[1] little pasture called Knowles, little croft out of New L., little meadow called Poplar M., 6 butts arable in the field towards Acton Burnell, 6 butts in Cross F. towards Golding and 10 butts in Evenwood F.; free common throughout the wastes and commons and free pannage for swine.

All tithes in Acton Burnell and Acton Pigott are due except the 3rd tithe sheaf of Acton Pigott (other than the demesne) which is paid to the parson of Cound.

Sep. 1685. Joachim Greaves, R; William Corfield and Thomas Botfield, CWs.

Land in Acton Burnell: Great New Tinding, Little New Tinding, Upper Hanfort, Lower Hanfort, Bucknalls Hatch, Linall M., Old Mills.

Land in Acton Pigott: yard, croft, Ash Fur., Broad L., New L., Hanging L., Knolls L., Popleton M.

21 July 1693. Isaac Bould and Richard Woodhouse, CWs.

28 June 1698. Joachim Greaves, R; William Cound and Richard Granger, CWs.

16 Aug. 1698. Joachim Greaves, R; William Crumpton and Thomas Botfield, CWs.

House of 5 bays with brew house 1 bay, corn barn 5 bays, wain house 1 bay, hay bay, 1 bay for tying cattle, little garden, fold yard, kitchen garden ¼ a., yard 2½ a. and land adjoining called Mintwell 1 a.

Land in Acton Burnell: Bucknalls Hatch 8 a., Upper and Lower Hoof Yard 12 a., Great New Tining 6 a., Little New Tining 4 a., Linells 9 a., Shoot M. 3 a., Old Mills 3 a., church-yard 1 a.

Land in Acton Pigott: house 3 bays, bake house 1 bay, hay bay adjoining the bake house, barn 3 bays, 1 bay for tying cattle, fold yard, hemp butt, yard 2 a., 2 crofts adjoining 2 a., Limener 2 a., Ash Fur. 2 a., Broad L. 6 a., Hanging Lee 2 a., Knowles 1¾ a., New L. 4 a., Poplar M. 2 a., small parcel of land to the S. of the house with 4–5 apple trees.

Memorandum: 'we do not butt or bound the Lands being all entire Inclosures, & well known by the names above specified'.

All tithes in Acton Burnell are due in kind except milk for which 1d per cow is due, gardens 1d, 1d smoke for wood and fuel burnt, colts 1d. In Acton Pigott all tithes are due in kind except 1d per cow for milk, ½d per calf and 1d per colt. The custom for hay is 4d per house except Farmers tenement which pays 10d p.a; tithe hay is due in kind for certain meadows [named]. Communicants pay 2d at Easter.

---

[1] 'Warden' was an old form of pear used for cooking: *O.E.D.*

Part 1 (Abdon to Llanfair Waterdine)

Surplice fees: marriage 1s 2d, burial 4d, churching 4d.

Clerk's wages were customary, but are now paid by the CWs and much augmented.

21 Oct. 1701. Joachim Greaves, R; Thomas Haynes and William Cound, CWs.

Tithes: in Acton Burnell 4d per stall of bees put down for honey is due.

2 May 1705. Joachim Greaves, R; Edward Collins and Thomas Cound, CWs.

23 July 1711*. Joachim Greaves, R; Edward Collins and Richard Graynger, CWs.

House in Acton Burnell of 5 bays with a brew house of 1 bay adjoining, little old stable with a shore for a fowl house, a corn barn 5 bays, wain house, tying for cattle, place for fodder and a hay bay adjoining and stable with a little place adjoining for common uses.

Land in Acton Burnell: Mintwell, Bucknalls Hatch, Old Mill, tithe M., Lynells in 2 parcels, Great New Tynings in 2 parcels.

Land in Acton Pigott: house of 3 bays, 2 sheds for tying cattle, hay bay, corn barn of 4 bays, common fold, hemp butt, small garden, yard; 2 crofts, Limner, Ash Fur., Broad L. in 2 parts, Knowles, New L., Poplar M., Hanging Lea, all bounded by good quick or other fences.

The chancel of a small chapel in Acton Pigott is maintained and repaired by the rector, the body and steeple by the inhabitants of the township; they have the right of morning prayer in the chapel from the first Sunday after All Hallows to May Day every Sunday before the time at Acton Burnell if requested, the right to the Lord's Supper every Easter morning before Acton Burnell and the right of baptism and marriage if required.

'All things in nature' are tithable in kind except 1d per cow, 1d per colt, honey 4d per stall of bees put down, 1d per garden 1d for house and smoke; in Acton Burnell the 10th calf is payable in kind unless compounded; in Acton Pigott ½d is due for every calf; there is a custom for hay on certain lands [named]; one-third of the tithe grain is due to the rector of Cound and two-thirds to Acton Burnell; a whole lamb is due at 10, or at 7 when the rector may take a lamb and pay 3d for each short of 10; under 7 the owner pays 3d per lamb; wool is paid at the tenth part by weight; 3 eggs are due per cock and 2 per hen.

Mortuaries are due in both townships. Communicants pay 2d at Easter.

Clerk's wages are 13s 4d p.a. paid by the CWs from the lewn; every cottager with a seat in church pays 2d; fees: making a grave 6d, tolling the knell 6d, churching 4d, marriage 4d, 2 eggs per cock in the week before Easter.

23 July 1718. Peter Studley, R; John Price and Humphrey Aderley, CWs.

Parsonage house new built or repaired with 6 rooms per floor, corn barn 5 bays, stable lately a wain house with 2 bays more for tying cattle, hay bay, small old stable, necessary house and small garden with a new brick wall.

7 July 1726. Peter Studley, R; Richard Boycott and Edward Coles, CWs.

1730. Peter Studley, R; Thomas Harrington and Thomas Haughton, CWs.

There is now a suit in the Exchequer to determine whether the townships of Ruckley and Langley are in Acton Burnell and to whom the tithes belong.

1733. Peter Studley, R; John Beyley and Thomas [?]Townsend, CWs.

Glebe terriers of Shropshire

23 June 1736. Peter Studley, R; Richard Aston and Thomas Lawrence, CWs.

1739. Peter Studley, R; Thomas Botfield and John Beyley, CWs.

18 Sep. 1742. Peter Studley, R; Thomas Haughton and Thomas Harrington, CWs.

1745. Peter Studley, R; Thomas Botevile and Richard Aston, CWs.

1748. Peter Studley, R; John Bayley and Thomas Harrington, CWs.

20 Sep. 1752. Peter Studley, R; Thomas Lawrence and Thomas Haughton, CWs.

13 Sep. 1756. Peter Studley, R; Thomas Price and William Haughton, CWs.

1759. John Lea, R; Thomas Price and William Townsend, CWs.

1763. John Lea, R; William Townsend and John Bayley, CWs.

1767. John Lea, R; Richard Hall and Thomas Haughton, CWs.

n.d. John Lea, R; Charles Everall and Thomas Haughton, CWs.

1775. John Lea, R; William Townsend and Daniel Bromley, CWs.

1779. John Lea, R; Thomas Lawrence and Daniel Bromley, CWs.

1783. John Lea, R; John Bailey and E. Bayley, CWs.

6 Aug. 1787. John Lea, R; Thomas Price and Robert Dawes, CWs.

24 Oct. 1792. John Lea, R; Thomas Haughton and Daniel Everall, CWs.

24 July 1797. John Lea, R; Richard Bailey and Daniel Everall, CWs.

1801. John Lea, R; Edward Haughton and Edward Hudson, CWs.

1805. John Lea, R; John Haughton and Edward Snapton, CWs.

2 Sep. 1810. Robert Maddocks, C; Joseph Lawrence and Edward Snapton, CWs.

14 Aug. 1845*. E[dward] Wainwright, R; Thomas Bray and G. Walker, CWs.
There is a suitable house in Acton Burnell on the glebe near the church with an entrance hall, 2 parlours, study, kitchen, brew house, pantry, knife house, 2 cellars, 4 best bedrooms, 3 servants' bedrooms and storeroom, small garden in front and large garden at the back with pump, barn, cow house, stable, carriage house and orchard to the S.
Farmhouse in Acton Pigott with kitchen, parlour, wash house, 3 bedrooms, barn, wain house, cow house, 2 stables and pigsty.
Land: at Acton Burnell: 2 closes called Lower and Upper Mintwell 5 a., 2 closes at the back of the turnpike gate on the road from Acton Burnell to Frodesley called Bucknalls Hatch and Radhurst F. 11 a.
Land at Acton Pigott: Baylisses M., Yard, Big Limners, Little Limners, Parkwell, Ash Fur., Giggs leasow, New L., Broad L., Hanging Lees, Poplar M., Lower Haughfoots, Upper Haughfoots; 90 a. leased at £120 p.a.
Tithes great and small are due in Acton Burnell; one-third of the tithes of Acton Pigott belong to Cound; the great and small tithes of Ruckley and Langley are claimed; commutation has been agreed at £230 p.a., but is not confirmed.

Payment of synodals[1] and interest to the governors of QAB amounts to *c.* £60.

Surplice fees: marriage by licence 10s, marriage by banns 5s, burial 5s, churching 2s, vault £5, headstone £3 10s, footstone £1 10s, mortuaries £1; fees are double for non-residents.

Clerk's fees: burial 4s, marriage by licence 5s, marriage by banns 2s 6d, baptism 6d.

The chancel is repaired by the rector and is in good repair.

Plate: silver flagon and silver chalice. There is an iron chest for the registers at the parsonage house.

Benefactions: Thomas Jones of Langley left £10 for the poor of Acton Burnell and Ruckley, the interest to be bestowed in bread on the feasts of Ascension and St Thomas; John Roberts of Langley left £5 to the poor of Acton Burnell and Ruckley, the interest to be bestowed in bread on the feast of St John; Edward Bayley of Kenley left 10s for bread on New Year's day.

There was an almshouse in Acton Burnell village which has been converted to a house and blacksmith's shop, thus depriving the poor of a poor house.

4 Aug. 1857. E[dward] Wainwright, R; Thomas Reynolds and Catherine Morris, CWs.

There is a schoolhouse on the glebe land in Acton Burnell village and a house purchased with parish money and rented by the parish clerk.

14 Apr. 1861.[2] E[dward] Wainwright, R; Thomas Reynolds, CW.

The poor house was purchased with charity money, but has been converted to 2 houses and there is now no poor house.

Acton Scott

26 Jan. 1589/90. Edward West and Richard Arndell, CWs.

Richard Acton of Acton Scott is undoubted patron.

There is a house and outhouses.

Land: 35 a. of pasture and meadow being Parsons Moor 7 a. ,Calves L. 4 a., Parsons Broomy Close, Parsonage L. 4 a., leasow near a common wood called Castle Hill, pasture near town field called Burfield 3 a., close called Espley, close called Barn Yard 1 a., close beneath Pool 1 a., Hale M. 2 a., dole of meadow near Bannes Wood 1 a., meadow of 1 a. [bounds]; the parson has common pasture in Ockwood for sheep and store cattle.

Adderley

24 Aug. 1682. Robert Adams, R.

Land: large meadow of 4½ a. in which the parsonage house stands, garden adjoining the house within the moat, little croft near the house called

---

[1] Synodals are defined by the *O.E.D.* as payments by inferior (i.e. parish) clergy to diocesan officials.

[2] Filed with the Acton Burnell terrier for 1861 is the abstract of title of Edward Joseph Smythe, bt., to the manor of Acton Burnell.

Parsons Croft ¾ a., 2 pieces of arable called Lichways *c.* 7 a. near the road to Audlem.

1 Oct. 1685. Andrew Dorrington and William Watkin, CWs.

12 Sep. 1693. Robert Adams, R.

9 May 1694.[1] Robert Adams, R; Robert Widdows and Joseph Mulliner, CWs.

Parsonage house of 4 bays with barn of 4 bays adjoining, cow house and stable 1½ bays, old kiln 1 bay and cart house.

Land: garden with 6 apple trees and moat within which the house stands, meadow around the garden 5 a. with house and garden, large fold with barn and little croft adjoining ¾ a, 2 closes called Lichways *c.* 8 a. with the road to Cheshire on the NE. [bounds].

Tithes on corn are due in kind throughout the parish; hay is taken by composition; modus on calves of 2d per calf, 1d per orchard, 1d per garden, 1d per smoke; tithe pigs, geese, wool, lambs, hemp and flax are due in kind.

17 Aug. 1698. Robert Adams, R; John Maulkin and Thomas Shard, CWs.

Parsonage house of 4 bays with barn 4 bays, cow house 1 bay adjoining, stable adjoining the cow house 1 bay and building of 2 bays standing alone 30 yd. NE. of the house.

Land: garden before the house within the moat, garden to the SW. of the house beyond the barn with fold yard adjoining, Little Croft ¾ a. NW. of the house, meadow around the house 4 a., 2 pieces called Lichways 8 a.

Tithes: 2s is customary for a calf at 7 and 1s at 5 which was reckoned half a calf; lambs, pigs, geese, hemp and flax are due in kind, and where there are not 10 pigs, geese or lambs, the parson has 1 at 7. 'There is a pretended modus for hay and small tythes of the demesne of Shavington' of £1 5s.

Offerings: 2d for each house.

Fees: churching 4d, registering a baptism, marriage or burial 4d.

21 Oct. 1701. Robert Adams, R; John Swanwicke and John Maulkin, CWs.

A single bay of building stood not long since in a meadow to the NE. of the house, but has lately been removed to the Barn Yard to the NW. of the house.

4 May 1705. Robert Adams, R.

Parsonage house encompassed with small moat and barn, cow house and stable joined together SW. of the house *c.* 40 yd. away, small building W. of the house *c.* 80 yd. away and small cart house.

Land: small garden within the moat, garden at the back of the barn SW. of the house, Glebe M. 3½ a. around the house, garden within the moat, a little croft NW. of the house ¾ a., Lichways beside the land towards Swanbach, Cheshire *c.* ¼ mile from the parsonage house 8 a. The yearly value of the rectory is *c.* £75.

25 July 1711. Robert Maulkin and John Maulkin, CWs.

---

[1] The Adderley 1694 and 1711 terriers are filed with the bishop's transcripts (LRO, B/V/7/1).

House of 4 bays with barn 5 bays and a little building standing by itself in the barn yard, all in good repair.

24 July 1718. Robert Adams, R.
The chancel belongs to the rectory and is in good repair.

7 July 1722. B[enjamin] Clive, R; William Browne and William Swanick, CWs.

6 July 1726. B[enjamin] Clive, R; Thomas Clayton and John Murhall, CWs.

6 Nov. 1734. B[enjamin] Clive, R; John Hudson, CW.

Jul. 1736. Henry Corbet, R; John Worrall and Joseph Moore, CWs.

30 Aug. 1739. Henry Corbet, R; William Gamall and Thomas Podmore, CWs.

26 Aug. 1742. Henry Corbet, R; William Gollins and Thomas Browne, CWs.
[Tithes copied from 1718].

9 Aug. 1748. Henry Corbet, R; John Blantorn and William Turner, CWs.

18 Sep. 1752*. J. Morris, C; Joseph Hudson and John Worrall, CWs.
Parsonage house is a good, new brick house of 3 bays standing on the bank of the meadow with barn and stable of 4 bays contiguous.
Tithes: composition for hay; small tithes are due in kind.

28 Aug. 1756. Robert Clive, R; Ralph Cooper and Gabriel Alman, CWs.

24 Oct. 1759*. Robert Clive, R.

13 Sep. 1767. Robert Clive, R; Joseph Hudson and William Turner, CWs.

9 Aug. 1824. William Cotton, R; William Duckers and John Kemp, CWs.
Parsonage house is a brick and tiled house 42 ft × 28 ft with stable and 2 cow houses contiguous.
Land: a garden, fold and orchard 1 a. adjoining, close called Billingham M. 3 a., close called Clays Yard 2½ a., close called Intack 6 a. adjoining the highway to Drayton in Hales [bounds].
Tithes great and small are paid in kind throughout the parish.

1841. William Cotton, R; John Kemp and John Duckers, CWs.
Rectory house is a brick and tiled house of 60 ft × 28 ft with stable, cow house and coach house contiguous 76 ft × 20 ft, laundry 22 ft × 15 ft.
Land: garden, fold and orchard adjoining the house 1 a., Billingham M. 3 a., Clays Yard 2½ a., the Field 4 a., Intack 6 a.
Fees: marriage by licence 5s, 2s 6d by banns, burials 1s, churching 1s; no Easter roll or mortuaries.
Clerk's fees: marriage by licence 5s and by banns 2s 6d, burials 5s to clerk and sexton; salary £6 6s p.a.
Tithes have been commuted for £666 16s including poor rates and land tax amounting to £33.
The repair of the chancel belongs to the rector and is in a good state.
Communion plate: 2 silver chalices, 2 silver patens and 1 silver flagon. There is an iron chest for the registers.
Benefactions: details of bequests made Revd Robert Adams and Thomas Reynolds are affixed to the wall of the church; [the following are on a

separate sheet] Revd Robert Adams by his will of 19 Oct. 1719 devised an estate at Winnington, Mucklestone, Staffordshire to the Bishop of Lichfield subject to a charge of £13 12s being £8 for Mucklestone, Adderley and Drayton in Hales alternately for setting forth a poor boy or girl apprentice, £1 10s for the use of a schoolmaster or schoolmistress to teach 6 poor children of Adderley until they can read English and say the catechism by heart, £1 10s for Mucklestone likewise and £2 12s for 12 penny loaves every Sunday at the beginning of divine service to 12 poor heads of families; he also bequeathed £20, the interest to be distributed every Whitsun; Thomas Reynolds of Dodcott and Wilkesley by his will of 5 June 1725 devised a tenement in Walgherton, Cheshire to trustees to pay half the rents on St Thomas's Day to the poorest housekeepers of Adderley and half to the poorest of Dodcott and Wilkesley.

13 Aug. 1845. John Kemp and John Duckers, CWs.

23 July 1849*. William Cotton, R; John Duckers and Thomas Hudson, CWs.
Rectory house with a range of brick and tiled buildings—saddle room, boot hole, cow house and coach house with hay lofts above, 34 ft × 20 ft.
Land: Stable Croft, Intake 6 a., fish pond, Pool Piece 5 a., The Piece 4 a.; 17 a. in all inclusive of the house and garden and all contiguous SE. of the house.
There are 3 bells and a clock in the tower.
Benefactions: Thomas, Viscount Kilmorey pays £1 per month for bread; the interest on £100 given by Thomas Clayton is given to poor widows every month.

26 July 1853. Frederick Broome, C; John Duckers and Thomas Hudson, CWs.

4 Aug. 1857. Frederick Broome, R; John Duckers and George Moore, CWs.

16 Apr. 1861. Frederick Browne, R; John Duckers and James ... [faded], CWs.

20 Apr. 1869. Athelstan Corbet, R; John Duckers and John Bourne, CWs.
Rectory house erected 1866–7 of brick and slate 94 ft × 37 ft with a range of brick and slate buildings including coach house, saddle room, stable and cow house with lofts above and pigsty adjoining.
Land: garden, croft and pasture field 16 a. gained by exchange in 1866.

1884*. Athelstan Corbet, R.
Tithe rent charge £666 16s.
Schedule of registers from 1692.
Plate: 2 plate and 1 silver chalice, 2 silver patens, plate flagon and brass alms dish.
Benefactions: Adams Charity of a house and 36 a. at Winnington rented for £49 10s 6d p.a., of which Adderley receives £9 18s 8d, Drayton Magna and Mucklestone the rest, the school £4, bread for the poor every Sunday £2 12s, apprentice money £3 6s 8d to bind apprentices every 3rd year; Reynolds Charity being £1,081 1s 8d yields £32 8s p.a., of which £16 4s goes to the overseers of Dodcott cum Wilkesley and £16 4s to the poor on

St Thomas's Day; Clayton's Charity being £131 7s 3d yielding £3 16s 8d p.a. for bread each month to poor widows.

Albrighton (near Shifnal)

22 Dec. 1612. Nicholas Barnes, minister; John Cleark and John Cooke, CWs.
Vicarage house of 6 bays with barn 3 bays, all in good repair; orchard, garden and hemp butt.
Land: pastures called Lincroft 3 a., Poole L. 4 a., pasture called Forlong 4 a., 4 a. arable in Hanstone and 3 lands in Clock F. ½ a., Garidge ½ a., ½ a. iu Wildicote F. [bounds].
Tithes: half the tithe on wool and all on lambs is due, also small tithes of pigs, geese, hemp, flax, apples, onions.
Oblations: 2d per person.
Fees: marriage 9d, burials 6d, churching 1d.

12 Nov. 1685. John Hilton and Thomas Howell, CWs.
Vicarage house and outbuildings, barn and stable, garden, orchard, hemp butt and fold of 2 a.
Land: 6 pieces of enclosed land being 2 meadows and 4 pastures lying together adjoining the vicarage house 20 a., enclosures called Lincroft 7 a., Ringle Marsh 7 a., Three Butts 2 a., dole of meadow ¾ a. in a meadow of Thomas Stokes at Wildecote, ¾ a. in an enclosure of John Jellicoe [bounds].

17 Aug. 1698. William Scott, V; Thomas Weightwick, CW.
Vicarage house of 4 bays with tithe barn, stable, yard for feeding pigs and geese and cow house.
Land: Tithe Barn Yard 2 a., Pool L. 3 a., Little Yard 1 a., Foxall L. 3 a., Little M. 1½ a., Long L. 4 a., Far M. 3 a., dole in the land formerly of Thomas Stokes, 3 butts amongst the lands of John Jellicoe, Rindle Marsh 7 a.; Lingcroft 6½ a. [bounds].
The impropriate tithes of corn except those on the lands of Major Waring were purchased *c*. 20 years ago with money left for pious uses by the Company of Haberdashers, London. A modus of 10s is due from Cosford Grange, £2 13s 4d from Pepperhill, £1 from Beamish Hall for small tithes and hay and 16s 8d from Bowling Alley; all small tithes are due in kind except hay; the tithe on wool and lambs is due on the 10th lamb or fleece and 'if the vicar tithe at the seventh lamb he allows the owner nine pence at three pence a lamb & if the owner have six tithe lambs or fewer he allowes & payes to the vicar three pence a peice or else counts on to the next yeare. If the vicar tithe at the seventh fleece he allows threepence & for any Number of fleeces under seven he either receives a penny a peice or counts on to the next yeare'.
Easter offerings: persons over 16 2d, every house for smoke 1d, every garden 1d.

1701. Thomas Wood, R; Robert Marygold, CW.
Land: Tithe Barn Yard 2 a., Pool L. 3 a., Little Yard 1 a., Foxalls L. 3 a., Long L. 4 a., Far M. 3 a., 1 a. dole worth 10s p.a. at Wildecott, 3 butts in a

field of John Jellicoe, 3 butts 1 a. in a field of Thomas Howell, Ringlemarsh 4 a., Lincroft 6 a. [bounds].

2 Aug. 1717. Thomas Wood, V; John Bridgen, CW.
Vicarage house and outbuildings with a small building used as a dairy.
Small payments are due for hay from particular meadows or livings.

7 July 1722. Thomas Wood, V; William Yeates, CW.

12 Oct. 1726. Francis West, V; Robert Marygould, CW.

29 Aug. 1730. John Devey, C; Joseph Jellicoe, CW.

9 Aug. 1733. Francis West, V; Richard Bridgen, CW.

15 July 1736. Thomas Wood, V; William Burny, CW.

17 Aug. 1739. Francis West, V; William Baylies, CW.

Aug. 1742. Francis West, V; Edward Shadwell, CW.

29 Aug. 1745. Francis West, V; Thomas Davenhill, CW.

9 Aug. 1748. John Hale, V; John Shelton, CW.

1 Aug. 1752. John Hale, V; Thomas Green, CW.

16 Sep. 1756. John Hale, V; Thomas Meeson, CW.

20 Sep. 1759. John Hale, V; Thomas Davenhill, CW.

6 Sep. 1763. John Hale, V; Thomas Watho, CW.

15 Sep. 1767.[1] [Signatories blackened and illegible].

7 Sep. 1772. John Hale, V; John Hewitt, CW.

21 Aug. 1775. John Hale, V; George Smith, CW.

6 Sep. 1779. John Hale, V; Addison Bromhall, CW.

Nov. 1787. H. Binfield, V; John Wightwick, CW.
Vicarage house with 2 parlours, brew house, storeroom and 6 chambers with 2 garrets.

23 Oct. 1792. [No signatories].

9 Aug. 1824. Thomas Lloyd, minister; William Pigott and John Meeson, CWs.
Commodious vicarage house in good repair with tithe barn, stable, cow house and cottage adjoining built by the present vicar.
Land: Tithe Barn Yard 2 a., Pool L. 3 a., Foxall 3 a., Lady M. 2 a., Long M. 4 a., Far L. 3 a., Ling Croft 5 a., half a meadow intermingled with George Pigott's land at Wildecotes, 3 short butts in the land of Thomas Oatley. The land tax was redeemed by the sale of Ringle Marsh to George Bucknall, the surplus being invested in consolidated funds in the name of Thomas Knapp, clerk to the Haberdashers' Company, patrons. 'Some alterations have been made in the sizes of the Leasows since the Glebeland

---

[1] The SRRC copy (P7/F/2/3) of the Albrighton 1767 terrier is labelled 1842 and has no signatories.

was measured or mapped. In the old terrier [of] 1779 Ling Croft is described as containing about six and a half acres, 'why . . . [as] it is no more than 5 acres is a mystery to the present vicar'.

Tithes: in 1665 Edmund Waring of Humphreston, Donington parish, Esq. sold to the Haberdashers' Company of London for £830 the rectory or parsonage impropriate of Albrighton with tithes and advowson; the purchase of this was made with money left by Dame Mary Weld of London by her will of 12 Feb. 1615.

The chancel and the pews in it belong to the vicar as impropriator of the great tithe.

Plate: flagon, chalice and plate of silver and a pewter plate. There is an iron chest for the registers in the vicarage house and an oak chest in the chancel.

Fees: marriage by licence 5s, by banns 2s 6d, funeral 1s, churching 6d.

1828. T. Franklin, V; William Pulteney Dana and John Bucknall, CWs. Copy of 1779.

9 Sep. 1841*. G. W. Woodhouse, V; Richard Yates and John Oatley, CWs.

Vicarage house is a good substantial building with sitting room, entrance hall, kitchen, laundry and offices on the ground floor, tithe barn, stable, gig house, cottage and small garden let for £4 4s p.a., garden and pleasure ground of 3 a.

Land: Three Butts 1 a., part of Headnall Oak F. or Long L. ½ a., croft 2 a., part of Dog Kennel M. ½ a., Greave 1½ a., Field 5 a., all leased; Lynne Croft let in cottage allotments.

Tithes: tithes are due on corn, hay, clover, potatoes, turnips, calves, lambs, wool and pigs. Cosford Farm pays no tithes but a modus of 10s p.a.; Humphreston Farm pays no tithes or modus; a modus of 16s 8d is due from Bowling Green M., £2 3s 4d from Pepperhill, 4s from Bishton, all belonging to the Earl of Shrewsbury; 2d is due from Mr Wood of Whiston, 4d from W. Oatley, 6d from Mrs Keeson, 5s from Beamish Hall, 2s from J. Yates of Benthall, Shropshire; £1 14s 2d is due from the Haberdashers' Company being interest on money held by them as trustees.

Fees: surplice fees, vaults £10–12, headstones £1 1s.

The Easter roll amounts to *c.* £1 12s.

Clerk's fees: marriage 2s 6d, burial 1s, churching 6d, 6d for each occasion of holy communion; salary £7 p.a. from the parish.

The minister has 14s 1d fee farm rent from the Crown, 14s p.a. from the Bounty Office.

Benefactions: John Chapman gave 13s 4d p.a.; Mr Bromley gave £100, William Scott £40, Thomas Davenhill £20 and Mary Waltho £20, all with interest for the poor.

13 Aug. 1845*. G. W. Woodhouse, V; George Causer and George Bucknall, CWs.

At commutation moduses will be treated as uncertain.

1884*. G. W. Woodhouse, V.

House with 3 sitting rooms, kitchen, laundry, scullery, 9 bedrooms, dressing room, brew house, coal house, stables with loft, coach house with loft and garden; total *c.* 2½ acres.

Land: various [unnamed] pieces of land, all leased; a parcel of glebe was exchanged for an equal amount of land with the Earl of Shrewsbury adjoining the churchyard and is now consecrated; *c.* 30–40 years ago an old dilapidated barn was burnt down and the insurance payment of £30 paid to the present incumbent was spent on general improvement of the buildings and some additional building.

Schedule of registers from 1555.

Plate: 2 chalices, 1 silver and 1 silver gilt, 2 patens, 1 silver and 1 pewter, silver flagon and brass alms basin.

Albrighton (near Shrewsbury)[1]

1884*. Frederick Walker, V.

House of brick and slate built in 1860, garden 1 a.

Income: farm at Wernddu, Hernant, Oswestry 35 a. rented for £30 p.a.; QAB £19 10s p.a.; fees average p.a. 15s; in 1881 Liverpool Corporation paid £40 for easement for water pipes through Wernddu, this is invested and yields £1 12s p.a.; £8 p.a. charge on the Betton Strange estate by the marriage settlement of George Scott in 1802.

Schedule of registers from 1663.

Plate: 1 silver and 2 plate chalices, 1 plate paten, 1 plate and 1 pewter flagon and 1 plate alms dish.

Annscroft[2]

1884. House with 6 rooms downstairs and 6 bedrooms upstairs, stable, coach house, piggeries and garden ½ a.

Income: £7 in lieu of small tithes from two farms at Great Lyth; Eccl. Com. £160; fees *c.* £1 10s p.a.

Schedule of registers from 1870.

Plate: 2 silver chalices, 1 silver paten and 2 silver flagons, all lent by Condover church.

Ash[3]

9 Sep. 1841. Timothy Gibson, perpetual curate; Richard Broom, CW.

House with 3 sitting rooms, kitchen and back kitchen on the ground floor, stable, gig house, pigsty and lodging rooms over, garden one-eighth a.

---

[1] Albrighton, Perrill and Broadoak were formed into an ecclesiastical parish from part the parish of St Mary, Shrewsbury in 1860: *P.O. directory of Shropshire* (1879), 272.

[2] Annscroft was formed into an ecclesiastical parish from parts of the parishes of Condover, Meole Brace and St Chad, Shrewsbury in 1872: *A History of Shropshire*, viii, ed. A. T. Gaydon (*The Victoria history of the counties of England*, 1968), 53.

[3] Ash parish was formed from the townships of Ash Magna, Ash Parva, Old Woodhouses and New Woodhouses in Whitchurch parish in 1844: *Kelly's directory of Shropshire* (1891), 257.

Part 1 (Abdon to Llanfair Waterdine)

Land: 4 pieces of freehold land near the house being House F. 2½ a., croft near the churchyard ¼ a., Great Socknall 3 a., Little Socknall 1 a.

No tithes are due.

Dividends on £500 and £377 in stock are payable to the curate; the rector of Whitchurch voluntarily pays £70 p.a.

Fees: burials c. 2s p.a., 1 headstone in the last year £1 1s, churchings c. £1 p.a.

Clerk's fees: burials c. 10s p.a., churching c. 7s p.a.; he also receives £7 10s p.a. paid by voluntary subscription.

The repairs of the chapel and chancel are charged on the above £377 and are in a good state.

Plate: silver cup and paten. There is an iron chest for the registers.

£500 in stock was bequeathed in 1837 by Mrs Elizabeth Langford to 4 trustees to pay dividends to the minister; there is an inscription in the church.

13 Aug. 1845. William Cole, perpetual curate; Richard Groom and James Hamnett, CWs.

Fees: no gravestones have been erected since the induction of the present incumbent.

2 tables with the Ten Commandments have been recently set up by subscriptions collected by the wife of the present incumbent.

23 July 1849. Martin Benson, perpetual curate; James Hamnett, CW.

26 July 1853. Henry Price, perpetual curate; James Hamnett, CW.

4 Aug. 1857. Henry Price, perpetual curate; Thomas . . ., CW.

16 Apr. 1861. Henry Price, perpetual curate; H. Hughes, CW.

£1,000 given by Archibald Millington was met by £1,000 from the Eccl. Com. and £500 from Lichfield Church Extension Society[1]; the board in the church as yet only records Mrs Langford's benefaction.

1884*. House with 4 sitting rooms, 10 bedrooms, housemaid's pantry, 2 kitchens, covered back yard with coal house, larder and dairy, harness room, 2-stalled stable, coach house, 2 loose boxes, cow house, bay for 4 cows, hen house and pigsties.

Land: 5 fields c. 30 a., 1 in front of the vicarage, the others to the E.

Income: £30 from the Eccl. Com.; £50 p.a. voluntary payment from the rector of Whitchurch.

Schedule of registers from 1837.

Plate: silver chalice, 2 silver patens, silver flagon and brass alms dish.

£500 in 3% consols was part of the endowment; £380 in 3% consols is the balance of subscriptions given towards the building of the church.

[1] The Lichfield Diocesan Church Extension Society was founded by Henry Ryder, Bishop of Lichfield, and George Hodson, Archdeacon of Stafford, in 1835: *A History of the county of Stafford*, iii, ed. M. W. Greenslade (*The Victoria history of the counties of England*, 1970), 70.

Ashford Bowdler

1589. Thomas Davis and William Coliar, CWs.
Mr Foxe of Bromfield is patron of the church which is annexed to Bromfield.
There is no house, only a barn.
Land: 6 a. in an arable field, 2 parcels of 1 a. in West F., ½ a. at Fish Pool
Hill, 1½ a. of meadow [bounds]; there is no pasture or commons.

8 Nov. 1627. William Higgens, incumbent; Thomas Chanelins, William
Pilson, CWs.
House with barn and garden.
Land: 13 a. arable in Wood F., 11 a. arable in Lower F., 12 a. arable in
Heath F., 3 enclosed pieces of meadow *c*. 3 a., pleck of pasture 1 a. by
Marbrook Side, all leased [bounds].

Astley[1]

1884*. A. Brooke, V.
House built *c*. 20 years ago with stable, coach house and yard 3 a.
Income: £75 tithe rent charge from Shrewsbury Grammar School; Eccl. Com.
£33 6s 8d in 1872; QAB £52; fees average £2 p.a.
Schedule of registers from 1695.
Plate: silver chalice, paten and flagon, silver gilt paten and pewter flagon.
Benefactions: Joseph Jones of Shrewsbury left 10s per month to the incum-
bent and £15 p.a. to Astley school; Thomas Bright of Shrewsbury left
£20 p.a. to the incumbent and £3 for repairs.

Astley Abbots

n.d. [?1589]. Thomas Asley and John Walker, CWs.
Francis Billingsley is patron of the donative.
There is no house, only a chamber at the end of a barn.
Land: close in which the chamber and barn stand 1 a. with the lane from
Astley Abbots to Bridgnorth on the W., 2 little closes 3 a. encompassed by
the land of Francis Billingsley, close near Depedale 3 a., close 3 a. near
Bach Brook, close adjoining the park of Francis Billingsley, close 2 a. near
the lane from Nordley to Bridgnorth [bounds]; there is no folding for sheep
and cattle.
Part of the tithe of corn and hay and the privy tithe belongs to the curate.

Aston Botterell

1589. David Myllichop, parson; Thomas Gitton and William Cruxon, CWs.
Edward Scriven is reputed patron of the rectory.
Land: 50 a., being 30 a. of enclosed arable adjoining the highway from
Aston Botterell to Shrewsbury, 8 a. of pasture S. of the parsonage house,

---

[1] Astley was a chapelry of St Mary, Shrewsbury: J. B. Blakeway, 'History of Shrewsbury
Hundred or Liberties', *Trans. Shropshire Archaeol. Soc.* 2nd ser. i (1889), 118–27.

other pasture 7 a., 3 a. of meadow with the lane leading to the Brown Clee to the S., 1 a. of meadow by Ash Brook and another 1 a. of meadow adjoining the rectory house [bounds]; common of pasture on the Brown Clee. Personal and predial tithes are due.

16 May 1607. David Millichope, parson; Robert Shipman, John Rawlins, William Millichop.

Hall house with parlour, buttery and kitchen with lofts over, barn 4 bays at the end of the house, stable with loft, wain house with loft, all built by the present incumbent; garden, orchard and backside 1 a.

Land: Low Pool M. at the N. end of the house 2 a., leasow 1½ a. with cow house, hay house and wain house of 3½ bays newly built, leasow of wood, leasow of 4 a., Siggfield 14 a., New Pool M. 2½ a., Moorebrooke 4½ a. with a way to Mr Scriven's mill through it, Lete Hill pasture 3 a., meadow 3 a. had by exchange with Rowland Lacon for which 3s 4d p.a. is paid [bounds]; common of pasture on the Brown Clee and liberty to fetch fern.

Aston Eyre *see* Morville with Aston Eyre

Aston on Clun

8 July 1589. Edmund Shorn and Morgan Bedow, CWs.
William Wigmore is patron.
Small house with chamber and barn of 2 bays.
Land: 6 a. in the fields of Aston [bounds]; common of pasture on Bringewood.

1594.
Land: 5 a. arable in Ashley F., 7 a. in Sowmeadow F. and 8 a. in Bettonlonds F., pasture called Hadalls, little meadow of ½ a. [very detailed bounds].

n.d. [early 17th century]. Richard Varnolls, parson.
House and close of *c.* 3 a.
Land: 8 a. of pasture and meadow in a pasture called Hadalls bounded by the lands of Mr Littleton, ½ a. meadow.

n.d. [early 17th century]. John Neale and Thomas Joanes, CWs; Richard Varnolls, parson.
House with kitchen, 2 chambers and 4 other rooms, barn and beast house of 5 bays, 2 orchards, garden, hemp butt, *c.* 4 a.
Land: 24½ a. arable in Betterton F., 11 a. arable in Ashley F., 11½ a. arable in Lower F.

10 June 1607. Richard Varnolls, R; Edmund Shorn and Robert Hopkins, CWs.

4 July 1637. Thomas Hopkin and John Tedstill, CWs.
Land: 14 a. arable in Betterton F., 17 a. in Sowmeadow, 17 a. in Astleys F.

17 July 1810. T. Hodget, R; John Lowe and Thomas Haynes, CWs.
House with garden and yard.

Land: pasture and orchard 1 a., meadow 3 a., pasture and wood 7 a., all adjoining the rectory house, 17 a. of arable in 5 parcels [bounds]; 8 a. of Aston Common recently enclosed in lieu of common rights.

Rectorial tithes are due and Easter offerings.

Fees: burials 1s, churching 1s.

The rector receives £4 p.a. being interest on £200 received from QAB until this sum is invested in land; a further £200 was received by parliamentary grant in 1809.

Atcham

1612. Robert Fareley, V; John Scantock and Richard [?]Brand [worn], CWs.

Vicarage house of 3½ bays with little barn 2 bays, 2 little houses 1½ bays, little garden behind the house, little orchard at the church gate, cottage of 'simple building' in the middle of the town of Atcham with garden, 1 end of the cottage being a dwelling, the other a stable, another cottage being the lowest house in the town next to the River Tern 3½ bays, little barn ½ bay and a close.

Land belonging to the vicarage beyond Berwick [bounds].

Tithes: wool and lambs are due in the whole parish except the manor of Atcham which belonged to Lilleshall Abbey and pays no tithe; no sheaf tithe but tithe of the home closes, i.e. closes of the townships of Uckington, Berwick, Emstrey, Chilton, Cronkhill and Atcham, but 2 of the best closes in Atcham 'are holden from the vicar . . . as wee thinke wrongfully as also the whom closes of a farme called Heathen Chilton are holden from him by one Mr Edward Cludd'. Tithe hay is due from some and money from others at 4d–12d per house; the township of Atcham will pay neither money nor hay; the Easter roll is due and the small tithes of pigs, geese, eggs and the fruit of orchards, some paying fruit, some 2d per orchard.

28 Jan. 1635/6. Roger Barbor, V; Thomas Russell and Thomas Proude, CWs.

Vicarage house and barn in sufficient repair and a cottage with ¾ a. of land let for £2 10s p.a., also cottage with 3 a. let for £1 6s p.a.

Land: at Berwick there are 3 several pastures near Greenway Bank called Vicar's Leasows 10 a.

A yearly pension of £4 is due from Mr Gaye by virtue of a decree in Chancery 1 Nov. 1612; 6s 8d is due from Tern Mill and 6s 8d from Duncocks Mill. Mortuaries are due according to statute.

Tithes are due on herbage, also small tithes, tithe of home closes, Easter roll (the grange of Atcham excepted).

Edward Burton Esq. of Atcham Grange is the right patron.

23 Aug. 1682. Abraham Butler, V; Richard Barnes and Thomas Grice, CWs.

16 Sep. 1685. Abraham Butler, V; William Harris and John Smith, CWs.

1693. Abraham Butler, V; William Jones and William Chilton, CWs.

1698*. Abraham Butler, V; William Calcott and Richard Price, CWs.

Part 1 (Abdon to Llanfair Waterdine)

Tithes are due on the home closes of 11 tenants of Uckington, varying amounts for calves, lambs, wool, geese and hay, 6s 8d for Doncott Mill and 1d per orchard in lieu of fruit [individual tenants are named with their differing liabilities]; in Berwick hay is paid in kind throughout the township except for 3 tenants; 6 tenants in Emstrey pay 4d per house for hay; at Chilton the vicar has the grass of a little meadow and tithe wool, lambs, geese and pigs from the whole township and from one tenant at Cronkhill; the vicar has 40s from Atcham Grange and £1 p.a. for hay and the home closes in Atcham; wool, lambs, hemp, flax, pigs and eggs are paid in kind throughout the parish; tithes of hay, clover, grass, geese, apples and pears are due except in Uckington.

Easter roll: house and garden 2d, man and wife 4d, widows 3d, manservant 4d, maidservant 3d, cow 1d, calf 1d, barren cow 1d, horse colt 4d, filly colt 2d, stall of bees 2d, boy and girl over 16 2d, manual or handicraft 4d, apprentice 2d.

Clerk's wages: 10s p.a. paid by the CWs.

20 Oct. 1701. Abraham Butler, V; Richard Brooke and Roland Evans, CWs.

2 May 1705*. Abraham Butler, V; Roger Pemberton and Thomas Lea, CWs.

£4 is due from Mr Gage for Atcham and Atcham Grange which was left as a legacy by one of Mr Gage's ancestors; £1 p.a. is in dispute between the vicar and the lord of Atcham, the vicar saying it is due for the home closes or tithe hay of Atcham which he has recovered since being vicar the past 20–30 years; 6s 8d is in dispute which the vicar finds by an old terrier is due from Tern Mills, Atcham.

Robert Burton of Atcham Grange is believed to be the rightful patron.

23 July 1713. Certificate from 15 inhabitants of Atcham ranging in age from 14 to 40 years saying that the small tithes of Atcham are due to the vicar and were so paid under former landlords.

23 July 1718*. Richard Colefax and Thomas Downes, CWs.

1718. Samuel Jones, V; Thomas Downes and Robert Clarke, CWs.

Clerk's wages: 10s paid by the CWs and 4d from every team land in the parish.

1722. Samuel Jones, V; Thomas Evans and Jonathan Rider, CWs.

7 July 1726. William Corfield, C; John Edwards and Robert Yeamans, CWs.

20 Nov. 1730. Samuel Fowler, V; W. Calcott and Humphrey Davies, CWs.

7 Aug. 1733. Samuel Fowler, V; Edward Gittins and Andrew Gittins, CWs.

1736. Samuel Fowler, V; W. Jones and William Jones, CWs.

1739. Samuel Fowler, V; William Phillips and George Watson, CWs.

Vicarage house to the E. of the church built of brick and tile 4 bays at 18 ft per bay with barn, stable, coalhouse of brick and tile lying together 3 bays; house in Atcham with a shop, stable and hay loft plastered and thatched 4 bays; small cottage 1½ bays now taken in as a stable of the Cock ale house paying the vicar 6d p.a.; 3 cottages lying together at the end of Atcham of 3–4 bays thatched and plastered with thatched barn of 1 bay, all leased.

17

1742. Samuel Fowler, V; Richard Lawrence and Richard Hall, CWs. [8 other signatories]. Land: Holdstones Yard 1½ a. at the end of Atcham near the Tern, Rowley Close or Atcham M., 2 closes beyond Berwick 4 a. and 3 a. (measured by Mr Meredith of Shrewsbury in 1733).

1745. Samuel Fowler, V; William Screven and Thomas Wright, CWs. [8 other signatories].

14 Oct. 1752. John Evans, C; William Gittins and William Davies, CWs.

1756. Samuel Fowler, V; William Jones and Rowland Calcott, CWs.

1759. Samuel Fowler, V; Thomas Yeomans and Richard Leake, CWs.

1763. Samuel Fowler, V; Richard Hall, CW.

1767. Samuel Fowler, V; Edward Gittins and Thomas Rudge, CWs.

14 Aug. 1845†. Henry Burton, V; John Williams, CW.
House of brick and tile at the E. end of the church with stable, cow house and barn of 2 bays adjoining the S. of the house, coach house, granary and pigsties suitable and convenient to the house, flower garden adjacent with yard of 2 a. and fold and stack yards adjoining the farm buildings.
Land: Dove House Yard 3 a., arable field of 4 a., Atcham F. 2 a., garden ½ a., Bonny Croft 7½ a., Chitwood F. 13 a., all in the occupation of the vicar.
Tithes: Cronkhill and Berwick pay hay and clover in kind, Duncott Farm likewise except for Warren ground which pays £1 10s 4d; small tithes are due throughout the parish except for Atcham Grange and Duncott Mill which pays 6s 8d; Chilton Grove Farm pays all small tithes in kind; Chilton town pays small tithes in kind, but 3 men pay for hay; Emstrey pays small tithes in kind and 4d per house for hay; Berwick pays all small tithes in kind; Atcham likewise but nothing for hay; in Uckington they pay a goose or 1s whether they keep geese or not, and all other small tithes in kind, except 1d per orchard for apples and pears. The 1698 terrier said sheaf tithe was due from 11 home closes, 8–9 a., in Uckington; 4, *c.* 8 a., in Berwick; 7, *c.* 8½ a., in Chilton; and 2 in Cronkhill, but these cannot now be identified. Tern Mill pays 6s 8d.
£4 is due to the vicar by way of a legacy of the Gage family of Atcham Grange, being £2 from the owners of Atcham Grange and £2 from the owner of the manor of Atcham.
Robert Burton of Longner Hall is patron.
Inventory: silver flagon, chalice and paten, pewter plate, 2 linen surplices, linen cloth for the communion table and 2 napkins. There is an iron chest for the registers in the vicarage house.

1884*. [Algernon Kingsford, V].
House of red brick with 3 sitting rooms, kitchen, back kitchen, dairy, larder, pantry, 8 bedrooms, 2 lumber rooms, stable, cow house, few small outbuildings, garden and vegetable garden *c.* 1 a.
Land: 30 a., 9 a. held by the vicar and 21 a. by Jeffrey Poole of Chilton.
Income: tithe rent charge £297; fees average p.a. £5.
Schedule of registers from 1621.

Plate: silver chalice dated 1721, 2 silver patens one dated 1675, silver flagon dated 1764 and brass alms dish.

Benefactions for the school: Jones's charity *c.* £25 (it varies acccording to the value of the land), Burton's charity £10, Countess of Harborough's charity £7, Hill's charity £3 2s 8d.

Badger[1]

n.d. [?1589]. [Dr Thomas Gwillim, minister]. Mr Kynnersley of Bagesore [Badger] nominates the next incumbent and the queen presents.

House of 3 bays with barn 2½ bays and little cottage 1 bay.

Land: 8 a. arable in the field to the S. of Badger Heath, little meadow yielding 1 load of hay, 2 little yards 'which will scant summer one cow', common for 40 sheep.

All tithes are due and 8s p.a. in money from Humphrey Blackman's house.

18 June 1607. Dr Thomas Gwillim, minister; Edmund Colin and Thomas North, CWs.

Land: 12 a.

26 June 1615. [Richard Froysell, minister] William Foxall and Sampson Morrall, CWs.

House with backside, orchard, garden, barn, cow house and other decayed buildings.

Land: close adjoining backside, pasture *c.* 3 a., pasture adjoining Beckbury F. 6 a., meadow 'continuallie enclosed' 1 a., furlong of leet ground in Cross F. adjoining Badger Heath 8 a., rent of half yardland in Badger 'concealed from its right uses', parcel of woody ground called Calves Leyes 1 a., 'an ancient cottage late decayed' in a home close of 1 a. with a little garden adjoining.

Baschurch
(*and see* Little Ness; Weston Lullingfield)

22 Oct. 1612. John Newton, V; Thomas Cotton and Richard Scotte, CWs; John Kynaston and Roger Higley, wardens of the chapel of Little Ness.

Vicarage house in Baschurch of 4 bays with a barn 3 bays, hay bay, 2 gardens, orchard and yard, *c.* 2 a. in all.

House in Little Ness 1½ bays with hay house, orchard and yard *c.* 2 a.

Land: leasow called Croft 5 a., dole of meadow 1 a. within Flowers M., 4 butts and a parcel of meadow in Woodfield and 8 other butts within the same field, 5 butts and Claypit Fur. in Peyrie F., 2 selions in Adcote Way Fur., 1 butt on Grymley Yate Fur., 2 butts on Leppydge Fur. and a butt or Eldertree Fur. in Heath F. [bounds].

---

[1] Badger was transferred from Hereford to Lichfield diocese in 1905: *Victoria history of Shropshire*, ii. 1. There are copies of the Badger terriers for 1589 and 1615 in SRRC 513/box 6.

1682. Samuel Tomkys and Robert Bayly, CWs.

Land: Chapel Croft or Winters Croft 8 a., 2 pieces of land on Tong Hill, Waltons Piece, Collys Headland, 2 butts in Yersmore, 2 butts in Long Fur., 2 butts in Croft M., 8 a.; total 16 a.

[Parish register 1 Apr. 1680–16 July 1682].

30 Sep. 1685. [No signatories].

21 July 1693. George Hudson, V; Richard Fox and Richard Ferrington, CWs.

House in Baschurch of 5 bays with barn of 2 bays with threshing floor and 1 bay shore, hay bay, small stable 1 bay, 2 gardens and orchard.

Small dwelling house in Ness Parva of 2 bays and 2 shores with barn 2 bays 'sustayned by forkes'[1], orchard and backside.

Land in Ness Parva: Waltons Stile, Collians Headland, 4 butts in Yardsmoor F. and small meadow to the S. of Little Ness chapel 8 a., 2 butts in Tongue Hill, piece of meadow in Flowers M. belonging to the house in Ness Parva 9 a.

16 Aug. 1698. George Hudson, V; William Reeves and . . . [blackened], CWs.

Tithes: 2 eggs per hen, 3 eggs per cock due in the week before Easter; 4d per man and wife, 2d per son or daughter over 21, or ½d if under 21, 4d per hired servant having 40s p.a., 3d if 30s p.a., and 2d if under this and of an age to receive the sacrament due at Easter (masters are to pay Easter dues for servants); 'every handicraft man payes a groate for his hand'; also due 1d per cow, ½d per calf, 1d per stall of bees put down, 1d per colt, 1d per garden, 1d for smoke; by ancient prescription Plat Mill pays 4s, Milford Mill 3s 4d, Adcote Mill 4s, Mr Coles's mill at Yeaton 3s 4d, Thomas Rogers's mill at Yeaton 2s 8d and Mr Chyers's mill at Walford 2s; tithes of wool and lambs are due at Midsummer, if there be 5lb of wool or 5 lambs, half is due to the vicar, if there be 7 he allows ½d to make up 10, if 11, 12, 13, 14 or 16, 1 is due, they allowing ½d over 10, if 15 1½ is due, if 17, 2 are due allowing 1½d; the vicar takes the whole tithe of wool together; if sheep are sold out of the parish, the parishioner pays herbage money for the period from Midsummer until they are sold; tithe geese, hemp, flax, pigs and hops are due to the vicar and paid as wool and lambs when pulled up or fit for eating; at Michaelmas 1s 8d in the £ is due for land grazed by those living out of the parish and parishioners pay for unprofitable cattle grown for the market.

Memorandum the vicar receives all these tithes from every township in the parish, also two-thirds of the tithes of Bagley, the rector of Hordley taking only one-third, and also two-thirds of Noneley tithes in Loppington parish and half the tithe of 3 tenements in Mytton in Fitz parish.

Surplice fees: baptism 1s, churching 1s, burial 1s, funeral sermon 6s 8d, marriage 5s.

2 May 1705. George Hudson, V; John Wikey and John Thornes, CWs.

Surplice fees: publishing banns 1s 2d, funeral sermon 6s 8d or 10s.

Mortuaries are due according to statute.

---

[1] The term 'forks' probably implies a cruck construction.

Part 1 (Abdon to Llanfair Waterdine)

The profits of the vicarage at present are about £40 p.a.

1718.[1] George Hudson, V; Thomas Evans and Edward Kinaston, CWs.

5 July 1722. George Hudson, V; Edward Tomkiss and Robert Batho, CWs.
Vicarage house with hay bay of 1 large bay of building and a shore adjoining for tying up cattle, 2 gardens, bean yard and orchard.
Tithes: if parishioners sell lambs before they are tithed they must allow for them out of those that remain, if they sell them before they are shorn they must pay a groat for every month they are kept in the parish from the Midsummer before they would be regularly tithed; hemp and flax must be paid on the butts where they are grown; pigs, sows and gilts are paid when they are fit to eat, geese between Midsummer and Michaelmas and hops when they are gathered; dove houses pay 6d at Easter.

1726. Stephen Parker, V; Thomas Davies and Thomas Sides, CWs.

1730. Stephen Parker, V; Richard Payne and Robert Fox, CWs.
Easter dues: a child over 16 pays ½d, a man of 21 and upwards 2d, the master pays 4d for servants with 40s wages, 3d for servants with wages of 30s and 2d if the servant is over 16 but the wages under 30s; artificers pay an additional 4d.
6s 8d is due for a grave in the church.
Madam Eleanor Harris left by will £1 to be paid to the vicar for the time being for a sermon on the Sunday after 11 Feb. every year in memory of her liberal benefaction to the parish.[2]

7 Aug. 1733. Stephen Parker, V; William Reeves and Daniel Parton, CWs.

21 June 1736. Stephen Parker, V; Thomas Cotton and John Smith, CWs.

14 Aug. 1739. Stephen Parker, V; Jonathan Martin and John Dacker, CWs.

25 Aug. 1742. Robert Jeffreys, minister; William Clayton and Francis Jones, CWs.

27 Aug. 1745. Robert Jeffreys, V; Edward Kynaston and Christopher Barnett, CWs.

1748. Robert Jeffreys, V; John Newns and William Weston, CWs.
Vicarage house: 5 rooms on the ground floor with a cellar below, 4 rooms and a closet on the first floor and 3 garrets above.

1752. Robert Jeffreys, V; John Bright and Robert Fox, CWs.

1756. Robert Jeffreys, V; Francis Higginson and Edward Harriss, CWs.

21 Sep. 1759. Robert Jeffreys, V; Thomas Jones and John Brayne, CWs.

---

[1] The Baschurch terriers for 1718, 1752, 1756, 1787, 1836, 1841 and 1845 are included in the printed parish register (Shropshire Parish Register Soc.).

[2] By her will of 1709 Eleanor Harris left lands at Stanwardine in the Fields for various annuities and for the education of poor boys and girls of Baschurch; when funds permitted, the boys were to be set apprentice and the girls were to be given marriage portions: S. Bagshaw, *Directory of Shropshire* (1851), 24.

1763. Robert Jeffreys, V; Thomas Evans and Thomas Payne, CWs.

1767. Robert Jeffreys, V; John Scott and John Crowther, CWs.

19 Aug. 1772*. Robert Jeffreys, V; Joseph Lee and Thomas Rusco, CWs.
Glebe land in the chapelry of Little Ness: house with 1 a., Flowers M. ½ a.,
Upper, Middle and Lower Lees 10 a., Cockpit L. 4 a., Collays Headland
2 a., Yarsmoor, Three Butts 2 a., Tongue Hill F. 2 a., Adcote or Cross
Meadow Butt ¼ a.

1775. Robert Jeffreys, V; John Lloyd and Thomas Orwell, CWs.
Little Ness.
House of 2 small bays with barn 2 bays and meadow adjoining the house, in
all 1 a.
Land: 3 closes 10 a., 2 furlongs in Tongue Hill F.,1 a., ½ a. in Flowers M.,
New Piece 4 a., 4 furlongs in Yarsmore F. 2 a., Colleys Headland 2 a., 1
butt in Cross M. ¼ a., all surrounded by the lord's land.
Tithes as Baschurch.

1779. Robert Jeffreys, V; John Jones and William Jones, CWs.

1783.[1] Robert Jeffreys, V; John Allport and David Edwards, CWs.
Tithes: if sheep are sold before they are shorn, 4d is due per score per month
they have been pastured in the parish since the last Midsummer; 1s 8d per
£ is due for every piece of land which any from out of the parish grazes and
from every householder who grazes only for the market.

4 Aug. 1787. Robert Jeffreys, V; John Randles and John Birch, CWs.

24 Oct. 1792. Robert Jeffreys, V; Thomas Morris and John Troy, CWs.

1797. Robert Jeffreys, V; A. Lateward and Thomas Evans, CWs.

n.d. [late 18th century]†. [No signatories].

1801. Henry Pickstock and Thomas Orwell, CWs.

1805. D. Morris, minister; Henry Smith and John Owens, CWs.

1810. David Morris, minister; John Jones and Richard Atcherley, CWs.

1824. G. Blakiston, V; Richard Scott and Benjamin Minton, CWs.

1828. G. Blackiston, V; George Belliss and James Teece, CWs.

1832. William Jones, minister; Thomas Evans and Samuel Onions, CWs.

1836. Henry Pickstock, CW.

1841*. William Jones, V; Richard Smith and Thomas Cotton, CWs.
Vicarage house with drawing room, dining room, study, 2 kitchens, pantry,
cellars, 4 bedrooms, 2 dressing rooms or closets, 4 garrets on the 2nd floor,
stables, saddle room, coach house, cow house and yard and close 1½ acres.
Land: house, garden and churchyard in Baschurch 3 a., allotment of 3 a. on
Baggymore in Stanwardine in the Fields, allotment of 1 a. on Baggymore
in Stanwardine in the Wood, allotment of 2½ a. on Baggymore in Weston.
The proprietors of the great tithe repair the chancel; it is in good repair.

---

[1] The Baschurch 1783 terrier is filed with the bishop's transcripts (LRO, B/V/7/1).

Part 1 (Abdon to Llanfair Waterdine)

Plate: 3 cups or goblets, large plate, and 2 smaller plates, all of silver. The registers are in an iron chest provided by the parish.

Benefactions (on tablets in the chancel): Thomas Baker of Sweeney left £4 p.a. rent charge, Revd J. Barnett £20 and Thomas Battersby £30 for the poor; Eleanor Harris left lands in Stanwardine in the Fields and Weston Lullingfields to found a charity school for poor children; Edward Tomkiss left £100, the interest to be spent on 6d loaves to be distributed at Christmas and Easter; Thomas Presland of Walford Esq. £20; Richard Watkins of Prescott Esq. £20; Mrs Sarah Atcherley £30; Mrs Elizabeth Waring of Shrewsbury £20, the interest to be given on the Sunday before Christmas to the poor of Eyton township; Joseph Mucklestone of Prescott Esq. left £50, the interest being for the poor at Christmas.

14 Aug. 1845. William Jones, V; Richard Smith, CW.

Land: 3 a. allotment on Baggymore in Stanwardine in the Fields, ¾ a. allotment on Baggymore in Stanwardine Wood, 2½ a. allotment on Baggymore in Weston, 4 a. allotment on Baggymore in Bagley in Hordley parish, these being leased; also 32½ a. in the fields of Little Ness in the hands of the vicar.

The vicarial tithes of Yeaton, Walford, Prescott, Eyton and Fenemere have been commuted for £100, of Baschurch, Newtown, Boreatton, Birch and Newhouse for £101 0s 5d, of Weston, Stanwardine in the Wood and Stanwardine in the Fields for £85 and of Little Ness for £35; two-thirds of the small tithes of Noneley in Loppington parish have been commuted for £12 6s; two-thirds of the small tithes of Bagley, Hordley are not commuted but are worth c. £12.

The poor rate and the highway rate are paid by the incumbent and also interest on instalments due on £605 11s obtained from QAB for repairs and additions to the vicarage house.

24 July 1849. William Jones, V; William Matthews, CW.

Two-thirds of the small tithes of Bagley in Hordley parish have been valued at £16.

Fees: churching 1s, burials 1s, marriage 5s, banns 1s 2d, funeral sermon 10s, vault £5, gravestone £1 1s, headstone 10s 6d.

27 July 1853. William Jones, V; Edward Birch and David Vaughan, CWs.

1857. William Jones, V; John Jebbe and Edward Birch, CWs.

20 Apr. 1869*. William Jones, V.

1884*. T. Rider, V.

Good sized house with dining room, drawing room, study, kitchen, scullery, servants' hall, pantry, cellars, 5 bedrooms, 3 dressing rooms, bathroom, 4 rooms on the 2nd floor, conservatory with boiler, 2 stables with 5 stalls and a loose box, saddle room with a room over, coach house, fowl house, cow house, 2 pigsties, boot room, coal place, lumber room and garden 1½ acres.

Land: 3 a. in Stanwardine in the Fields, 2 fields each of 1 a. in Weston Lullingfields, Mill Green 1 a., Bagley Marsh in Hordley 4 a.

Tithes are commuted for £346.

Income: £42 from the Eccl. Com.; 32 a. of glebe at Little Ness was sold in
1884 to Alfred Darby for £1,500 which was invested with the Eccl. Com.
Fees are voluntary except for 6d for the clerk, burial 4s, marriage 7s 6d,
banns 1s 6d, vault £3, reopening a vault £1 10s, gravestone £1 1s,
headstone 10s 6d; average receipts £4 p.a.
Plate at Baschurch: silver chalice, flagon and alms tray, a silver gilt and a
pewter paten.
Plate at Little Ness: silver gilt chalice, silver gilt and amethyst chalice, 2
silver gilt patens, silver flagon, and plated brass alms tray. [Full details of
age and size].
Benefactions: Eleanor Harris in 1720 gave lands at present let for
£399 13s 8d p.a. to endow the school [schedule of lands]; Baker Charity
£4 charged on the Sweeney estate for the poor; the Edwards' bequest of
£200 is invested in the Mersey Docks and the interest given to 4 farm labourers being churchmen of good character with garden and dwellings
neatly kept. [Other small bequests].

Battlefield

4 Apr. 1694. Roger Eddows, C; Robert [?]Rider, CW.
There is no house or land.
Tithe is due on wool and lambs in kind and the 10th goose or pig if there are
7 or more; 1½d is due for every cow and calf, 1d per barren beast, the late
minister gathered all the tithe of grain and corn by gift of the patron, but
the present minister is paid by the patron who gathers these tithes.
Offerings: 6d for man and wife at Easter, 2d for smoke and garden, 2d for a
single person over 16 years.
Surplice fees: burial 1s, baptism and churching 1s, marriage with banns
2s 6d, marriage by licence 5s.
26 Apr. 1699. Roger Eddows, C; Andrew Reynolds and John Simmonds,
CWs.
There is no parsonage house or tithes in kind.
The king pays £3 p.a. to the minister but deducts 7s 6d p.a. which he
demands as a fee; Roger Corbett of Albright Hussey Esq. 'spontaneously
and for the present' makes up the king's allowance to £10.
21 Oct. 1701. Roger Eddows, C; Thomas France, CW.
Fees: burial in the churchyard with coffin 1s, without coffin 6d, in the church
with coffin 2s, without 1s.
12 June 1705. Roger Eddows, C; Joseph Roberts, CW.
23 July 1718. Roger Eddows, C; William Young, CW.
Clerk's wages: 10s p.a. paid by the CWs.
The impropriator for some years past has given £12 p.a. to the minister, but
at his pleasure.
5 July 1722. Roger Eddows, C; Thomas Young, CW.
7 July 1726. Roger Eddows, C; Thomas France, CW.

Part 1 (Abdon to Llanfair Waterdine)

1733. Richard Phillips, C; Thomas France, CW.

1736. Richard Phillips, C; William Young, CW.

1 Sep. 1739. Richard Phillips, C; William Young, CW.

18 Sep. 1742. Richard Phillips, C; William Young, CW.
The Queen's Bounty was annexed last year.

10 Sep. 1745. Richard Phillips, C; Richard France, CW.
There are no Easter dues.

14 Sep. 1748. Richard Phillips, C; Robert Leigh, CW.
The patron, John Corbett Esq., gives £12. 5% interest, £2, is due on £200 from the Queen's Bounty.

21 Sep. 1752. Leonard Hotchkis, C; Robert Leigh, CW.
Interest on £400 is paid to the curate by the governors of QAB who have twice augmented his salary; in December last £200 more was paid to the governors by J. Corbett Esq., impropriator and parson and £200 by John Windsor of Shrewsbury in conjunction with the governors.

14 Sep. 1756. Leonard Hotchkis, minister.
£3 from the Crown is paid by the Auditor of Land Revenue who 'unreasonably' deducts 7s 6d out of this.
Land: one farm in Sutton, West Felton is let at £40 p.a. and another for £2 p.a. (6s 8d chief rent is due to Lord Craven), a farm at Llanfyllin, Montgomeryshire was leased in 1752 for 21 years at £5 10s p.a.; these three estates were purchased for £1,200 in 1745 by the governors of the Bounty, being 2 lots by the Bounty £400, John Corbett £200 and £100 from him in the name of his agent Mr Windsor, £100 from Leonard Hotchkis and £400 from the Bounty on account of the benefactions.

Sep. 1767. Leonard Hotchkis, C; Richard Higginson, CW.

Sep. 1772. Robert Leigh, C.

Aug. 1787. Edward Kynaston, minister; John Moreton, CW.

8 Sep. 1792. Edward Williams, minister; Henry Leigh, CW.
[Parish register 15 June 1787–8 Sep. 1792].

5 Aug. 1824. Edward Williams, minister; Edward Webster, CW.
Land: farm of 147 a. with house and cottage; estate of 29 a. and a house near Llanfyllin.

7 Aug. 1828. Edward Williams, minister; John Walmsley, CW.

6 Sep. 1836. John Hopkins, minister; John Walmsley, CW.
Land: farm and 2 cottages at Whixall had by exchange with William Owen Esq. in 1829 for Sutton, West Felton leased for £200 p.a.; estate at Llanfyllin called the Pant leased for £25 p.a.
[Copy of 1718 terrier included].

7 Sep. 1841. John Hopkins, minister; John Moreton, CW.
Clerk's salary £2 p.a.
Plate: silver paten, 2 silver cups and metal flagon.

Benefactions: £50 legacy [no details], the interest being distributed to the poor.

14 Aug. 1845. John Hopkins, perpertual curate; John Moreton, CW.
The chancel is repaired by the patron, Mrs Corbet of Sundorne Castle.
Surplice fees: marriage by licence 5s, marriage by banns 2s 6d, publishing banns 1s, certificate of marriage 6d, burial in churchyard 1s 6d, burial in church 2s 6d, churching 1s.
Clerk's fees: marriage by licence 2s 6d, marriage by banns 2s 6d, burial 1s 6d, grave and bell 1s 6d, banns 6d, baptism 6d.
Benefactions: details of £50 legacy are in the register; there is no public record in the church.

24 July 1849. John Hopkins, perpetual curate; Edward Moreton, CW.

1884*.
House with 10 rooms, stable, cow house, coach house and 2 pigsties; 3 a. surrounding the house is rented for the nominal sum of £2 p.a. from the owner, Revd J. D. Corbet of Sundorne Castle.
Land: farm with house, stable, granary, shed, turnip house, 2 cart houses, 3 cow houses, barn and 4 pigsties at Whixall 152 a. leased.
Income: tithe rent charge £26; pension of £2 11s 2d; QAB £32; fees average p.a. 16s.
Schedule of registers from 1665.
Plate: 2 silver chalices, silver paten and silver flagon.
Benefactions: a sum in Lloyd's Bank yields £1 13s 9d p.a. for the poor; £56 1s 1d left by Richard Winnall yields £1 16s p.a., 1 guinea of which is for the vicar for a sermon on 17 July in memory of the testator's mother.

Bayston Hill[1]

1884*.
House, garden and adjoining field *c*. 2 a.
Land: 54½ a. in the angle between Lyth Hill and the road to Lythwood Hall.
Income: Eccl. Com. £59; fees averaging £1 10s p.a.; £320 is invested in the Midland Railway Co. and £60 in the North British Railway Co.
Registers from 1846.
Plate: 2 silver chalices and 2 silver patens.
Benefactions: £76 5s 11d in the Savings Bank for repairs of the church and churchyard; £1,500 invested for the school; £300 invested for the poor.

Beckbury[2]

n.d. [?1589]. William Stringer and Richard Rudge, CWs.
Mr Grey of Enville is reputed patron.

---

[1] Bayston Hill ecclesiastical parish was formed from parts of the parishes of St Julian, Shrewsbury and Condover in 1844: *Kelly's directory of Shropshire* (1891), 263.
[2] Beckbury was transferred from Hereford to Lichfield diocese in 1905: *Victoria history of Shropshire*, ii. 1.

Part 1 (Abdon to Llanfair Waterdine)

House of 2 bays with barn 2½ bays and sheepcote 1 bay.
Land: 16 a. of arable and 2 yards of *c.* ½ a.; common for 50 sheep, some young beasts and little horses.

18 June 1607. Dr Thomas Gwillim; John Jones and Francis Smeth, CWs.
Land: 10 a.

Bedstone

1589. Griffith Tayler and John . . ., CWs.
Rowland Barker, Robert Ireland and Rowland Jenins are patrons.
Land: 2 a. arable in North F., leasows of 4 a. and 2 a., 2 leasows of 1 a. and 4 a. at Marsh, 1½ a. arable in South field. [More details about the land and bounds are given, but the document is damaged].
Tithes: [document damaged].

8 Dec. 1604. Thomas Ellies, minister; William Wacklen and Griffith Tayler.
Small house of 3 bays with old ox house adjoining, old barn and sheep cote, garden and orchard.
Land: enclosed lands being Lat Oaks 2 a., Stocken 2 a., Hollonbroke L. 2 a., Meare L. 2½ a. and The Acre; 5 a. arable in North F. and 3 a. enclosed in the same, Dunstall in West F. 4 a., Twenty Ridges in South F. 9 a. [bounds].

1634. George Lloyd, R; Charles Wacklen and Edward Spencer.
House of 4 bays with barn 4 bays with a cutt end which this rector has built, cow house 2 bays with a cutt end and a little room built near the N. side under the eaves, hay house 2 bays, garden, fold and backside.
Land: enclosed pastures in North F. being Hollowbrook L. 3 a., another adjoining, 2 a., New L. 2 a., Oaks 1½ a., Royall 1 a., furlong of arable in the open field 3 a.; enclosed arable in South F. alias Mussell F. being Stockin 2 a. and Parsons Acre. open arable at Mussell Brook 2½ a., furlong of arable called Dunshill 3 a. in West F., Sandpits 2 a. [bounds].
All tithes belong to the rectory, also the tithe of grounds called Broomes, Sheepfield, Mathews fields and Royals reputed to be in Leintwardine; 4d is due for every Welsh cow depasturing in these grounds in summer, 1½d for every farrow cow, and the whole tithes of wool and lambs for sheep wintered there.

n.d. [early 19th century]†. [No signatories].
House with barn, stable and cowhouse.
Land: Lower Hollowbrook 2½ a., Middle Hollowbrook 4 a., Adleymore Acre 1 a., Marsh F. 3 a., all arable; Hopton M. 4½ a., Upper Hollowbrook and Tine Acre meadow and pasture 4½ a., Crosier 2 a., Stocks M. 2½ a., Harry M. and Dunstall 4 a., Mirrall M. 3 a., barn yard and butts 3½ a., Hodges Close 2 a., garden 1 a.; total 39 a. worth £105 2s 10d p.a.; Royals was given up in exchange with Mr Bennett for Hodges Close in front of the house; all should be permanent pasture and if let to the different occupiers of the land adjoining, the glebe would be advantageous to the incumbent; Cwm Coldbach Farm, Mainstone being old enclosed land 67 a., 20 a.

allotted by enclosure and freehold 11 a. with unlimited right of common on Clun Forest is let for £90 p.a. by lease due to expire in 1822; the timber on the lands is valued at £95.

Schedule of tithes [with names and payments due]; total £102 2s.

With deductions for the poor rate of £4, visitation fees 10s and assessed taxes £9 1s 6d the net value of the living is £284 2s 6½d.

Benthall[1]

n.d. [?1589]. Raffe More, Thomas Trump, CWs.

The queen is patron.

Land: 30 a. of glebe, taken by jury for the queen's use 'by what title we know not'; no commons or privileges are known.

Berrington[2]

1 Oct. 1685. [John Hughes, R] Richard Blakeway and Richard Maddocke, CWs.

House and outbuildings of 11 bays with 2 gardens, orchard and backside.

Land: Hawthorn L. 2 a., meadow 1 a., furlong in Mill F. adjoining the highway to the mill 2–3 a., another furlong in the same 3 a., 4 butts in Church F. ½ a., 2 furlongs in the same, Crowsmore Fur. in the same 1 a., Crabtree Fur. 2 a. [bounds].

21 July 1693. John Hughes, parson; Thomas Davies and Thomas Wareing, CWs.

House with 2 barns, yard, hemp butt, 2 gardens and orchard, all contiguous.

Land: Brickhill M., Hawthorn L., Park L., 20 strikes sowing in Church F., 1 strike sowing in Cross F., 2 strikes in Wheatall Bank, 16 strikes in Mill F.

1730. [John Lloyd, R] Richard Rider and William Edwards, CWs. [8 other signatories].

House of 4 bays with outbuildings 7 bays, orchard and backside 2 a.

Land: Hawthorn L. 6 a., Oaks 2 a., Churchpitt M. 1 a., land in Church F.

Tithes: Cantlop is all tithable to the rector; in Eaton the rector has one-third, the impropriator the rest; in Brompton and Betton certain [named] properties only are tithable; lambs are due at 10, or 7 when the rector pays 1½d.

Easter duties: master, mistress, son or daughter 2d, manservant 4d, maidservant 3d (unless born in the parish when it is 2d), Welsh cow 1d, calf ½d, garden 1d, house 1d, colt 3d, bees if killed or put down 3d, tradesman 6d for his hand or trade; in Betton 1d is due for hay that grows in stall meadowing; Cantlop Mill pays 6s 8d.

---

[1] Benthall was a chapelry of Much Wenlock and was slow to become fully independent: *A History of Shropshire*, x, ed. G. C. Baugh (*The Victoria history of the counties of England*, 1999), 255.

[2] Berrington was transferred from Lichfield to Hereford diocese in 1905: *Victoria history of Shropshire*, ii. 1.

Part 1 (Abdon to Llanfair Waterdine)

Surplice fees: marriage by banns 1s 2d, publishing banns 1s, burial 6d, registering 4d, churching 6d.
The rector provides bread and wine at Easter and a feast on Easter Monday for the parishioners.

1733. [John Lloyd, R] John Maddocks and Richard Kilvart, CWs. [13 other signatories].
Land: Church Hill M. 1 a., Hawthorn L. 6 a., Oaks 2 a., Church Pitt M. 1 a., parcels of 2 a., 4 a., 2 a., 4 a., 1 a., and ½ a. in Church F., 1½ a. in Atcham F. and 1 a. in Wheatall F.

23 Oct. 1736. [John Lloyd, R] Richard Bromley and Edward Bennet, CWs.
[The tithable lands in Betton and Brompton are described in great detail].
Small tithes: lambs and wool except in Eaton where they are divided between the rector and the impropriator; pigs are due except a gilt or sow in its first 'faith'; 2 eggs are due per hen or duck and 3 for a cock or drake.
Clerk's fees and wages: every inhabitant pays from 2d to 6d, graves 6d, attending the clock 10s, 2d cake for baptisms.

1739. [John Lloyd, R] William Rider and Jonas Rudge, CWs. [9 other signatories].

18 Sep. 1742. [John Lloyd, R] Thomas Whitefoot and Samuel Meire, CWs.

n.d. [?1745]. [Daniel Austin, R] Thomas Houghton and John Dale, CWs.

1752. Daniel Austin, R; Edward Snaxton and Thomas Calcott, CWs. [6 other signatories].

1756. Thomas Kilvart and William Bromley, CWs. [9 other signatories].

21 Sep. 1759. Daniel Austin, R; John Waring, John Cleaton, CWs.

1763. [Daniel Austin, R].

1767. Daniel Austin, R; Samuel Meire and Thomas Horton, CWs.

1772. [Daniel Austin, R] John Hoggins, CW.

18 Aug. 1775. [Daniel Austin, R] Richard Calcott, CW.

1779. [Daniel Austin, R] James Rider and Abraham Beddow, CWs.

1783. Daniel Austin, R; Edward Ditcher, CW.

1787. Rowland Chambre, R; Andrew Davies and Edward Clark, CWs.

1792. [Rowland Chambre, R] John Ditcher and John Wigley, CWs.

25 July 1797. G[eorge] Scott, R; John Meire and Daniel Onions, CWs.

1801. [Hon. Richard Noel-Hill, R] Joseph Calcott and John Wigley, CWs.

1805. Richard Noel-Hill, R; John Elsmere and Thomas Harris, CWs.

25 Mar. 1805.
Mortgage to raise £800 for a new rectory house under the act of 17 Geo. III[1] signed by the Bishop of Lichfield, Lord Berwick and Richard Hill.

---

[1] Clergy Residence Repairs Act, 1776 (sometimes known as Gilbert's Act), 17 Geo. III, cap. 53.

Declaration by Joseph Bromfield, architect 22 Feb. 1804 that the rectory house being mostly made of timber is so decayed it would be better to take it down and rebuild at an estimated cost of £2,300.
Letter of permission from Bishop of Lichfield.
Coloured elevations of the new house and a plan of the ground floor.

1810. Richard Noel-Hill, R; Edward Ditcher and John Langford, CWs.

1824. Richard Noel- Hill, R; John Elsmere and Edward Pugh, CWs.

1828. [Richard Noel-Hill, R] John Dixon and Timothy Ditcher, CWs.

1832. Richard Noel-Hill, R.

1835. [Richard Noel-Hill, R] Thomas Poole and Thomas Whitfield, CWs.

1836. [Richard Noel-Hill, R] John Elsmere and Richard Lawrence, CWs.

7 Sep. 1841. Richard Noel-Hill, R; Edward Ditcher, CW.
The repair of the chancel belongs to the rector and is in a good state.
Communion plate; cup and paten of silver and pewter dish. There are 2 chests in the church, 1 of iron in which the registers are kept.
Benefactions: in 1631 John Smith of Withington left £1 charged on 3 pieces of land in Withington to be paid half-yearly to 10 of the poorest households; in 1723 Richard Wellings of Berrington left £20, the interest to be yearly distributed to the poor; Mrs Margaret Thomas left £6, the interest to be used to buy bibles for poor children.

18 Aug. 1845. Berwick [Hon. Thomas Noel-Hill], R; Thomas Poole, CW.
Rectorial tithes have been commuted for £526; the Earl of Liverpool of Pitchford Hall has £28 13s and Richard Williams of Eaton Mascott Esq. £45.

1849. T[homas] Noel Hill, R; Thomas Elsmere and Samuel Meire, CWs.
[Land, house and tithes described as in earlier terriers, though house rebuilt and tithes commuted].

1884*. George S. Flack, R.
House with 2 drawing rooms, dining room, library, kitchen, butler's pantry, still room, school room, servants' hall, larder, scullery on the ground floor, 4 bedrooms, 3 dressing rooms on the 1st floor, 6 bedrooms on another floor, 3 attics on the 2nd floor, 3 bedrooms over the stables, stables, coach house, granary, workshop, dairy, brew house, 2 greenhouses and gardener's cottage.
26 a. glebe land.
Income: tithe rent charge £546; fees £3 p.a. average.
Schedule of registers from 1559.
Plate: 2 silver chalices, 2 silver patens, 1 silver flagon, 1 pewter and 1 brass alms dish.
Benefactions: John Smith of Withington left £1 charged on Leeberries, Green Bank and Loppet in Withington for the poorest housekeepers; Richard Wellings in 1753 left £20, the interest for the poor; Mrs Margaret Thompson left £6, the interest to be spent on bibles for poor children.

Part 1 (Abdon to Llanfair Waterdine)
Betton Strange[1]

1884†.
There is no house, land or tithes.
£31 p.a. is paid by QAB.
Schedule of registers.
Plate: silver chalice and paten, electro-plated flagon and wooden alms basin.
No charities.

Bettws y Crwyn

n.d. [late 16th/early 17th century]. Thomas Hanley, parson; Richard Yssmore and Roger Broke, CWs.
There is no glebe land.

Bicton[2]

7 Sep. 1841*. William Sandford, minister.
The chapel is in the parish of St Chad, Shrewsbury.
Land: small cottage and 57 a. at Cyffronydd, Welshpool let for £30 p.a.
Income: rent charge of £5 on the Onslow estate paid by John Wingfield Esq., rent charge of 10s on lands in Bicton paid by John Strange; £3 10s paid to the minister by the CWs of St Chads; interest on money from QAB and parliamentary grant of £20 5s 2d; total £59 5s 2d.

14 Aug. 1845. Humphrey Sandford, perpetual curate; R. Blakemore, CW.
The incumbent receives £17 4s being interest on £430 received for the sale of timber at Cyffronydd; interest of £13 p.a. is paid on a royal bounty of £400 and £7 5s 2d on a parliamentary grant of £242 3s.
Plate: plate and 2 sacrament cups of silver.
Benefactions: £6 p.a. was left by Mr Taylor for bread for the poor; £1 being part of Gabriel Rogers's bequest is payable by the CWs of St Chads for bread for the poor, the rest, £4, is payable to the minister; Revd Humphrey Sandford has £54 in his hands left to the poor by his late uncle Edward Sandford.

1884*.
Income: a legacy of J. Fownes charged on the Onslow estate yields £3 18s; Gabriel Rogers's legacy yields £2 1s 2d and is paid by the CWs of St Chad's, Shrewsbury; Eccl. Com. £132 14s 6d; QAB £26 5s 2d; fees averaging *c.* £6 p.a.
Registers from 1853.
Plate: 2 chalices and 1 paten, all of silver.
Benefactions for the school: Mrs Wingfield of Onslow gave £12 2s 4d p.a.

---

[1] Betton Strange ecclesiastical parish was formed from part of the parish of St Chad, Shrewsbury in 1860: *Kelly's directory of Shropshire* (1891), 265. In 1929 it was transferred from Lichfield diocese to Hereford: *Victoria history of Shropshire*, ii. 1.

[2] Bicton parish was formed from parts of the parishes of St Alkmund and St Chad, Shrewsbury in 1853: *Kelly's directory of Shropshire* (1891), 266.

Benefactions for the poor: rent charge of £6 p.a. charged on lands at Bicton to be spent on bread; Gabriel Rogers gave £100 security for the late house of industry and this yields £1 for bread; the interest on £400 in consols is spent on bread in St Chad's, Frankwell, Bicton and Oxon.

Billingsley

n.d. [?1589]. Thomas Rea and John Rea, CWs.
Thomas Aston of Aston, Esq. is patron.
Land: 8 a. of arable and pasture, 1 a. of meadow.

1607. John Burton, clerk; Thomas Burnell, Edward Rea, John Smithes.
Parsonage house, barn and garden S. of the house.
Land: L. at the Brook W. of the church 2 a., 2 little pastures 3 a., little pasture called Fishpole F. 1½ a., New Tining ½ a., pasture at Little Yeate 2 a. [bounds].
Tithes of corn and hay are due and Easter duties.

12 Feb. 1636/7. Ralph Hyde, R; William Wyer and Thomas Walters, CWs.
House of 3 bays with barn 3 bays and stable.
Land: Lower Cook Yard 1½ a., parcel adjoining 3 a. allotted to the glebe by exchange for a parcel now part of Harps L., 3 pastures adjoining the parsonage house on the NW. 8 a., orchard, 2 gardens adjoining [bounds].
Tithes of corn and hay and all small tithes are due.
Memorandum by Ralph Hide: the exchanges were made by the last incumbent, Mr Burton.

Bishops Castle

1 July 1607. [Walter Stephens, V] Edward Thomas, bailiff; Henry Boole and Rowland Gwilliam, CWs. [11 other signatories].
House with barn 3 bays, stable, garden, cow house and hay barn.
Land: 12 a., being 9 a. arable in 14 parcels in Novers F., 2½ a. in 3 parcels in Hope F. and ½ a. in Hurlemynd F. [bounds]; 1s p.a. rent is due to the vicar for 3 parcels in Woodbach Bryn and a meese place by the toll board.

Bitterley

1589. John Fraunse and Walter Bowhouse, CWs.
Henry Anders is patron.
House and barn.
Land: pasture called Hendles Hill, 7 days' math of meadow in 4 parcels *c.* 14 a., 31 a. arable in the common fields, further 19–20 a. with a barn [bounds], common of the fallow of the town.
All tithes are due from Bitterley, Hilluppencott, Snitton and Henley; £1 p.a. and personal oblations from Cleeton; the 3rd sheaf, privy tithe and oblations from Middleton; 6s 8d from Ledwyche; the tithe of a farm called Aston and another called Court of Upper Bitterley.

32

Part 1 *(Abdon to Llanfair Waterdine)*
Bolas Magna

16 Oct. 1612. Roger Bendbowe, parson; Thomas Brooke and Fowke Sockett, CWs.

Parsonage house of 3 bays and about 6 yd. in breadth with stable, barn 4 bays with a shore for a cow house, ox house and sheepcote 3 bays, bake house 1½ bays with an oven and kiln; 2 little gardens on the street and a yard or backside of *c.* 2½ a.

Land in Bolas: Fourde M. with the River Tern on the N., dole of meadow below the parsonage house known as Parson's Ford M., little pieces called the Parson's Hooks with the River Meese on the W. *c.* 2 a., pasture called New L. in Heath Marsh F. 4 a., little pasture in Old F. 2½ a., strips of arable in Heath Marsh F., Cross Hill F. and Nobridge F., Bolas.

Land in Meeson: 2 little butts in Marsh F., little pasture in Bridge F., 1 a. in Red Marl Pitt F., cottage of 1 bay with barn and backside [bounds].

Tithes: all tithes and oblations in Bolas and Meeson are due to the rectory.

4 Oct. 1635. Isaac Martin,[1] R; Michael Walker, Richard Dios, CWs.

Parsonage house of 2 bays 'floored over head' with 2 bays of cross building floored over and with 2 shores, 2 gardens and little hemp butt next to the bake house, bake house with oven and kiln floored over-head, barn near the river with 3 bays and shore, 2 barns 3 bays, ox house with a shore to tie cattle in and bing in between; cottage 2 bays with dwelling house, chamber, barn for corn, orchard and backside of about 1 old strike seedness.

Land: 8 parcels of arable in Nobridge F., 2 parcels in Mill F., 5 parcels in Cross Hill F., 2 in Meeson Further F.; enclosed ground being a backside of 10 new strikes seedness of rye with a dole of meadow, leasow towards Meeson L. of 18 new strikes seedness of rye, Ox L. of 7 new strikes seed-ness of rye and little croft at Meeson Bridge of 1 old strike; meadows being Ford M. by the River Tern beyond Little Bolas bridge, Homes M. beyond the River Tern, 2 little meadows called Hooks, both of 1 day's math by the River Meese [bounds]; the rector has free liberty of commons for sheep and turves for the fire on Bolas Heath like the other freeholders.

Tithes are due on corn, hay, wool, lambs, hemp, flax, pigs, geese, apples and pears, all in kind except calves.

The Easter Book is paid according to custom 'as some suppose'.

'If anyone . . . claims any Butt or Lands exprest in this Terrier under pretence that they have formerly belonged to other livings in Bolas and were other mens lands, yt binn known that the Rectorie enioyeth those Lands by an exchange made long agoe in the Time of the former Incumbent and those parties had full satisfaction out of the auncient glebe for them and therefore cannot be taken away without manifest token of sacriledge, the auncient Church grounde being nowe not certainly knowne. And we doe nott doubt but the curse of god will pursue that man to the utter extirpation of him

---

[1] Isaac Martin was ejected from Bolas Magna in 1650 for refusing to sign the Covenant: introduction to the printed parish register (Shropshire Parish Register Soc. 1912).

and his posterity for ever whosoever shall attempt to do it. Sic faxit Deus Amen'.

25 Aug. 1682. John Tourneour, R.
Parsonage house of 3 bays situated W. of the church with bake house N. of the house, 8 bays of other building S. of the house, yard below the house with the River Tern on the W.
Land: Barn L. with the River Tern on the W. and a lane on the E., a meadow beyond the river and another on the same side as the church, a garden between the house and the church.
There are 2 townships in the parish—Bolas and Meeson.
Tithes: Bolas and Meeson both pay all tithes in kind.

20 Sep. 1689. John Tourneour, R.
Parsonage house is a large, ancient house of 4 bays W. of the church with barn and stable 5 bays W. of the house, 4 bays of other building S. of the house, bake house 1 bay N. of the house, 1 little garden to the W. and 1 to the N. between the house and the bake house yard with the river on the W.
Land: Barn L. with the river on the W., Cliff L., a meadow beyond the river, meadow on this side of the river, Mill L., cottage belonging to the rectory with the street to W. and N.

12 Sep. 1693. John Tourneour, R.
Parsonage house: the house and outbuildings are in good repair.

17 Aug. 1698. John Tourneour, R; William Smith, Walter Key, CWs. [6 other signatories].
Parsonage house of 4 bays with barn 5 small bays, hay barn 2 small bays with cow house for 12 cows and bing under the same roof, small stable for 4–5 horses, coal house for 8–9 stacks of coal, bake house for baking and malt kiln for drying 10 strikes of malt and 'withering'[1] floor; small house in Bolas with dwelling room and 2 small lodging chambers on the ground floor and small hovel at the end for fuel.
Land: churchyard, garden and fold yard, well yard with the River Tern to N., together 7 a., Barn Close W. of the well yard 8 a., Cliffe L. SW. of Barn Close 5½ a., Mill L. with the River Meese to the S. 8½ a., 1 butt by Nobridge Lane ½ a., Upper M. with the River Tern to the W. 2½ a., Lesser M. 2½ a., yard belonging to the cottage ½ a., Bridge Lane ½ a.; total 38 a. [bounds].
Tithes are due in kind, there is no modus except on calves and colts, the rector having only 1½d per cow and calf, 1d for a barren cow and 3d for a colt; pigs, geese and lambs are due at 7 with 1½d for odd lambs between 7 and 10. At Easter every house or cottage pays 6d or 4d per house and 2d per garden.
Surplice fees: 8d per marriage after banns and 5s after a licence, 10s per funeral sermon, 4d per burial or churching, baptisms nothing.

---

[1] 'Withering' meant drying (*O.E.D.*); the 'withering floor' was the second floor of a malthouse where the malt was dried before being put in the kiln.

Part 1 *(Abdon to Llanfair Waterdine)*

Clerk's wages: customary, being 4d from every living with a plough land and 2d per cottage; fees: 1s per wedding after banns and 2s 6d after a licence, 1s for making a grave in the church or chancel, 6d for making a grave in the churchyard if it is a coffin grave or otherwise 4d, 1s for the passing bell.

1701†. [Copy made 1865]. John Tourneor, R; Thomas Betteley and John Wild, CWs.

7 July 1722. John Tourneour, R; William Smith and Thomas Walker, CWs. Clerk's wages: £1 10s p.a.

6 July 1726. John Tourneour, R; Thomas James and Richard Whittingham, CWs.

29 Aug. 1730. John Tourneour, R; John Walker and Thomas Walker, CWs.

9 Aug. 1733. John Tourneor, R; Philip Heaynes and John Eddows, CWs.

15 July 1736. John Tourneor, R; Benjamin Bettely and Thomas Walker, CWs.

21 Nov. 1739. John Tourneor, R; Thomas Hitchins and Thomas Growcock, CWs.

17 Sep. 1742. Thomas Griffith, R; Thomas Walker and John Eddows, CWs.

10 Sep. 1745. Benjamin Wase, sequestrator; Thomas Picken and Thomas Growcock, CWs.

9 Aug. 1748. Benjamin Wase, R; John Massey and Thomas Walker, CWs.

1 Aug. 1752. Benjamin Wase, R; John Eddows and Thomas Growcock, CWs.

16 Sep. 1756. Benjamin Wase, R; George Bate and Thomas Bladen, CWs.

n.d. [probably 1759]. Borlase Wingfield, R; John Walker and Thomas Growcock, CWs.
[Folded inside is a visitation return for Lilleshall 14 Aug. 1759].

6 Sep. 1763. Thomas Griffith, R; Thomas Smith and John Slack, CWs.

15 Sep. 1767. Borlase Wingfield, C; Thomas Growcock and Robert Eddows, CWs.

7 Sep. 1772. Borlase Wingfield, C; [CWs' names illegible].

21 Aug. 1775. R. Morgan, C; Thomas Growcock and Thomas Betteley, CWs.

6 Sep. 1779. Creswell Tayleur, C; John Slack and Joseph Slack, CWs.

4 Aug. 1783. Creswell Tayleur, C; Thomas Betteley, CW.

6 Aug. 1787. Creswell Tayleur, C; John Slack and Joseph Slack, CWs.

23 Oct. 1792. Creswell Tayleur, C; John Walker and John Growcock, CWs.

24 July 1797. Robert W. Hill, C; R. Rogers, CW.

26 Aug. 1801. Robert W. Hill, minister; John Preston and John Growcock, CWs.

1 July 1805. Robert W. Hill, minister; Edward Austin and Samuel Minor, CWs.

25 Mar. 1810. Edward Scott Dickenson, minister; Joseph Slack and John Arkinstall, CWs.

6 July 1824*. Edward Scott Dickenson, minister; Samuel Bodenham, CW.

1830*. Robert W. Hill, R; Samuel Slack, CW.
Parsonage house is in the occupation of Mrs Mary Slack.
Land: garden ½ a., Well Yard 7 a., Barn Yard 8 a., Cliffe L. 5½ a., Mill L. 8½ a., butt by Nobridge Lane ½ a., Upper M. 2½ a., Lower M. 2½ a., allotment of 12 a. on Bolas Heath, all in the occupation of Thomas Taylor.

Aug. 1832. John Hill, R; John Taylor, CW.
Parsonage house leased to Thomas Taylor.

7 Sep. 1836. John Hill, R; Thomas Taylor, CW.

9 Sep. 1841. John Hill, R; Samuel . . ., CW.
Parsonage house newly erected near the church in thorough repair with stable and cow house, gardens and shrubberies.
Land: Well M. 3 a., M. 3 a., Well Yard 4 a., orchard ½ a., The Butt ½ a., Barn Yard 6½ a., Nomans Land ½ a., Lower M. 2 a., Cliff M. 6 a., Mill L. 8½ a.
Tithes have been commuted for £330 including £12 on account of the rectory glebe.
In 1836 £657 was borrowed from the governors of QAB for rebuilding the parsonage house on the usual terms; this has been regularly paid.
The repair of the chancel belongs to the rector and is in a good state.
Plate: silver chalice, paten and plate and pewter flagon. There is a good iron chest for the registers.
Clerk's wages: £2 12s p.a.
Benefactions: £20 was left in 1723 by Elizabeth Walker of Meeson to be invested and the interest given to the poor every Sunday; John Whitfield, servant of Sir Rowland Hill left £10, the interest to be distributed on St John's Day.

13 Aug. 1845. John Hill, R; Thomas Taylor, CW.

23 July 1849*. John Hill, R; John Taylor, CW.

26 July 1853. John Hill, R; William Axon, CW.

17 Apr. 1861†. [John Hill, R] Thomas Bellingham, CW.
Parsonage house; also cottage and garden in Bolas leased.
Every house and cottage pays 6d at Easter.
Fees: marriage by banns 8d, marriage by licence 5s.
Clerk's salary £2 paid by the church wardens.
Clerk's fees: marriage by banns 1s, marriage by licence 2s 6d, grave in church or chancel 1s and in the churchyard 6d, passing bell 4d.

20 Apr. 1869*. [Richard Turner, R] Thomas Growcock, CW.

1884*. [Richard Turner, R].
House with 3 sitting rooms, kitchen, back kitchen, pantry, 2 larders, coal shed, 2 privies, pigsties, adjoining this a block with 2-stalled stable, coach house, saddle room, loose box, cow house, 2 pigsties and garden 1 a.

Land: 38 a. with barn, cow shed and turnip house.
School with 4 roomed cottage held by the school committee.
Income: tithe rent charge £330, average fees p.a. 2s 4d.
Schedule of registers from 1590.
Plate: silver chalice, paten and alms dish and pewter flagon.

Boningale[1]

1733. Robert Danbrie, R; George Nock, chapelwarden.
Boningale is a chapelry belonging to the rectory of Stockton. There is no
building belonging to the chapelry.
Land: 8 a. arable in 2 pieces called Parsons Heath and Parsons Hill, 3 a.
meadow, all leased [bounds].
Tithes and Easter dues are the same as Stockton.
Clerk's fees are the same as Stockton with the addition of 6d per hour for
tolling the bell after the first hour.
Clerk's salary: 3d–6d is due from each farmer according to the quantity of
his land and 2d from each cottage.
Repairs of the chancel belong to the rector.

15 July 1736. Robert Danbrie, R; Alexander Shenton, chapelwarden.

1739. Robert Danbrie, R; John Nock and William Newton, chapelwardens.

17 Sep. 1742. Jeremiah Whitehouse, C; Thomas Watho, chapelwarden.

1745. Richard Stanley, C; John Sheinton, chapelwarden.

1748. Robert Danbrie, R; Richard Stanley, C; Richard Parsons, chapelwarden.
[Register of baptisms, marriages and burials 29 Sep. 1745–22 May 1748].

19 Sep. 1752. Robert Danbrie, R; Thomas Jellicoe, chapelwarden.

16 Sep. 1756. Richard Stanley, C; John Nock, chapelwarden.

20 Sep. 1759. Richard Stanley, C; Thomas Jellicoe, chapelwarden; Benjamin
Shenton, late chapelwarden.

1763. Richard Stanley, C; John Nock, chapelwarden.

1832. Copy of 1752.

1884*. C[harles] P. Isaac, V.
There is no house or buildings.
Land: arable fields 3½ a. and 4 a., meadows 1 a. and 2 a., all leased at
£26 7s p.a.
Income: tithe rent charge £234; average fees p.a. 5s.
Schedule of registers from 1698.
Plate: chalice and 2 patens of silver, pewter flagon and brass alms basin.
Benefactions: Littleford and Sheinton charity £30 invested by the freeholders
of the parish in building 2 cottages *c.* 1812 and 30s paid to the poor from
the rent of these; 6s 8d from Wood Farm, Donington; the total £1 16s 8d is
distributed among the industrious poor [an added note says that the 6s 8d

[1] Boningale is also included in the 1612 and 1730 terriers for Stockton.

from Wood Farm has been redeemed]; the Kidd charity pays £5 p.a. to the poor at Christmas.

Bridgnorth St Leonard[1]

18 Oct. 1803†. [Copy made in 1856]. John Williams, C; Robert Langford, Edward Gittos, CWs.

There is no parsonage house.

Curate's income: £2 5s p.a. from the Audit Court every October, £5 from the Corporation of Bridgnorth every Michaelmas, £10 p.a. from the estate of Henry Lee of Coton every Christmas; half the rent of *c*. 20 a. of land at £60 p.a. left by the will of Archdeacon Wheeler in 1687 after deducting £10 for the poor of Bridgnorth, £2 for the curate of Maisemore, Gloucs. and 10s p.a. for the poor of Willey (this 20 a. of land is in the parish of St Mary Magdalene, Bridgnorth having the turnpike from Bridgnorth to Shifnal on the N. and E. and the Severn on the W.); the bailiffs and burgesses are trustees of Archdeacon Wheeler's will which also requires a sermon on the feast of St James the Apostle; 10s from the rent of a house near the Friars is paid for a sermon 22 Jan.; William Pennell left £1 for a sermon every 21 Oct.

Land: small house called Littleton's tenement with barn, beast house, garden, orchard and 5 a. of land in Highley leased for £14 p.a.; house with beast house, garden, orchard and 15 a. of land near Old Wood Common, Tenbury leased for £15 p.a.; 9 a. near Leominster leased for £9 p.a. [bounds]; 13s 4d from an estate in Bobbington; 6s 8d from the rent of a house in Hungary St., Bridgnorth.

Fees: marriage by licence 7s 6d, by banns 5s, publishing banns 1s 6d, burial in the chancel 3s 6d, in the church 2s 6d and in the churchyard 1s (but if a pauper only 6d), churching 6d, register entry 6d, copy thereof 1s.

Clerk's fees: marriage by licence 5s, by banns 2s 6d, putting up banns 1s, burial in church or chancel 2s, in the churchyard 1s, digging the grave 1s, tolling bell 1s per hour, directing the mason opening a vault in the church or churchyard 2s, churching 6d, digging grave, tolling the bell and assisting at the funeral of a pauper 2s.

The church is an ancient building 77 ft × 65 ft excluding the chancel.

Inventory: crimson velvet cloth and cushion for the pulpit, 2 surplices, folio bible of 1717, 2 folio prayer books, 2 books of office, stone font with small earthen basin in it, 2 tables of 10 Commandments, 1 table of the Creed and 1 of the Lord's Prayer, 3 large benefaction tables, the king's coat of arms, 2 benches, organ, gallery at the W. end for the children of the charity school, old wood communion table with green cloth cover, several green cushions, 3 old kneeling forms, 1 towel, 1 napkin, flagon, chalice and 2 plates of silver, old chest, 2 large boxes, poor box, 4 shelves for bread, old book stand, 6 bells, clock and chimes and register books from 1656.

---

[1] Bridgnorth St Leonard, formerly a peculiar within the diocese of Lichfield, was transferred to Hereford diocese in 1905: *Victoria history of Shropshire*, ii. 1.

Benefactions: £5 left in 1687 by Archdeacon Wheeler for bread; £10 left by John Learn in 1691 for apprenticing children; £50 left in 1699 by Henry Bourne to buy land and use the income for bread; £100 left in 1709 by Edward Jackson to buy land and the income to be used for bread every Sunday; the interest of £25 left by Mr Guest in 1777 for bread; £10 left in 1793 by Revd Thomas Littleton of St Leonard's, Bridgnorth to be divided among poor inhabitants not receiving parish relief; £20 left in 1796 by Mr Guest jr. for bread; land at Highley leased at £28 5s for the poor in bread (this appears to have been purchased partly with legacies from Bourne and Jackson); a few years ago some timber on this land was sold for £136 and was used by the overseers of the poor; an annual rent charge of £5 on land in Bobbington is given in bread and is supposed to have been left by Mr Bennett; a house in the churchyard is let for £1 10s, a house in the High St. for £23 and a garden and pigsty adjoining Pound St. for 2s 6d.

Gifts and legacies to the almshouse, hospital, Sunday schools and Blue Coat school are listed on the benefaction tables; there are 12 almshouses funded, it is supposed, by the Corporation for 12 poor women, a hospital founded by Revd Palmer, rector of Sandy, Beds. in 1686 for 10 poor widows of St Leonard's parish, a free grammar school for the sons of burgesses, 2 Sunday schools, 1 for boys and 1 for girls and a charity school for boys of St Leonard's and St Mary's parishes.

Bromfield

n.d. [?1589]. Richard Hill, V; Thomas Wates and William Mylward, CWs.
Charles Fox of Bromfield is reputed patron.
There is no glebe or common pasture.

1622. Richard Bulkeley, V; Thomas Nash and Richard Browne, CWs [also 13 other signatories].
House with garden, backside, orchard, barn and cow house.
Land: 1 little meadow and 6 a. arable.
The vicar receives a pension of £2 13s 4d from the parson or farmer, Sir Charles Fox.

Broseley

n.d. [?1589]. Richard Langley and Edmund Wylcokes, CWs.
James Clifford is patron of Broseley and of Linley chapel.
House with barn, backside and yard.
Land: Colliers Helde L. 1½ a. and Clencheacre L. 1½ a. being former arable in the common fields of Broseley [names given for those responsible for hedging], parcels of 9, 6 and 4 ridges in East F., parcels of 2 and 2 ridges in South F., parcels of 6 and 4 ridges in West F.; total arable *c.* 8 a. [bounds].
All tithes are due.

n.d. [early 17th century]*.[1] Thomas Langley, Richard Ould, William Wilcockes.

House with barn and backside called Parson's Yard.

Land: pastures called Colliers Helde 1½ a. and Clenchacre 1½ a., 3 parcels of arable in East F. alias. Strangmarsh F., 2 parcels of arable each of 2 butts and a pasture called Birch L. being 4 butts taken out of South F. and leased by James Clifford, lord of the manor, 6 butts in Cross F. and 5 little lands in a parcel lately enclosed [bounds].

The chapel of Linley has a small parcel of meadow annexed called the Churchyard.

Broughton

29 Sep. 1693. Richard Lloyd, minister; Harry Jukes and John Price, CWs.

The minister has no house, tithes or glebe land; they are all in the hands of the impropriator, Richard Lyster Esq. who pays the minister £4 6s 8d p.a.

1698. Richard Lloyd, minister; John Newton and Richard Wodd, CWs.

Surplice fees belong to the minister: burial 1s, baptism and churching 1s, marriage 2s 6d.

1701. Thomas Clarke, minister; Thomas Cotton and John Prise, CWs.

The impropriator, Thomas Lyster, pays the minister £10 of which only £4 13s 4d is the right of the church and the rest a gift for as long as he pleases.

2 May 1705. Richard Snedley, minister; George Yeoman and George Burrey, CWs.

23 July 1718. Samuel Pearson, C; Thomas Cotton and Hugh Edwards, CWs.

1733. Richard Phillips, C; William Cotton and Thomas Yeomans, CWs.

16 July 1736. Richard Phillips, C; Thomas France, CWs.

1742. Richard Phillips, C; John Maddox and John Nichols, CWs.

£5 p.a. has been obtained from the Queen's Bounty.

14 Sep. 1748. Richard Phillips, C; Richard Hales and Edward France.

Richard Lyster, the patron, gives the minister £7 and £3 belongs to the church from time immemorial; £8 6s 8d is received from the Queen's Bounty.

There was a house for the minister but it was pulled down.

21 Sep. 1752. William Bagley, minister; Richard Hales, CW.

25 Sep. 1756. William Bagley, minister; John Freeman and Richard Cotton, CWs.

There has been a house, barn and glebe, but the minister now has only £4 6s 8d from the patron, Richard Lister, who adds £5 13s 4d of his own free gift.

---

[1] The SRRC copy (P44/F/1/1) of the early 17th-century Broseley terrier is listed as 18th-century.

Part 1 (Abdon to Llanfair Waterdine)

There is a small estate worth £6 p.a.

7 Sep. 1763. William Bagley, C; Roger Wood, CW.
There is an estate in Montgomeryshire worth *c*. £8 p.a.

14 Sep. 1767. William Bagley, minister; John Miles and Roger Wood, CWs.
The impropriator has the tithe of corn and hay.
The patron pays the minister £10 p.a.; QAB in 1718 paid by lot £200 which was used to buy an estate worth *c*. £7 p.a. in Guilsfield, Montgomeryshire.

8 Sep. 1772. William Bagley, minister; John Maddox and W. Cartwright, CWs.
A second augmentation in 1767 was invested.

22 Aug. 1775. John Miles and George Yeomans, CWs.

7 Sep. 1779. William Bagley, minister; John Miles, CW.

1783. Thomas Lyster, minister; John Miles, CW.
The minister receives £10 p.a. from a farm in Guilsfield.

1787. Richard Howell, minister; John Miles and Charles Micklewright, CWs.

8 Aug. 1828. Francis Salt, minister; John Bate, CW.
'I never saw any terrier for the parish of Broughton'.
Income: the patron pays £4 p.a., *c*. 15 a. near Welshpool is worth £15 15s p.a., 6½ a. near Wem £24 p.a. and 16½ a. at 'Bergeddin', near Welshpool £24 13s.
Surplice fees: marriage by licence 7s 6d, marriage by banns 5s, burial 1s 6d, churching and baptism 1s, in all amounting to only a few shillings p.a.

Aug. 1832. Francis Salt, incumbent; Thomas [?]Eburey, CW.
The patron, Sir Rowland Hill, pays £4 p.a.

6 Sep. 1836. Francis Salt, incumbent; Peter Bate, CW.

1857. John Wood, incumbent; John Heatley, CW.
An estate at Wern, Guilsfield is worth £33 6s 8d, one at Cae Long, Guilsfield £20 and one at Wem £14 p.a.

1884*. John Wright, V.
Income: £4 p.a. from the patron, rent from 6 a. of land near Wem and 16 a. at Bergeddin, Welshpool; fees average only a few shillings p.a.
Schedule of registers from 1708.

Bucknell

n.d. [?1589]. Christopher Mason, R; John Mason and John Davis, CWs.
John Broome is patron.
Land: arable in Knowle, Teme and Hope Fields [bounds given, but the document is torn].; the only common feeding is in the town fields.

n.d. [late 16th century]. Ambrose Cooke, V. [12 other signatories].
Two houses, 1 called the vicarage and another little house in the churchyard with 2 barns, stable, ox house, cow house, sheepcote, backside, 2 gardens.
Land: 11½ a. in 5 parcels in Teme F., *c*. 5 a. in 8 parcels in Hope F. and *c*. 10 a. in 9 parcels in Reicroft F. [bounds]; common of estover in the lord's woods.

25 May 1607. Ambrose Cook, V. [8 signatories, no office given].

Mansion house and 1 other house in the churchyard, 2 barns, backside, stable, sheepcote, ox house.

Land: *c.* 45 a. in small parcels in Crosfield, Cold Fur. and Temes F. [detailed bounds].

Tithes are due except sheaf, and hay of Coxall.

21 May 1616. John Freemantle, V; Hugh Hagley and John Paramore, old CWs; Christopher Marrett, Howell Blucke, new CWs.

House with 2 barns, stable, ox house, cow house, garden and close of ½ a., depasturing in the churchyard, ox house and garden in churchyard.

Land: pasture close called Priestshale, 4 a., 3 a. pasture, leasow of arable called Crosshealde 7 a., arable close called Cold Fur. 6 a., Vicar's Close 3 a., enclosure of 2 a., ½ a. of pasture inMeadow Heads, ½ a. arable within enclosures of other men at Adlaughton, 3 a. woodland in Adleymoor, 1 a. arable adjoining, 8½ a. arable in Hope F., 2 a. arable in Barrow F., 2 a. arable in Langley F., 2 a. arable in Knowle F., 8½ a. arable in 5 parcels in Teames F. [bounds].

Tithes: grain of all home closes, tithe hay, wool, lambs, cheese, small tithes except from the lord's wood from which the vicar has wood for burning, tithe grain of Stall M. when sown.

26 Oct. 1639. Francis Couser and William Davies, CWs; there is no vicar or curate.

Old house with 2 barns, garden and backside near the churchyard, new house with buttery and garden.

Land: Priesthale meadow or pasture, parcels of 5 a. and 2 a., Cubleys Bank 2 a., Crossheld 3 a., pasture called Marsh F. 2 a., Could Fur. pasture 5 a., Deyside Acre 1 a., Hore 2 a., pasture of 2 a., Two Acres, 8 a. arable in 3 parcels in Teme F., 3½ a. in Hayes F., 5½ a. in 3 parcels in Mark F., 4 a. in Knowle F. [bounds].

Tithes of geese, pigs, wool, lambs, hemp, flax and cheese are due.

Buildwas

4 Aug. 1857. William Thorp, C; William Lewis, CW.

¾ a. glebe and cottage, rent £16 2s 6d.

Surplice fees and Easter roll amount to *c.* £3 p.a.

1884*. Henry Graham, V.

There is no parsonage house, but a double cottage with garden, coach house and stables belongs to the vicarage, half the garden is held by the vicar and half leased.

Income: £16 2s 6d tithe rent charge; £86 13s 4d from the Eccl. Com.; average fees p.a. £3 16s.

Schedule of registers from 1659.

Plate: silver cup, paten and alms basin, all given by Acton and Walter Acton Moseley.

Part 1 (Abdon to Llanfair Waterdine)

Benefactions: £5 p.a. charged on an estate in Much Wenlock purchased by the late Mr Forester to be given to 4 of the poorest and oldest inhabitants of Buildwas, 4 of Leighton and 4 of Sheinton; £100, the interest for 10 of the poorest families; £3 5s 6d p.a. interest from £109 5s 9d given by the will of Mrs Pritchard of Broseley (formerly Miss Wilkinson of Buildwas Abbey) to be spent on warm clothing for 10 poor women on St Thomas's Day with preference to those not on parish relief.

Burford: 1st Portion[1]

n.d. [?1589]*. Thomas Lane; John Penson and Richard Cooke, CWs. [Signatures of 6 sidesmen].
Thomas Cornwall is patron.
House with back house, barn, cow house, orchard and 2 gardens.
Land: 10 a. arable in West F., 8 a. in Conniger F., 10 a. in Hopes Moor, 3 a. of meadow; 12 a. pasture, no feeding for sheep on the commons.
Tithes: half the tithes of Whitton chapel, half the tithe of Burraston [Boraston], part of Nash chapel and half of Burford are due.
[On the reverse is a note saying that the terrier was used as evidence in a case of 22 Aug. 1700 between James Bayley and Ambrose Sparry, pls. and Sir Francis Charlton et al. defs].

10 Jan. 1613/4. [John Gawen, parson]; Richard Angel and George Hughes, CWs.
Land: 11 a. arable in West F., 12 a. in Conninger F., 10 a. in Hopes Moor, 6 a. in 2 places by Lewis's house, 7 a. in Pond Close, 2 little plecks; feeding for 14 sheep on the commons.
Half the tithe of Whitton chapel, half of Boraston, half of Nash (except Weston), half of Burford and part of Norton and Harthall is due.

10 Jan. 1616/7*. John Cleobury, 1st portioner; Richard Angell and George Hughes, CWs.
Lands before the exchanges: 5 a. in Rye F., 2 a. near the orchard, 4 ridges next to Pound Close, 3 a. of meadow in Castle M.
Land after exchanges: 11 a. arable in West F., 12 a. in Cunninger F., 20 a. in Hopes Moore, 6 a. in 2 parcels near Lewis's house, 7 a. in Pound Close and 2 little plecks adjoining, one arable, the other meadow; feeding for 15 sheep in the common fields.

18 Feb. 1678/9. Thomas Lane, 1st portioner; John Penson and Richard Cooke, CWs.
House with backhouse, barn, cow house, orchard and 2 gardens.
Land: 10 a. arable in West F., 12 a. in Conninger F., 20 a. in Hopes Moor, 3 a. meadow, 12 a. pasture, no commons.
Half the tithes of Whitton, Boraston and Burford are due and ¼ of Nash.

---

[1] Burford was one of only three Shropshire parishes in which the glebe land and tithes were divided between two or three rectors known as portioners (see also Pontesbury and Westbury): Anthea Jones, *A Thousand years of the English parish* (2000), 110–12.

43

Glebe terriers of Shropshire
Burford: 2nd Portion

1589. Richard Deykins, parson; John Penson and Richard Cooke, CWs. [6 sidesmen].
The patron is Thomas Cornwall.
House with kitchen, barn and close adjoining.
Land: leasow 4 a., Long Close 2 a., Hart F. 3 a., 10 a. arable in 5 parcels in West F., 4 a. in Conninger F. and 7 a. in Ree F.
Part of the tithes of Stoke, Greete, Harthall and Weston are due.

1615. [William Hughes, 2nd portioner].
House with kiln, barn, stable, garden, orchard, fold and close adjoining *c.* 2 a.
Land: close 3 a., Long Close 2 a., 2 plecks in Harte F. 2 a.; arable land [detailed description but document faded and damaged].

Burford: 3rd Portion

1589. John Smythe, clerk; John Waties, Richard Burnell, CWs.
Thomas Cornwall of Burford is patron.
House with kitchen, barn, close and pasture adjoining *c.* 1½ a.
Land: 8 a. arable in West F., parcels of arable 3 a. and 4 a. in Coningray F., parcels of 2 a. and 1 a. arable in Nash F., pasture called Birch 1 a., 2 a. pasture in Hughemores, 1 a. pasture called Hartes F., 1 a. in Middledale, 5 a. pasture at Burford town end adjoining the highway on one side, 2 a. in Nash F. [bounds]; no meadow nor feeding for sheep, only the common fields.
Half the tithes of Burford are due, half the predial and personal tithes of Nash, Boraston and Whitton, half from a farm house called Richard Cookes of Hartall and half of Norton.

1678. William Bishop, clerk, 3rd portioner; John Penson and John Eaton, CWs.
House in Boraston with enclosure of 1 a. adjoining where Thomas Bishop, tailor dwells.
Land: 6 a. arable and 1 a. meadow called Priest's M. in Over F., 7 a. arable in Lower F., 6 a. enclosed arable in Leith Hill F., ridge called St Matthew's Ridge in Collybach *c.* one-third a. [bounds], Boraston churchyard 1 a., ¼ Burford churchyard, ½ Whitton churchyard.

Burwarton

n.d. [?1589]. Fowcke Smithe, parson; John Redding and John Dun.
Sir Andrew Corbet was patron, but now his executors.
House and barn in a close.
Land: *c.* 20 a. of arable, meadow and pasture in closes.

Calverhall[1]

2 June 1840. R. Clay, perpetual curate; John Whittingham, chapelwarden.

---

[1] Calverhall parish was formed from Calverhall and Willaston townships in Prees parish in 1858: *P.O. directory of Shropshire* (1879), 293.

44

Part 1 (Abdon to Llanfair Waterdine)

The minister has no parsonage house or tithes.

The minister has a fixed income of £65 10s p.a. from a rent charge of £10 on the manor of Cloverley in Calverhall, £21 on the manor of Oldcastle in Malpas, Cheshire, £28 from the rent of 13 a. of land in Edgeley, Whitchurch and £6 10s interest on a grant of £200 from QAB. QAB gave a grant in 1726 which was used the buy the Cloverley rent charge; in 1741 they gave £400 and the founder of the chapel £200 for the rent charge on Oldcastle; in 1821 they gave a further £200 and with a benefaction of £200 in 1822 from John Whitehall Dod 13 a. of land at Edgeley was purchased; in 1829 a further £200 was given and is in the hands of the governors of QAB.

Surplice fees and Easter offerings are payable to the vicar of Prees.

Clerk's fees: churching 6d, burials unknown; he also receives £3 3s p.a. from the patron.

The repair of the chancel belongs to the patron and is in good repair.

Plate: paten and chalice of silver. There is an iron chest for the registers.

There are no benefactions for the poor, the minister or the repairs of the chapel.

1849. Edward Mainwaring, incumbent; Owen Owen, CW.

House with garden and croft of 3 a.

Land: £28 rent from land at Edgeley, £24 p.a. from land at Dodington, Whitchurch, £10 rent charge on land at Cloverley, £21 rent charge on land at Oldcastle.

15 Apr. 1861. Edward Mainwaring, incumbent; John Newnes, CW.

1869. Edward Mainwaring, incumbent.

Rent for the 13 a. in Edgeley formerly £28 is now £20 and Dodington formerly £24 now £18, reduced because of cattle plague.

1884*. Edward Billings, V.

House with 3 sitting rooms, 7 bedrooms, kitchen, servants' hall, dairy, stabling for 2 horses, loose box, 2 coach houses with rooms over, wash house, 2 cow houses, piggeries, garden and close 3½ a.; part of the glebe has been thrown into the school playground.

Income: field at Alkington, Whitchurch 12 a. let for £27, 3 fields at Heath Lane, Whitchurch c. 12 a. let for £24; rent charge of £10 p.a. on the Cloverley estate; rent charge of £21 p.a. on the Oldcastle estate, Cheshire; Eccl. Com. £53 6s 8d in 1868 and £88 in 1874; interest on £400 from QAB; fees average p.a. 19s 4d.

Schedule of registers from 1771; the church was consecrated in 1726.

Plate: silver chalice, paten and flagon and brass alms dish.

Benefactions: Hon. Catherine Kerr's charity £10 p.a. for the schoolmaster and £2 p.a. for coal to heat the school; she also gave the land for the school and playgrounds and the almshouses founded by her 17 Mar. 1738/9 and rent charges of £40 and £10 on the manor of Oldcastle for the support of the school and almshouses; Caroline Dod gave £1,000 to the almshouses which is invested in N.E. Railway stock.

Cardeston

n.d. [late 16th/early 17th century]. William Williams, R; Roger Harryes and John Spensor.

Land: pasture called Black Fur. 14 a., close of arable 5 strikes seedness, ridges and 11 strikes seedness in Edge F., 7 strike seedness in Wyston F. [bounds].

22 Apr. 1636. George Peate, R; Barnabee Marston, CW.

House with barn of 3 bays, garden and hemp yard.

Land: pasture called Black Fur., Harmer Pool Close, 7 hoops sowing in Hogmore, furlong in Sandie F., butts in Edge F., 1 butt of Harton Fur. [bounds].

Tithes are due from Cardeston, Corston and Wattlesborough.

Cardington

26 June 1589. Edward Hayle and Francis Cock, CWs.

William Leyeston of Plaish is reputed patron.

Land: 30 a. of meadow and pasture, viz Thornes Leasows 4 a. and 3 a., New L. 4 a. surrounded by the town field called Standell F., pasture 4 a., Over Standell M. 5 a., Nether Standell M. 5 a., Crosse L. 2 a., 3 a. pasture in Gretton F.

1 June 1607. William Watkis and Thomas Langford, CWs.

Land: pasture called Swyre Glatt with little close 5 a., Upper Standell M. 3 a., 1 dole of meadow and pasture adjoining called Middle Standell 4 a., Byrd Acres lately enclosed 6 a., Crosse Croft (leased) 1 a., 3 a. arable in field towards Gretton, 3 a. arable in field toward Willstone, croft at the cross adjoining the way towards Enchmarsh 5 a., dole of meadow in Gervase Smith's meadow 1 a., Plaish 1 a., dole of common or waste called Vicars Birch 10 a., common of pasture for cattle on the commons of Cardington, Willstone, Comley and Enchmarsh.

Caynham

1589. Thomas Haull, V; John Couper and Thomas Jukes, CWs.

The prince[1] is patron.

Convenient house with 3 little barns, houses for cattle, home close and 2 orchards.

Land: 10 a. of arable being ridges in Boke F., Ridge F. and Castle F., 3 a. of meadow, 7 a. of pasture in closes [bounds]; feeding for sheep and other cattle on the Clee 'being Common without ratement'.

All tithes are due except of corn and hay on the demesne of the Court of Caynham.

[There is also an undated copy of this terrier].

---

[1] i.e. the queen (in 16th-century usage a 'prince' could be a female ruler: *O.E.D.*).

Part 1 *(Abdon to Llanfair Waterdine)*
Chelmarsh

1 July 1589. [William Wood, V].
The queen is patron.
House with home close, barn and hay barn.
Land: 7 lands and 27 butts in 8 parcels in Church F., 29 little butts enclosed and 3 other parcels in Nether F., 7 parcels of butts and ridges in Over F. [bounds].
Tithes of corn and hay of meese places are due [further details illegible].

7 June 1607. Thomas Acton, V; Thomas Nycols and Thomas Aston, CWs.
An annuity of £1 6s 8d is paid by the late queen's Auditor.
Land: parcels in Church F., Nether F. and Over F. and a parcel enclosed out of Nether F. [bounds]; common in the fields according to the acres.
There is tithe corn and hay only of the home closes, tithe hay of the demesne of the manor of Chelmarsh and Nether Court, 2 closes in Hempton excepted; the vicar pays Rowland Lacon 6s 8d p.a. for the tithe corn of Normestall ground; predial or privy tithes are due.

Cheswardine
(and see Sambrook)

11 July 1635. Thomas Wellens, V; John Meeson and Richard Boyden, CWs.
Vicarage house of 3 bays boarded with lofts throughout and in good repair with a new kitchen, barn 2½ bays in good repair, little yard between the house and the barn, cow house, stable and cote 3 bays under 1 roof in good repair and a draw well at S. end of the house.
Land: yard taking 3 measures of rye at the E. end of the house with the lane from Cheswardine to Chipnall on the W., 12 butts in Marsh F. for about 16 measures of rye, 15 butts in Birch F. for about 20 measures of rye, 15 butts in Castle F. for about 25 measures of rye; one of the butts in Castle F. has an ancient cottage at the S. end with 2 little gardens and some apple trees [bounds]; 1 day's delf of turves p.a. in a common heath between Great Soudley and Chipnall called Lipley Heath, free pannage and common of estovers in a common wood called Haywood and in other waste ground of Cheswardine township and common for all animals through the whole commons and wastes of Cheswardine lordship by ancient deeds from Lord Strange.
All tithes are due to the vicar except corn.

n.d. Bartholomew Cooke and Thomas Badnall, CWs. [13 other signatories].

n.d. Francis Butter, CW.

12 Sep. 1682. John Cooke and John Hallam, CWs.
Vicarage house of 4 small bays with barn 3 bays, wain house and sheep cote 2 bays, stable and beast house 2 little bays, backside, hemp butt, orchard, garden, and close called Vicars L. or Pool Head adjoining the park pale.
Land: 10 butts in Castle F. 1 with a cottage, 13 butts in Marsh F. and 15 in Birch F. [bounds]; the vicar has privilege of common of pasture, turbary and the liberty to get wood on the commons.

Easter roll: 2½d per house and garden, 2d for every householder, 2d for every person living in the parish who is or has been married, 2d for servants over 16, 2d for all others except those over 16 who are still under the tuition of their parents, ½d; 1½d for a cow and calf, 1d for a barren cow, 1d for a colt, 1d for a stall of bees taken down; Chipnall Mill has anciently paid 4s p.a. to the vicar, Westcott Mill 1s, Ellerton Mill 2s and Sambrook Mill 1s.

Tithes are due on wool, lambs, pigs, geese, hops, eggs, hemp, flax and trees in kind and on hay, some in kind and some in money; tithe herbage is due from those not living in the parish who hold grounds or depasture cattle in the parish according to statute.[1]

Surplice fees: churching 4d, marriage 1s 2d (if the woman is a parishioner and marries elsewhere she still pays 1s 2d to the vicar), certificate of publication of banns 6d, for registering baptisms 4d, burials 4d. Mortuaries are due according to statute.

1685. Samuel Orpe, V; Thomas Savage and John Garmson, CWs.

Vicarage house 4 bays with barn 3 bays, beast house, bing and stable 2 bays, hen house, pigsty, turf house on forks and house of office, backside, garden and orchard 1 a.

Land: enclosure called Vicars Close abutting the park pale 3 a., 9 butts in Castle F. *c.* 4½ a. with a cottage on one of the butts, 13 butts in Marsh F. *c.* 6½ a., 1 flatt and 9 butts in Birch F. *c.* 7 a.; common of turbary on Lipley Heath and of wood in Haywood.

18 Sep. 1693. Samuel Orpe, V; Thomas Smallwood and John Ellerton, CWs.

Land: enclosure called Vicars Pool Head Close with the old park on the E. 3 a., 2 little crofts in Castle F. with the castle on the S. 2 a., 5 butts and a pike in Castle F., enclosure in Birch F. 3½ a., enclosure in Marsh F. called Snape Cross 2 a., large enclosure called Birch Fur. or Marsh Piece 8 a., 2 butts ½ a. at Hill Cross in Marsh F. [bounds].

Some pay tithe hay in kind, some by custom; hives of bees pay 1d when killed or sold.

8 Sep. 1698. Samuel Orpe, V; Henry Jervis and Obadiah Adams, CWs.

Land: Pool Head Piece 3 a., Castle Croft with Castle Pitt on the E. being 5 butt ends lately enclosed 2½ a., Greengore Piece 3½ a., Snape Gate Croft 2 a., Birch Fur. Piece 8 a., butt near Hill cross ½ a.; 36 perches which could not be agreed when the 3 fields were enclosed lie part in John Grendon's land for which he pays 1s 6d p.a., part in Thomas Smallwood's land at 2d p.a. and part in Samuel Ellerton's land at 4d p.a. [bounds].

Tithes: the custom for hays is for the vicar to receive 1d p.a. per £1 math of land in the parish occupied by men of other parishes; Cheswardine township pays tithe hay in kind except for Joseph Butter; grass let in Cheswardine park is payable in kind; certain persons [named] in Chipnall, Goldstone, Ellerton, Sambrook and Soudley pay by various compositions or moduses.

---

[1] Tithe pasture according to statute (Cheswardine 1682).

Part 1 (Abdon to Llanfair Waterdine)

Clerk's wages: 2d per house and 4d for houses reckoned as plough lands, payable at Easter for labour and cleaning the church; fees: burials 4d, marriages 4d, graves in the churchyard 4d and in the church 1s.

8 Oct. 1701. Samuel Orpe, V; John Butter and Henry Earp, CWs.

Land: enclosure called Vicar's Poolhead Close, 3 little crofts enclosed in Castle F. 2½ a., 5 butt ends lately enclosed in Castle F. 1½ a., enclosure in Birch F. 3½ a., enclosure in Marsh F. called Snape Croft 2½ a., a large enclosure called Vicars Marsh Piece 8 a., 2 butts lately enclosed on Hill Cross in Marsh F. jointly with Francis Spender ½ a; John Spender, Henry Jervis and Thomas Smallwood have some glebe land enclosed with their land; common of Lipley Heath and Haywood; cottage lately erected with a garden and hemp butt in a croft adjoining Castle Pit where there was an old cottage on forks which rotted and fell down about 6 years ago.

Tithes: some hay is due in kind in Cheswardine but elsewhere by custom [individual moduses and compositions given]; Chipnall Mill pays 4s, Westcott Mill 1s, Ellerton Mill 2s and Sambrook Mill 1s.

23 Apr. 1705. Samuel Orpe, V; John Butter and John Wollams, CWs. [9 other signatories]. The vicarage house and about 20 a. of glebe are valued at £10 p.a.

Tithes: hay in Cheswardine is due mostly in kind, Soudley Park in kind; there are moduses in some of Cheswardine and the rest of the parish worth £6 15s 6d p.a.; wool and lambs are due in kind and are worth £9 p.a.

Easter roll: mill money and herbage £4 18s 6d; eggs, apples, pears, pigs, geese, hemp, and flax are due in kind and are worth £3 14s 6d.

Surplice fees and mortuaries are worth 16s 8d p.a.

Total £35 6s 2d p.a.

23 Apr. 1705. Samuel Orpe, V; John Butter and John Wollams, CWs.

Cottage on the site of an old one built on forks is walled with stone and rented at 5s p.a.; Thomas Orpe, son of the vicar, is now parish clerk and lives in the cottage.

Land: Snape Croft 2 a., Birch Fur. on Marsh Piece 8 a., ½ a. at Hill Cross, ground which could not be equalled in the exchange of the 3 town fields, all now enclosed, being 36 perches in the lands of Thomas Smallwood who pays 2d p.a., Henry Jervis 4d p.a. and John Spender 1s 6d p.a. 'until they are exchanged, if ever'; the vicar has common of turbary and wood, though none is now to be found.

Tithes: Cheswardine pays in kind except named lands [described in detail], Chipnall, Goldstone and Soudley Magna have moduses.

Tithing [added note]: the vicar is to have a tithe pig at 7 and a goose at 7 and 2 geese at 17, a tithe lamb at 7 and 2 at 17, allowing the owner ½d for odd lambs from 7 to 10 and 17 to 20, the owner paying the vicar ½d for odd lambs under 7 and from 10 to 17.

Clerk's fees: burial 4d, making a grave 4d, penny loaf of white bread at churching.

13 July 1714. Samuel Orpe, V; John Butter and John Wolloms, CWs.

Glebe terriers of Shropshire

19 Aug. 1718. Samuel Orpe, V; William Butter and John Wolloms, CWs.
Tithes: compositions for hay include Obadiah Adams for the old mill 'before the forge was built'.

14 July 1722*. Samuel Orpe, V; Richard Deane and Humphrey Palmer, CWs.
The clerk has no set wages only 13s for looking to the clock, 2d per cottage and 4d for every plough land, also an ancient customary payment at Christmas called keech money[1] paid by certain people for cleaning their seats, also by ancient custom 2 eggs per cock and drake at Easter.
Clerk's fees: 2d for churching or 2 white loaves, for marriages 'as much money as he can get'.

2 July 1726. Edward Maddox and Joseph Cooke, CWs.

15 Aug. 1730. Henry Jervis and Roger Haines, CWs.

23 Sep. 1732. Samuel Pearson, V; Henry Jervis and Roger Haines, CWs.

27 Sep. 1735. Samuel Pearson, V; Henry Jervis and Roger Haines, CWs.

13 Sep. 1738. Samuel Pearson, V; Joseph Butter and Richard Deans, CWs.

7 Sep. 1741. Samuel Pearson, V; Joseph Butter and John Butterton, CWs.

30 Aug. 1744. Samuel Pearson, V; John Ward and Thomas Brisbourne, CWs.

29 Aug. 1747. Samuel Pearson, V; John Bold and Edward Tatnall, CWs.

7 Sep. 1776. Thomas Hayward and John Butterton, CWs.

1 Oct. 1782. William Butterton and John Arkinstall, CWs.

25 Oct. 1786. John Arkinstall and Joseph Butter, CWs.

27 Aug. 1791. John Sutton and William Lewis, CWs.

1 Aug. 1795. Andrew Martin and William Jefferys, CWs.

23 July 1800. John Butter and William Butterton, CWs.

13 Oct. 1805. Samuel Venables and William Butter, CWs.

4 Sep. 1809. Samuel Venables and William Butter, CWs.

24 July 1828. James Benbow and Thomas Hazledine, CWs.

31 July 1832. John Icke and Owen Bennion, CWs.

31 Aug. 1841*. John Healey Bromley, V; John Icke and George Marsh, CWs.
Vicarage house with a pleasure ground.
Land: Pool Head 3 a., Castle Croft with a cottage 2 a., Pickley ¾ a., Greengore 3½ a., Snape Croft 2 a., Hill Cross ½ a., Haywood 7 a.
Tithes have been commuted for £200 p.a. with £7 10s charged on the glebe land.
Part of the chancel belongs to the lay rector and part to the parish; it is in good repair.
Communion plate: 2 silver cups, flagon and salver, all of silver. There is an iron chest for the registers.

[1] The meaning of 'keech' in this context is obscure; according to the *O.E.D.* it meant a lump of congealed fat.

There is a table of benefactors in the church; benefactions have been laid out on land at Forsbrook, Staffordshire and Hinstock, Shropshire and the rent is given to the poor in corn; land left for the repair of the church was leased to Mrs Beeston of Drayton to pay off the outstanding debt for the rebuilding of the church.

18 Aug. 1845*. John Healey Bromley, V; Henry Stanley and William Boffey, CWs.

[Vicarage house still has a turf house among the outbuildings]. Lands left for the repair of the church are let at £18 p.a.

1884*. J. E. Hughes, V.

Land: 22 a., also 7½ a. in Soudley for which there are no title deeds; 14 a. in Forsbrook and 11 a. in Hinstock parish belonging to the poor.

Tithe rent charge £209 4s 6d; fees average £10 p.a.

Schedule of registers from 1558.

Plate: silver chalice, paten and flagon.

Benefactions: £973 18s 10d in consols for the poor; £2 10s p.a. charge on Chipnall Mill bequeathed by John Butter; £1 6s p.a. charge on Soudley Park Farm; £2 8s p.a. interest on £50 lent to the CWs on the security of 2 cottages at Soudley belonging to the church; £20 in the savings bank at Newport.

Chetton[1]

1589. John Richard.

Sir John Savage is patron.

House with kitchen and barn.

Land in Chetton: Pynne Fur. and Pool M.

Land in Laughton chapelry: 1 headland and 1 beast's grass in Thomas Loughton's pasture; common on the Brown Clee.

Tithes are due after the custom of the parish.

3 Nov. 1615. John Wrednall and John Harries, CWs.

House with parlour and chambers of 4 bays with backhouse 2 bays, barn 3 bays, hay barn and stable 1 bay, garden and yard ½ a.

Land at Chetton: close to N. of the barn 1 a., meadow on W. 3 a., meadow called Hickley Acre 1 a., Pool Close M. ¼ a., 1 a. arable called Pynne Fur. with the lands of John Overton surrounding it.

Land at Loughton: there was a common field called Old F., now enclosed, and the parson was to have pasture for 2 little beasts and 1 great as long as there was any keeping for them; the parson was also to enter common on the Brown Clee for a strake of 20 sheep.

Tithes of corn from Chetton are due and also of Loughton chapel; other tithes by custom.

Loughton chapel: yard and garden ¼ a.

---

[1] Chetton is mentioned in the Cound terrier for 1705.

Chetwynd
(and see Sambrook)

21 Oct. 1612*. Roger Harper, parson; Richard Foxe, Davie Mathews and William Cherrington, CWs.
Parsonage house of 2½ bays with kitchen 1 bay, barn 3 bays with cow house at one end and turf house at the other.
Land: a garden in which the house stands, a pasture called Parsons Croft with Mear F. on the W., Gorsty Croft, 2 little crofts on the bank above the mill, 7 butts in Woodford F., 5 butts in Larton F. and 6 butts in Danfords F.

1636*. Roger Harper, parson; John Rylands and Roger Okeley, CWs.
Parsonage house of 2 bays with a shore at the end, barn 3 bays and a shore, kitchen of 1 bay, cart house; these with garden, hemp yard and backside are worth £1 6s 8d.
Land: Gorsty L. worth £1 p.a., Haselhurst Close £1 6s 8d, 2 crofts called Parsons Crofts and 9 butts, 4 lands in Sambrook are worth 12s p.a.
The tithe of the whole parish is worth £24 p.a.

1682. Thomas Unton, parson: Richard Bishop and Richard Fordoe, CWs.
Land: hemp yard and churchyard worth £2 p.a., pasture near Haselwood £2 10s, a pasture near Hoggins gate £2, cottage in Sambrook and several lands and butts in Sambrook £1 12s.

1685. Thomas Unton, R; Thomas Phillips and John Ragg, CWs.
Parsonage house with backside, barn and Haselwood L. worth £4 p.a.; Poole L. £2 p.a.; also a house, garden, field butts and croft in Sambrook worth £1 10s.
[Baptisms for 1685 included].

1693. [No signatories].

25 Apr. 1699*. Francis Skrymsher, R; Richard Bishop and Thomas Jones, CWs.
Parsonage house at Chetwynd of 2 bays with a barn of 2 bays.
Land at Chetwynd: Parsonage Yard 2 a., Corfields L. 5 a., Hawkins Gate Piece 4½ a.
Land at Sambrook: cottage and 9 a. of field ground being 9 butts in [?]Feel F., 8 butts and 2 headlands in Danford F., 3 butts and 1 enclosure in Woodford F.; the forge pays £2 p.a. for making the pool by consent of the present rector [bounds].
Tithes on corn are due in kind; there are moduses for hay at Pilson [Puleston], Howle and Sambrook; all other tithes are due in kind; Easter tithes are 2d on everyone over 16, 1s per colt, 1½d per cow and calf, 1d per stall of bees, 2d per smoke and garden.
Fees: marriages 2s 6d, burials 8d, churching 8d, burials in the chancel 7s.

1701†. [Copied 22 Oct. 1752]. Francis Skrymsher, R; Thomas Fox, Edward Greenfield, CWs.
House of 2 bays with barn 2 bays and parsonage yard 2 a.
Land at Chetwynd: Corfields L. with the common field on the E. 5 a., Hoggins Piece 5½ a.

Part 1 (Abdon to Llanfair Waterdine)

Land at Sambrook: 9 a. field land; £2 p.a. is paid by the tenant at the forge for damage caused by access.

13 June 1705*. Francis Skrymsher, R; Robert Richards and John Bishop, CWs.

Land at Sambrook: cottage with garden and hemp butt and 12 a. enclosed by the previous rector.

Tithes: Chetwynd demesnes pay £10 p.a. for all tithes by composition.

27 Aug. 1730. William Saunders, R; John Talbot and Thomas Sutton, CWs.

Land at Sambrook: cottage, garden and hemp butt, Brickkiln Butt ½ a., 2 crofts called Smithy Crofts 2½ a., new enclosures in 4 parts 6 a. [bounds].

Tithes: there are moduses for hay at Pilson, Howle, Sambrook and Brooke's old farm at Chetwynd End.

There are no seats in the chancel but the minister has 2 in the church.

16 Aug. 1733. William Saunders, R; John Lowe and William Chaliner, CWs.

10 July 1736. William Saunders, R; Samuel Wild and John Talbot, CWs.

Tithes: calves, lambs, pigs or geese are due at 7; 1s is due per colt, 1½d per cow and calf.

Clerk's wages are uncertain, some houses paying 4d, others more or less.

26 Aug. 1739. William Saunders, R; George Bromley and Thomas Ansel, CWs.

10 Sep. 1742. William Saunders, R; William Jackson and Samuel Leek, CWs.

9 Sep. 1745. William Saunders, R; William Whistons and Edward Bagshaw, CWs.

6 Sep. 1748. William Saunders, R; Richard Greenfield and Francis Read, CWs.

1752*. William Saunders, R; William Taylor and Thomas Plant, CWs.

2 Sep. 1756. William Saunders, R; John Stubbs and Thomas Meakin, CWs.

3 Sep. 1759. William Saunders, R; William Hallen and Francis Hudson, CWs.

15 Sep. 1767. William Pigott, R; John Adderley and John Griffith, CWs.

Land at Sambrook: cottage and 9 a. in many small parcels in Heath F., enclosed butt near Forge Pool for which the owners pay the rector £2 p.a. for the drowning.

19 Nov. 1801. William Pigott, R; John Bishop and Thomas Barrow, CWs.
[Tithes and surplice fees only].

1884*. Large, roomy house with coach house and 8 a. land surrounding.

Land: 18 a. at Hinstock rented.

Schedule of registers from 1586.

Plate: silver chalice, paten, flagon and alms basin.

Benefactions: £50–60 to the school; £7 p.a. for the poor and the purchase of bibles and prayer books; George Pigott gave £2, Thomas Pigott £5, Walter Pigott £10, Thomas Pigott of Stafford £3, Honor Dryden £50, Ann Pigott £50, Robert Pigott £10 and the interest of £50 for poor householders at Christmas, Thomas Baddeley £20.

Childs Ercall

17 Aug. 1698. Richard Cooke and Edward White, CWs.
Surplice fees are according to custom.
The curate's salary is £20 p.a.
There is a small patch of land worth 5s 8d in rent p.a. paid to the CWs and used by them to pay the clerk for looking to the clock; other than this the clerk has what the parishioners choose to give him, the amount is uncertain.

24 Nov. 1701. Andrew Corbett, C; Francis Garmwell and Cornelius Yeomans, CWs.
Childs Ercall is a donative. Lady Frances Corbett possesses all the tithes and pays £20 p.a. to the curate; he also has the surplice fees which may be worth 7s p.a.
5s 8d p.a. is paid for Clerk's Dole in Horse Pasture; Ladycroft in the hands of Thomas Hand of Hungry Hatton is worth 2s p.a.

3 May 1705. Andrew Corbett, C; Thomas Clay and William Cooper, CWs.
All tithes belong to Lady Frances Poole. 'I hope yo. Ldship will be pleas'd to order me an augmentation by my churchwardens made out of her Ma'ties most Gracious Bounty to the Clergy'.

19 May 1708.[1] Andrew Corbett, C; Edward White and Thomas Bold, CWs.
A dole in a horse pasture called Clerk's Dole pays 5s 8d and Thomas Hand of Hatton 2s for Lady Croft to the CWs.
The tithes are in the hands of Sir Robert Corbett of Adderley; he pays the minister £20 p.a. and also allows him the surplice fees and the churchyard.

24 July 1718. George Felton, C; Jeremiah Mason and Thomas Hand, CWs.
The churchyard is the only land belonging to the church.

19 Nov. 1734. J. Dickenson, C; Edward Roycroft, CW.
Sir Robert Corbett is the impropriator.
There is no parsonage house.

19 June 1736. J. Dickenson, C; William Cooke and William Poole, CWs.

31 Aug. 1739. J. Haynes, C; Mackworth Young and Thomas Clay, CWs.

27 Aug. 1742. John Haynes, C; Thomas Clay and George Andrews, CWs.

29 Aug. 1745. J. Haynes, C; Thomas Clay and Richard Hatherton, CWs.

9 Aug. 1748. J. Haynes, C; Thomas Bealey and Richard Bealey, CWs.
Sir William Corbet of Adderley is impropriator.
Surplice fees: registering baptism 6d, churching 4d, registering burial 6d, marriage with licence 5s, marriage with banns 2s 6d, publishing banns 1s.

1 Aug. 1752. John Lea, C; William Dawes and Thomas Wall, CWs.

[1] The Childs Ercall 1708 terrier is filed with the bishop's transcripts (LRO, B/V/7/1).

Part 1 *(Abdon to Llanfair Waterdine)*

14 Aug. 1756. John Power, C; Thomas Worrall and Thomas Wells, CWs.

15 Aug. 1767. William Dawes, CW.

7 Sep. 1772. Edward Watkins, minister; Thomas Woodhouse and Joseph Higkins.

21 Aug. 1775. William Dawes, CW.

6 Sep. 1779. T. Lloyd, minister; Thomas Sherratt and William Perrin, CWs.

9 Aug. 1824. C. Hodgkin, C; Thomas Heatley and Edward Bourne, CWs.

11 Aug. 1828†. [Copy made in 1838]. Horace Chevasse for Revd Charles Hodgkin, C; Thomas Heathley, CW.
Andrew Corbet, baronet, is patron and the devisees of Sir Corbet Corbet impropriators.
The minister has £20 from these devisees and an estate of 24 a. called Long Hill at Audlem, Cheshire.

9 Sep. 1841*. John Kynaston, C; John Freeman and Richard Heatley, CWs.
Land: farm of 25 a. belonging to the benefice called Long Hill Farm at Audlem, Cheshire purchased by a grant from the governors of QAB, a dole of meadow called Clerk's Dole worth 5s 8d paid to the CWs, little croft called Lady Croft worth 2s p.a. also paid to the CWs.
Tithes: the impropriator pays £30 p.a. as a composition in lieu of tithes.
Surplice fees: marriage with licence 5s, marriage with banns 2s 6d, publishing banns 1s, baptism 1s, burials 1s, upright headstone 10s 6d, flat headstone £1 1s, vault £5 5s and upwards.
Clerk's fees: marriage with licence 2s 6d, marriage with banns 2s, burial 5s, baptism 6d; the impropriator allows a further £4.
The repair of the chancel belongs to the impropriator; it is in good repair.
Communion plate: cup of silver, chalice and 3 plates of pewter. There is an iron chest for the registers.

13 Aug. 1845*. Bertie Johnson, C; Richard Heatley and John Freeman, CWs.
There is no house at present; it is the intention of the impropriator to obtain augmentation from the Bounty Board to build one.
Land: an estate at Audlem was bought in 1788, 1791, 1803 and 1807 with funds from the Bounty Board with a contribution of £200 on the last occasion from the late Sir Corbet Corbet. Nothing has been received from Clerk's Dole and Lady Croft for the last 30 years.
The 1841 terrier says that the £20 paid by the impropriator to the minister was increased to £30; this increase has not been received.

4 Aug. 1857.[1] Bertie Johnson, perpetual curate; Richard Heatley, CW.
House with garden, stables, coach house, barn and pigsty.
Land: 22 a.
£30 composition in lieu of tithes.

---

[1] The copy of the 1857 Childs Ercall terrier in SRRC (P61/F/2/6) is a rough copy only.

Glebe terriers of Shropshire

1884*.[1] J. Padmore Noble, C.
Schedule of registers from 1569 and Poor Book 1699–1783 are in an iron wall safe in the vicarage.
Plate: 2 silver chalices, silver paten and flagon, 1 plate and 1 brass alms dish.

Church Aston[2]

1701. Dryden Pigott, R; Christopher Carsual and Andrew Jourdane, CWs.
Land in Church Aston: 11 selions and an enclosed croft in Windmill F., 14 selions in Moor F., 8 selions in Hill field.
Land in Chetwynd Aston: 9 selions in Port F. [bounds].

1705. Dryden Pigott, R; Richard Smith and Henry Bullock, CWs.

1718. Dryden Pigott, R; Roger Holmes and Thomas Smith, CWs.
Land: Priest Croft 1 a., Hill Piece 3 a., Upper Goosehook 4 a., Port F. 13 a., all enclosed.
Tithes are all due in kind; calves, lambs and pigs at 7; 1½d for a cow and calf, 4d per colt.
Fees: burial 6d, churching 4d, marriage by licence 5s, publishing banns and marriage 4s.
Clerk's wages 16s p.a.
The minister has no seats or burial places; there are 6 seats in the chancel erected *c.* 30 years ago. The rector repairs the chancel only and no part of the churchyard wall.

1722. Theophilus Holbrooke, C; Richard Smith and John Adams, CWs.
There is no rectory or vicarage house.
Glebe land belongs to the rector [of Edgmond]: an old enclosure near the churchyard 1 a., 4 new enclosures each of 4 a., 1 enclosure in Chetwynd Aston.
The curate has the tithes of Church Aston and £4 p.a. allowed by the rector; the tithes of Chetwynd Aston are leased for £50 p.a. for the life of the present rector; hay and corn are due at the 11th, calves at the 7th or 1½d for each cow and calf below 7; 1d is due for a barren cow, 4d for a colt; lambs are due at 7, the minister paying the owner 4½d each under 7, the owner to pay 1½d for each lamb; pigs and geese are due at 7 and 2 at 17.
Surplice fees: marriage by banns 2s 6d, marriage by licence 5s, burial 1s, baptism 6d, churching 4d.

1726. The. Holbrooke, C; William Brockhurst and William Brown, chapelwardens.
Land: all leased.
Tithes are all due in kind, there is no modus in the chapelry.
Clerk's wages of £1 are paid by the CWs.

---

[1] The Lichfield copy of the 1884 Childs Ercall terrier includes a plan of the parsonage house, garden and glebe.
[2] Church Aston parish was formed from part of Edgmond parish in 1860: *P.O. directory of Shropshire* (1879), 297. See also the Edgmond terriers for 1682 and 1694.

Part 1 (Abdon to Llanfair Waterdine)

1730. Theophilus Holbrooke, C; Edward Cotton and William . . ., CWs.

1733. The. Holbrooke, C; Richard Smith and John Bullock, CWs.
Land: *c.* 13 a. in Portfield, 8 a. in Moor F. with land belonging to the poor of Newport on the W., 3 a. in Windmill F., croft called Priest Croft 1 a. [bounds].

1736. The. Holbrooke, C; John Lowe and Henry Earp, CWs.

1739. The. Holbrooke, C; Nathaniel Wynn and Henry Earp, CWs.

1742. The. Holbrooke, C; John Nayler and William Bullock, CWs.

1745. The. Holbrooke, C; Nathaniel Wynn and John Garmeson, CWs.

1748. Theophilus Holbrooke, C; Nathaniel Wynn and John Garmeson, CWs.

1751. The. Holbrooke, C; Thomas Justice and John Bullock, CWs.

1763. The. Holbrooke, C; Nathaniel Wynn and John Garmeson, CWs.

1884*. Edward Ventris, V.
House built 1861 and since enlarged with garden ¾ a.
Income: tithe rent £122 18s; £66 132 4d from the Eccl. Com. granted in 1863 and 1878; £5 6s 4d from QAB; average fees p.a. *c.* £5.
Schedule of registers from 1620.
Plate: silver chalice, paten, flagon and alms dish.
Benefactions: Mary Broughton gave £600 by will in 1728 to be spent on bread worth £1 twice p.a, and on the education and apprenticing of 1 boy and 1 girl p.a.; Francis Watson £20; Geoffrey Leech gave 4s in 1666 for bread every Good Friday.

Church Pulverbatch

n.d. [?1589]. John Baylie and Richard Ryder, CWs.
Sir Phillip Butler is patron.
Land: 4 a. pasture in Wrentnall F., 2 a. pasture in Castle Pulverbatch, 1 a. pasture in Church Pulverbatch adjoining the churchyard, 1 a. meadow in Wrentnall F. and arable in Wrentnall F. [bounds].
There are no buildings or tithes.

1607. Richard Crosse, R.
Land: Parsons Lye pasture 10 a., orchard 1 a., New L. pasture 4 a., Five Acres pasture 3 a., Berarton pasture 3 a., ½ a. in Broad Oak L., parcel in Harp Close, Ox M. 1 a., ½ a. meadow adjoining Harp Close, Parsonage M. 1 a. with a new barn erected by the present rector, 2½ a. in the common fields [bounds].

Church Stretton[1]

n.d. [?1589].[2] William Harries, clerk. [9 other signatories].
Sir Rowland Hayward of London, alderman, is patron.

---

[1] There is a map of the glebe of Church Stretton dated 1776 in SRRC, D3651/B/122/1.
[2] There is a copy of the Church Stretton 1589 terrier in SRRC 1709/203.

There is a decent house with hall, 2 parlours, 2 butteries, 5 chambers, kitchen, bolting house, malt chamber, stable, ox house all under 1 roof, barn and sheep cote 5 bays, garden to S. and backside on W. 1 a.

Land: Hollen F. 5 a., Bercheacre 5 a. with Burway Lane on S and Long Mynd on S. and N., Shippen hill 2 a. with Watling Street on E., pasture 1½ a., Winley M. 1½ a., Pool M. 2½ a. with Watling Street on E., ¼ a. dole of meadow in Winley M., 10 a. arable in Nashcockes F., 1½ a. in Upper F., ½ a. in Snatch F. [bounds]; estover of wood and timber in lord's wood, common for housebote, firebote and hedgebote.

Tithes are due throughout the parish.

12 Sep. 1699. Henry Clayton, R; Thomas Poston, CW.

Hon. Henry Thynne, son of Thomas Viscount Weymouth is patron.

Land: Coneyborough adjoining W. of house 40 a., close in Hollen F., Long Hills 5 a., New Inclosure 3 a., 3 a. reputedly in Nasbrooke F., close called Bechacre 5 a. with Burway Lane on S. and Long Mynd on W. and N., close called Netherhill 5 a., close called Shippenhill 2 a. with Watling Street on E., Winley M. 1 a., Pool M. 2½ a., ½ a. arable in Snatch F. [bounds]; wood and timber in the lord's wood, common for housebote and hedgebote.

Churchstoke[1]

4 July 1744. Samuel Oakeley of Stepple leases the tithes from the warden and poor men of the hospital of Clun.

Tithes in the townships of Hopton Isaf and Bachaethlon on grain are due in kind, also on wool and lambs; the 10th lamb or fleece is due; if there are 10 lambs in a parcel, the owner takes 2 then the titheman the 3rd, if between 7 and 10, the tithe man takes 1 and allows the owner as many as make up 10 in the year following, if under 7 they are carried on until the next year; hemp, flax, eggs, apples and pears are due in kind, also 1 pig from a litter if there are 5 or more and 1 goose from a flock of whatever number; 1½d is due for a cow and calf, 1d for a barren cow, 4d for a colt, 1d garden, 1d smoke, 1d for a stall of bees killed, ½d for every sheep sold before tithing and half the tithe if depastured out of the parish, 1d for a day's math of hay; clover or rye grass are due in kind, also potatoes and turnips; the lessee of the tithe finds bread and wine for the sacrament at Easter; 5 a. called Broad F. belonging to the Pentrenant estate is abbey land and the 13th sheep is due; the tithes of Hopton Uchaf belong to another but each communicant pays 2d at Easter; the tithes of Mellington are as Hopton Isaf except for a modus of 1s for a day's math of hay and 1d for a colt; Church Stoke and Hurdley are as Hopton Isaf except Great Weston Farm which pays 12s p.a. in lieu of tithe hay; Rhiston is as Hopton

---

[1] Churchstoke parish was only partly in Shropshire, the larger part was in Montgomeryshire.

Isaf except 1d per colt is due; Brompton is the same except for several meadows [named] which pay a modus for hay.

Clee St Margaret

22 June 1801. Richard Fleming, sub-curate; Israel Colton and Samuel Jones, CWs.
Sir Henry Pelham is the impropriator of all the tithes great and small.
House with farm buildings, yard and garden.
Land: 29 a. of meadow, pasture and arable at Holdgate purchased with QAB by the late curate.
£1 4s 8d p.a. is paid out of 2 estates at Clee St Margaret for a sermon by the rector or curate of Holdgate on Whitsunday.
Each communicant pays 2d at Easter.

Cleobury Mortimer

n.d. [?1589]. Thomas Ellis, John Wildsmith, CWs. [6 other signatories].
The queen is patron.
The minister has a house and close but no glebe.

Cleobury North

9 July 1589. William Browne and John Yeaton, CWs.
Humphrey Hill is patron.
House and cottage near Lady Wood.
Land: 8 a. arable in 4 parcels in the field S. of the town, 7 a. in 6 parcels in the field W. of the town, 8½ a. in 9 parcels in Stubbe F., 30 a. of pasture; total 61½ a. [bounds]; common of pasture on the Brown Clee.
Tithes and duties are due; money payments are due for hay [added in a different hand].

12 Dec. 1604. Richard Browne, parson; William Mynd, Thomas Haswell.
Parsonage house with kitchen, barn, stable, cow house, wain house, garden, pasture on the backside called the Moor 34½ a., cottage formerly a beasts' house with garden and meadow adjoining 1 a.
Land: Lydiates L. 1½ a. with a new house built on it by by the parson in the last year for the curate with 2 small butts called Parnells Yard 1 a., Ock Wood L. 2½ a., White L. 2 a., pasture called Hartley 6 a., pasture called Lye 6 a., Clybrooke M. 1 a., New Tyning 2 a., 7 a. in Stubbe F., 7 a. in Over F. towards Ditton, 4 a. in the field towards Burwarton, Park and Park M. 2 a., Hollow M. ½ day's math, Haymore M. 1 day's math [bounds].
Tithes and oblations are due.

Glebe terriers of Shropshire
Clive[1]

1784.[2]
£18 6s 8d is due to the minister from the Free School in Shrewsbury; £1 4s is
charged on an estate in Clive the property of the Earl of Exeter; the minister also has £8 p.a. being a half share of a tenement and 29 a. of land in
Guilsfield, Montgomeryshire purchased for £200 by QAB, (the other £8
going to Broughton).

1884*. [John Wood].
House and land 1 a.
Income: rent of land at Guilsfield held jointly with Broughton £20; rent of
£6 6s from 5 a. near Wem bought in 1820 by QAB; £1 4s rent charge on the
land of Mrs M. Puleston; tithe rent charge £102 7s 6d; Eccl. Com. £50 in
1877; fees average c. £3 p.a.
Schedule of registers from 1671.
Plate: silver chalice dated 1598 and silver paten [illustrated with drawings].

Clun

n.d. [late 16th/early 17th century]. Robert Johns, clerk. [12 signatories, no
office given].
House with barn and a small cottage built by the present vicar.
Land: 16 a. in 6 parcels Cockford F., 3 a. in Sydenall F. [bounds, but the
document is torn]; no meadow or feeding for sheep.
The farmer has the tithe of corn and lambs; the rest belongs to the vicar.

8 Dec. 1604. Erasmus Powell, V. [Signatures of 16 parishioners].
House with kitchen and cow house under the same roof, barn 4 bays, stable,
orchard and garden.
Land: 4 a. arable adjoining the backside, 4 a. arable and wood called Vicar's
Park, 3 day's math in Spoad M., 1 day's math in Lord's M., Bicton, 9
swathes of hay in Doley, Whitcott Evan; 9 a. in 3 parcels of arable in Clun,
5 a. of arable dispersed exchanged for 5 a. in an enclosure called Cockford,
free burgage of ½ a., 2 a. arable in Cockford F., 2 separate acres in
White L. lately enclosed, 3 a. arable in Sydnalls F., 1 a. meadow in
Loser M., 1 a. pasture in the leasow under the hurst, 1 a. in a leasow in
Penshop, 1 a. in Brenhynbren, 1 a. in Croviard F., 1 a. by the highway
from Clun to Clunton, 1 a. on top of Croviard, 6 a. pasture in Croviard L.,
3 a. pasture in Upper Kylmock intermixed with other men's land, 3½ a.
arable in Lower Kylmock F., 6 a. arable in Mouldre [bounds].
The inhabitants of houses, burgages and land on the left side of St George St.
on passing from the bridge to the church pay rents and services to the
vicar.

---

[1] Clive was originally a chapelry of St Mary, Shrewsbury: Blakeway, 'History of Shrewsbury Hundred', *Trans. Shropshire Archaeol. Soc.* 2nd ser. ii (1890), 333–58.
[2] The terrier is included in the printed parish register (Shropshire Parish Register Soc.
1906).

Part 1 (Abdon to Llanfair Waterdine)

16 May 1607. Erasmus Powell, V. [8 signatories, no office given].
Land: 74 a. [details and bounds, but the document is very faded].

Clunbury

22 July 1628. William Hayle, minister; Thomas Richards and Henry Morris, CWs.
House with barn, garden and small backside.
Land: 1 meadow.

6 Mar. 1636/7. George Barkley, C; Hugh Edwards and John Lucas, CWs.
Clunbury is reputed to be a chapel of Clun which is a vicarage; Clunbury has only a curate at the charge of the proprietor of the rectory of Clun, Humphrey Walcot, who holds the church, chapel, glebe and tithes from the king in fee farm.
House with backside, garden and barn in Clunbury, being 1½ bays of new building built by the present incumbent.
Glebe: little meadow in Kempton, Clunbury.

Clungunford

n.d. [late 16th/early 17th century]. [Very faded].

11 May 1607.
House with 2 barns, hay house, garden and orchard of 2½ a.
Land: Calder M. 1 a., 3 a. in Dagedalls, 1 a. meadow at Holen on the River Clun, close round the churchyard 1 a., 12 a. arable in 4 parcels in Nether F., 9 a. arable in 10 parcels in Middle F., 6½ a. arable in 7 parcels in Upper F., arable in Mill F. [details and bounds, but document damaged].

26 Apr. 1638. Philip Mullart and John Harper, CWs.
Land: Home close, 4 a. meadow in Dogdale near R. Clun, pasture called Weaver L., ½ a. in Abcott M., 4 a. enclosure of arable formerly in Nether F., enclosed arable called Peamwall L. 5 a., enclosed arable called Upper L. formerly part of Upper F. 8 a., enclosed meadow called the Dole, 6 a. arable in 3 parcels in Nether F., 4½ a. arable in 5 parcels in Middle F., 11½ a. in 6 parcels in Mill F., 11½ a. arable in 6 parcels in Abcott F., 5½ a. arable in 8 parcels in Abcott F. called Weamore, 7½ a. arable in 10 parcels in Abcott Middle F., 2 parcels arable in Abcott North F. called Dogdale, 7 a. glebe in 6 parcels in other men's lands [bounds]; common of pasture in the fields of Clungunford and for 1 beast on the aftermath in Lingen M. and Cow M.; free pannage in Abcott Wood for all the parson's swine, in Shelderton Wood for 6–8 swine and in Goatalls for 2 hogs.
Tithe fish are due from Heath Pool, tithe wood from Saddle Hill and other coppices and underwoods as often as felled.
First fruits are valued at £16, subsidy at £1 8s, procurations to the chancellor at 6s 8d and to the archdeacon 6s 8d, synodals at 1s.

1589 [Copy]. Edward Hotchkis and John Corne, CWs.
House of 2 bays with hay house and cote.

Land: Sande Madow, 3 a. of meadow at Dogdale, 1 a. of meadow called Howney, ½ a. in Abcott M., close adjoining the churchyard, 5 a. arable in 3 parcels in Nether F., 9 a. arable in 10 parcels in Middle F. called Peamewall, 5½ a. arable in 6 parcels in Upper F., 17½ a. in 17 parcels in Mill F., 10 a. arable in 18 parcels in Abcott F. called Winmore, 8 a. arable in 13 parcels in Abcott Middle F., 10½ a. in 21 parcels in Abcott North F. called Dogdale [bounds]; common of pasture in the fields of Clungunford and for 1 beast on the aftermath in Lingen M. and Cow M., free pannage in Abcott Wood for all swine and in Sheldertons Wood for 6–8 swine and in Goatalls for 2 hogs.

Cockshutt[1]

7 Sep. 1841*. Samuel Burrows, C; William Haycocks, CW.
No house.
Land: 27 a. at Woolston, West Felton rented at £40 p.a., 13 a. at Kinnerley rented for £20 p.a. and another 4½ a. at Kinnerley rented at £8 p.a.
The seats in the chapel have immemorially been the property of the minister and are let by him for his salary.
QAB gave £200 and the land at Treginfert, Kinnerley was bought, also £200 in conjunction with Lady Dowager Gower who as executrix of the Earl of Thanet gave £200, the money being laid out on land at Woolston, West Felton. The Bounty Board gave a further £200 in 1791.
Surplice fees: no marriages take place in the chapel, burials 1s 6d, vaults £2–5 depending on size, churching 1s, the fees are treble for non-residents;
Clerk's fees: burial 2s, churching 8d.
The chancel and chapel are in good repair.
Plate: flagon, chalice and paten of silver and a pewter plate. There is an iron chest for the registers.
Benefactions: F. Lloyd of Crosemere by will 1791 left 6s p.a. to the poor of Cockshutt, Crosemere and Frankton from the rent of a croft in Frankton; Roger Jones by will 1789 left £20 for a clock; Mrs Ann Harris of Ellesmere in 1778 left a bible in 2 volumes; F. Lloyd of Domgay in 1796 left £20 for an altar piece; Joseph Cotton, clerk in 1800 gave a marble font; F. Lloyd of Crosemere left £6 6s, F. Lloyd of Domgay £6 6s, B. Hatchett of Lee £4 4s and Mrs Hatchett £4 4s, the interest on these being for repairs of the church and the money was invested in 1781 in the name of Bulkeley Hatchett, but was later spent on new bellframes.

1884*.
There is no parsonage house, only a house rented from Lord Brownlow, the patron, for £25 p.a.
Land: parcels of 4 a. and 12 a. in Kinnerley are let for £9 and £20 and 25½ a. in West Felton for £50.

---

[1] Cockshutt was made into an ecclesiastical parish in 1872 from part of Ellesmere parish: *Kelly's directory of Shropshire* (1895), 70.

In 1867 Lord Brownlow gave a tithe rent charge of £71 11s 6d and in 1882 £10 and the Eccl. Com. granted £50 to meet this; in 1791 £6 10s p.a. was granted by QAB; fees amount to *c.* £5 p.a.on average; total income £222 1s 6d p.a.
Schedule of registers from 1773.
Plate: silver chalice, paten and flagon, the gift of Francis Lloyd of Crosemere in 1776.
Benefactions: F. Lloyd of Crosemere in 1791 gave 6s p.a. by will for the poor of Cockshutt, Crosemere and Frankton from the rent of a croft in English Frankton; John Parker by will in 1839 gave the interest of £200 for the poor of Cockshutt; both these are given in bread on the first Monday each month.

Cold Weston

n.d. [?1589]. [Roger Bucher, parson]; Oliver Heynes and Thomas Slade.
Richard Hopton is patron.
House of 2 bays.
Land: 2 a. of meadow, 20 a. of arable in the 3 leet fields of Weston, Well F., Middle F. and Springwall F. [no bounds]; common pasture on Weston Hill and the Brown Clee.

1607. Roger Bucher, parson; Oliver Peynes and Robert . . . [faded], CWs.
House of 1 bay with a little close of pasture on which the house stands, yard, barn 1 bay and 1 a. of pasture adjoining.
Land: 1½ a. in Hongrell being part meadow and part arable, small parcels of arable and pasture in Reall F. and Middle F. [bounds].

1630. [Simon Cotton, parson]. Thomas Bent, CW; William Cockes, sidesman.
House with barn and garden.
Land: 10 a. arable, wood and pasture in Reall F., 8 a. of arable, wood and pasture in Elverlong F., 4 a. of arable, wood and pasture in Little F.

22 June 1801. Richard Fleming, minister; Robert Heighway, CW.
Small house with cow house.
Land: 3 a. of meadow, 6 a. of arable and 7 a. of pasture lying together [bounds].

Colemere *see* Lyneal cum Colemere

Condover[1]
(and see Annscroft; Bayston Hill; Dorrington)

24 Oct. 1612. Timothy Price, V; Thomas Heynes and William Lateyardes, CWs.

---

[1] Condover was transferred from Lichfield to Hereford diocese in 1905: *Victoria history of Shropshire*, ii. 1. See also the terriers for Longnor 1701–30. For a plan of the vicarage and glebe land in 1784 see SRRC 1977/2/7.

Parsonage house with old barn and some other old buildings, 1½ a. of ground adjoining.

The tithe hay of Dorrington is due to the vicarage and the hay of a certain dole of meadow falls to the vicarage 1 year in 3; tithes of the home closes; white tithes.

' . . . for those thinges that are in doubte when wee come to knowledge of them you shall further have knowledge'.

30 Sep. 1680. [Henry Brickdale, V] Humphrey Smyth and Richard Wood, CWs.

House of 2 bays with barn of 3 bays, small stable, small yard and orchard of *c*. 1 a.

9 Sep. 1682. Henry Brickdale, V; Richard Steventon and Thomas Stevens, CWs.

House with barn, backhouse, garden and home close worth £3 p.a.

[On a separate sheet]. Judy Owen gave 12d weekly for bread for the poor; Edward Owen the like; Henry Haynes 1s 6d to be given on St Thomas's Day; William Haynes 6d per week; Richard Lateward and George Hodges have each given £2, the interest to be given in bread at Whitsun to the poor who have no weekly pay.

21 Oct. 1701†.[1] Richard Podmore, C. [Henry Brickdale, V].

House of 4 bays with small barn, stable, 3 strikes sowing of barley, small orchard and garden.

Tithes: mainly wool and lambs and other vicarage tithes and home closes; Dorrington pays tithe hay; Lythwood is said to belong to a forest and only pays offerings;[2] all the parish except Lythwood pays mortuaries by statute; 2 home closes in Stapleton pay tithes to Condover; Longnor has a private chapel which pays greater tithes to the impropriator, but pays no vicarage tithes 'for what reason I know not', neither do they communicate at the parish church at any time. Mortuaries are also due from Frogley [Frodesley] and Stapleton.

2 May 1705. Henry Brickdale, V; Roger Blaynes, CW.

House new built by the present vicar of 3 storeys with good cellar and brewing house of 4 bays, stable, coal house 1½ bays, Vage land 1 a.; new court before the house taken out of the waste by the consent and kindness of the lord of the manor.

Tithes are principally of wool and lambs with all other vicarage tithes; tithe hay and clover are due in Dorrington; corn and iron mills pay 6s 8d.

Longnor inhabitants do not communicate at the parish church 'which sure is a great wrong to the Vicar & fit to be redressd'.

Land tax has been assessed at £20 p.a.—higher than the neighbours.

1706.

Certificate of exchange of land: Vicar's Yard exchanged for Widnold 4 a.

---

[1] The 1701 terrier for Condover is included in the printed parish register (Shropshire Parish Register Soc. 1906), 197.

[2] Forest land was accounted extra-parochial and paid tithe only to the king or his lessee: Burn, *Ecclesiastical law*, ed. Fraser, iii. 378.

Part 1 (Abdon to Llanfair Waterdine)

30 May 1711. [George Lluellen, V; no signatories].

26 June 1718. George Lluellen, V; Bartholomew Pool and Thomas Bucknall, CWs.

Sep. 1722. George Lluellen, V; John Hancock and Richard Bowen, CWs.

28 Aug. 1730. George Lluellen, V; William Brethen and John Gough, CWs. Glebe land 9 strikes sowing.

7 Aug. 1733. George Lluellen, V.

16 July 1736. George Lluellen, V; Richard Preece and Vincent Lewis, CWs.

14 Aug. 1739. William Pugh, C; William Griffiths and Samuel Wood, CWs.

1742. Roger Barnston, V; William Daker and Thomas Gould.

11 Sep. 1745. Roger Barnston, V; Thomas Easthope and James Hartshorn, CWs.

14 Sep. 1748. Richard Podmore, C to Roger Barnston; Richard Easthope and Richard Wood, CWs.

20 Sep. 1752. Richard Podmore, C; John Parsons and Thomas Elks, CWs.

1756. Richard Podmore, C; William Easthope and Thomas Weeks, CWs.

1759. Richard Podmore, C; Joseph Pryce and Richard Bowen, CWs.

1763. Richard Podmore, C; William Whitefoot and Peter Deakyn, CWs.

1767. Richard Podmore, C; David Edwards and William Phillips, CWs.
Upon failure of males in the family of Owens, patrons, there fell to the vicar an annuity of £69 payable out of the estate of Thomas Berrington Esq. in Meole Brace, but the land tax and the weekly largess of bread to the poor reduce this to £60 p.a.

8 Sep. 1772. Richard Podmore, C; John Williams and Thomas Weeks, CWs.

21 Aug. 1775. Richard Podmore, C; Edward Thorns and Thomas Deakin, CWs.

7 Sep. 1779. Richard Podmore, C; Thomas Cund and William Wood, CWs.

1792. Thomas Bowen, CW.
[Parish register 26 Oct. 1787–15 Oct. 1792].

1801. Forester Leighton, V; John Goff and Thomas Price, CWs.

1805. Forester Leighton, V; George Hopton and Joseph Crane, CWs.

1810*. Richard Scott, V; Thomas Parr and Hugh Lloyd, CWs.

18 June 1825. L[awrence] Gardner, V; Thomas Parr and Philip Wilcox, CWs.
Parsonage house in the village of Condover 21 yd. × 6 yd. with stables, coal house, yard, walled orchard, kitchen garden and a small piece of ground in front of the house with the turnpike from Shrewsbury to Ryton on the E.; this is not the ancient vicarage house, the site was changed according to a deed of 1787 in the church chest.
Land: 2 pieces 4 a. with the turnpike from Condover to Atcham on the N.

An annuity charged on Moat Hall by the late Thomas Berrington Esq. in 1824 amounted to £66 3s; £2 16s was paid in land tax and £2 12s in bread for the needy.

12 Aug. 1828. Frederick Leicester, V; James Turner and John Boothby, CWs.

1832. Henry Burton, V; Edward Yardley and William Francis, CWs.

1884. House with drawing room, dining room, school room, study, kitchen and back kitchen on the ground floor, 6 bedrooms and 2 dressing rooms on the 1st floor and 2 bedrooms on the 2nd floor and garden ¾ a.
Land: Hither Glebe 2½ a., Further Glebe 1 a.
Income: rent charge of £69 p.a. on Moat Hall, Pontesbury; tithe rent charge was £211 5s, but is now £203 13s 3d as the charge on some lands at Great Lyth was given to Annscroft; fees average £6 p.a.
Schedule of registers from 1570.
Plate: 2 silver chalices and patens, 1 silver flagon and brass alms dish.
Land and cottages known as the Church Estate was sold in 1877 for £708 17s 5d and the money vested in the Charity Commissioners.
Benefactions: parcel of land leased for £20 p.a. for the use of the incumbent; Joseph Pryce bequeathed a sum in 1824, the interest of £6 16s 1d to educate 6–8 children of Dorrington; £2 12s 0 p.a. from Justice Owen's Charity of 1598 for bread every Sunday; £1 6s p.a. from Brickdale Charity of 1700 for bread on Sundays; Vicar's Bread charity of 1786 being £2 12s p.a. for bread every Sunday; £1 11s 5d interest from Plumer's Charity of 1811 for bread on St Thomas's Day; Henry Haynes by will in 1659 left £1 6s p.a. for bread on St Thomas's Day; Benjamin Price left £13 2s 8d by will in 1797, the interest for bread on St Thomas's Day; George Hayward left £15 9s 10d, the interest for bread on St Thomas's Day and 17 Feb.; Daker's Bread left money for 40 6d loaves on St Andrew's Day.

Coreley

n.d. [?1589]. Edward Cotynge and Roger Nashe, CWs.
Richard Oteley is patron.
Land: 3 a. arable in Coreley F., 3 a. in Broomy Hill, 4 ridges in Bradeley F., parcel of meadow in Diches M., 4 a. arable near Diches M., many other ridges and butts in very small parcels, piece of woodland, Stockwalls Close [very detailed bounds].

Cound[1]
(*and see* Cressage)

24 Oct. 1612. Richard Wood, parson; Richard Mollard, CW, and Thomas Dodd, surveyor.
House with 2 barns, cow house, stable, garden, 'young' orchard and yard.

---

[1] Cound was transferred from Lichfield to Hereford diocese in 1905: *Victoria history of Shropshire*, ii. 1.

Part 1 (Abdon to Llanfair Waterdine)

Land in Cound: little meadow called Halleway M., 2 doles of meadow Oxen Hole, little yard called Parsonage Yard, pasture called Leese F., ridges and butts of arable land in Church F., Upper Cound F., Harnedge Hill F., Broadewall F. and Pool F.

Land in Cressage: tenement with barn, house, backside, chapel yard, pasture, close called Bridgwall, meadow called Pool M. and arable land at Belswardine Hill, Gold Eye Pit, in the field towards the grange and in Lords Oak F. [bounds].

There is a chapel at Kenley with tithes said to be a 'member of Cound the possession thereof we have not neyther know certenly the houses or gleabe thereof'.

1682. James Cressett, R.

Land in Cound: Bannat Hill Yard, Holloway M., Oxen Hole, 2 doles of meadow, pasture called Lees F., ridges in Church F., Upper Cound F., Harnage Hill F., Broadwall F. and Pool F.

Land in Cressage: house, barn, backside, yard, chapel yard, pasture, Bridgewall M., Dole M., ridges and butts in Dole F., the field towards the Grange and in Lady Oak F. [bounds].

11 Jan. 168–. Adam Ottley, R; Samuel Dod and Thomas Brooke, CWs.

House and outbuildings of 12 bays.

Land in Cound: Bannittree Yard, Dovehouse Close, large piece of arable called Great Church Fur., and small piece of arable adjoining called Little Church Fur., 2 pieces of pasture called Colepit Fur., Holloway M., butts and pikes in Pool F. alias Vineyard F., little meadow called Vineyard Mewadow, 3 furlongs in Harnage Hill F., Hurst M. towards the Severn, 2 pieces of pasture adjoining Cound Moor called Lees, small parcel in Ryton F. leased for 4s.

Land in Cressage: house, barn, garden, hemp butt, yard, chapel yard, pasture called Homer, small Pool M., meadow in the field towards Belswardine called Long Lands, 3½ a. in Lady Oaks F. called Briery Fur., Grange 3 a., piece adjoining Bromley Moor called Withimore Poole, butts called Dichbury Sych.

18 Sep. 1695. Adam Ottley, R; Richard Bentley and John Farmer, CWs.

Parsonage house with 2 barns, ox house, stable, barn with cow house, sheepcote, granary, orchard, yard and dove house.

Land in Cound: Dovehouse Close, Bannittree Yard, Little Church Fur., Middle Church Fur., Great Church Fur., Hoggins Croft, Hurst M., land in Ryton F., Rough Fur. and Vineyard Fur. in Lower Cound F., 4 furlongs in Pistle F., Hollow M., Cole Pit Fur. and New L. adjoining, house and yard at Harnage called Long Croft, house and yard adjoining Cound Moor, 2 pieces of land called Lees adjoining the Moor.

Land in Cressage: parsonage house with barn, yard, orchard, garden and piece of land at the town's end, pasture called Holmer adjoining the Severn, chapel yard, Whitmore Pool, Gridnal Bank, 3 pieces towards Belswardine called Long Land, butt in John Mullard's land leased, Pool M.

Tithes: one-third of the tithes of grain of Acton Pigott (glebe excepted) is due.

A corrody is due from Acton Round in Hereford diocese being 14s paid by Sir Edward Acton of Aldenham; also a corrodie of 5s from the rectory of Chetton and 3s 4d from the rectory of Easthope.

28 Aug. 1698. Adam Ottley, R; Samuel Dod and John Granger, CWs.

28 Apr. 1705. Adam Ottley, R; Robert Dod and Gilbert Cole, CWs.

House of 6 bays with 2 barns 6 bays, stable 1 bay, new stable 2 bays, cow house, sheepcote, barn and granary 3½ bays, garden and orchard ½ acre, churchyard 1 a., fold ½ a., dove house and yard 1 a.

Land in Cound: Bannittree Yard 4 a., Little Church Fur. 4½ a., Middle Church Fur. ½ a., Great Church Fur. 7 a., Hoggins Croft ½ a., Hurst M. near the Severn 1 a., ½ a. in Rytons F. leased, enclosure called Rough Fur. 12 a., Vineyard and Vineyard Fur. belonging to Lower Cound and Harnage 2 a., 4 furlongs 4½ a. in Pistle F., Hollow M. 1½ a., Coalpit Fur. 4 a., New L. 5 a. (ancient enclosure), cottage in Harnage of 2 bays and yard 3 a., Long Croft 2 a., cottage and garden adjoining Cound Moor ½ a., Lees between Cound Moor and Springwell Brook 13 a.

Land in Cressage: house and stable 3 bays, barn 3 bays, garden, orchard ½ a., chapel yard 1 a., Holmers pasture butting on the Severn of 1 day's math, ½ piece at the town's end 3½ a., Whitmore Pool 1½ a., Gridnall Bank 5½ a., butt in John Mullard's land leased.

Tithes are payable in kind in the whole parish except a piece by Cound Lane which belongs to St Giles's Hospital, Shrewsbury which is claimed to be free of tithes, but enquiry into it is needed, tithe of hay for Golding Farm which pays 3s, Langley's house 3s 4d Ottley's tenement 2s, 2 tenements in Lower Cound, 3 in Harnage and 26 in Cressage [named] pay small amounts; half the tithe grain from Acton Pigott is due to the rector; a pension of 14s due from Acton Round was formerly paid by Wenlock Priory, now by Sir Edward Acton of Aldenham; 5s is due from Chetton and 3s 4d from Easthope.

Easter roll of Cound: 2d per communicant, 1d per cow, 4d per colt, 2d per stall of bees, 4d per score of sheep sold, 1d per house in smoke, 1d per garden; calves are due in kind except from certain tenements in Lower Cound and Harnage which pay a modus for hay which they reckon includes calves.

Easter roll of Cressage: as Cound except only ½d is due on calves except where they pay 1 calf p.a. except 4 parishioners [named] who pay 1 calf every other year—'we must enquire into this'.

Surplice fees: burial 4d, churching 4d, marriage 2s 6d.

Clerk's wages: 8d from every team land p.a.

The rectory has £10 in stock.

18 May 1708. Adam Ottley, R; Thomas Snaxton and Thomas Juckes, CWs.
Stable of 2 bays lately built.

1 Oct. 1722. James Jones, R; Thomas Snaxton and John Lloyd, CWs.
House at Cressage of 3 bays with stable 3 bays and another lately built of 2 bays, garden, orchard and yard ½ a.

Part 1 (Abdon to Llanfair Waterdine)

Land at Cound: Bannittree Yard 4 a., Little Church Fur. 4½ a., Middle Church Fur. 5 a., Great Church Fur. 7 a., Hoggins Croft ½ a., Hurst M. near the Severn 1 a., ½ a. in Ryton's field let for 5s p.a., Rough Fur. enclosed 12 a., Vineyard Fur. in Wetpit F. 2 a., 4 furlongs in Epistle F., Hollow M. 1½ a., Coalpit Fur. 4 a., New L. 5 a., cottage in Harnage of 2 bays with yard 3 a., Long Croft 2 a., cottage and yard at Cound Moor ½ a., Lees 18 a.

Land at Cressage: Chapel Yard 1 a., Holmere 1½ day's math, 3½ a. at the town's end, Whitmore Pool 1½ a., Gridnall Bank 3 a., 3 pieces towards Belswardine 5½ a., 1 butt in John Adams land let for 5s p.a., Pool M. let for 1s 6d.

7 July 1726. James Jones, R; William Higginson and John Grainger, CWs.

28 Aug. 1730. John Paschond, C; William Higginson and Jonathan Jones, CWs.

7 Aug. 1733. John Paschond, C; Edward Granger, Allen Whitesides.

23 June 1736. John Paschond, C; Allen Whitesides and Edward Phips, CWs.

We have a bond of £100 from the late Dr Ottley, Bishop of St Davids, but the payment is uncertain because one of his executors put all his effects into Chancery; also £16 in the hands of Robert Dod of Harnage and £5 in the hands of Thomas Langley Esq.

14 Aug 1739. Edward Cressett, R; Francis Yeates and Andrew Snaxton, CWs.

18 Sep. 1742. John Paschoud, C; Francis Yeates and John Ballen, CWs.

27 Aug. 1745. Edward Cressett, R; John Newcomb and Thomas Powell, CWs.

14 Sep. 1748. Edward Cressett, R; John Richards, CW.

26 July 1748.

Deeds concerning exchange of glebe land by Edward Cressett, Dean of Hereford, patron and rector of Cound for some of his own lands; the Bishop of Hereford's survey said that this would be of benefit to the rectory.

14 Sep. 1752. E[dward Cressett, Bishop of] Landaff, R; John Newcombe, CW.

14 Sep. 1756. W[illiam] Adams, R; John Grainger and Richard Bryan, CWs.

16 Sep. 1759*. W[illiam] Adams, R; Samuel Phipps and Abraham Oliver, CWs.

7 Sep. 1763. W[illiam] Adams, R; James Farmer and John Richards, CWs.

21 Sep. 1779. [William Adams, R; no signatories].

12 Aug. 1828. E[dward] Owen, R; Edward Ditcher, CW.

1849. Henry Thursby, R; T. Meire and John Norris, CWs.

Tithes of Cressage, 1,784 a., have been commuted for a rent charge of £208 15s 10d.

Tithes of Cound, 3,500 a., have been commuted for £622 rent charge including £20 moduses on hay (except 14 a. by Cound Lane which belongs to St Giles's Hospital Shrewsbury); the tithe of hay in Golding now belongs to the Earl of Liverpool.

Land at Cound: cottage and Coppice Ley 6 a., Brickkiln F. 3 a., Barretts L. 6 a., house and garden called Banky Croft 1 a., Calves F. 1 a., Yewtree L. 1 a., Pit L. 1 a., Upper Leys 6 a., Little Leys 3 a., Lower Common Piece 2 a., Upper Common Piece 1 a., Baynuttree Yard 3½ a., parsonage house, yards and outbuildings 3 a., pleasure grounds and gardens 1 a., church and yard 1 a., Church Fur. 4 a., wood and marsh 3 a., Pasture Patch 4 a., Bottoms 2 a., Brook L. 6 a., Pointed Slang 6½ a., Little Church Fur. 4 a., Patch 3 a., Hardibutt 5½ a., Little F. 5½ a., Cow Pasture 9 a.; total 95½ a., value £175 p.a.

Land at Cressage: churchyard 1 a., Townsend 3 a., Townsend 1 a., Long Lanes 5 a., Long Lane 2 a., Homer F. 2 a., Bromley Moor 2 a., F. 3 a., cottage and patch 1 a., Quillet 1 a., small close 1 a.; total 23 a., value £45 6s p.a.

1884.

House built in 1882 with beer and wine cellar in the basement; entrance and staircase hall, porch, WC, drawing room, dining room, library, servants' room, china pantry, kitchen, scullery, dairy, coal store, servants' WC, outdoor WC on ground floor; 6 bedrooms, bathroom, WC on 1st floor; 3 bedrooms, box room, housemaid's closet and linen store on 2nd floor; 2-stalled stable, 2 loose boxes with hay loft over, saddle room, men's room over, wash house, coach house with granary over, workshop, cow house for 4 cows, 3 pigsties, game shed, fowl house; gardener's cottage with parlour, kitchen, back kitchen, pantry, 2 bedrooms, lobby, potting shed and tool house; parish room 50 ft × 20 ft with laundry and wash house; Glebe Farm House with cellar, kitchen, best kitchen, shop, back kitchen, dairy, pantry, 4 bedrooms, granary, coal store, cow house, 3-stalled stable, barn, 2 pigsties and fold.

Land: Bannet Tree Yard 3 a., house and garden 4 a., Dove house, close and yard 3½ a., Church Fur. 4 a., Hardy Butts Wood 5 a. being 20½ a. in the hands of the vicar; Little Church Fur. 4 a., parcel of 2 a., Wood Patch and Cutlers L. 5 a., house and croft ½ a., house and buildings ½ a., Barn L. 4 a., Hardy Butts 10 a., Upper Bottons 2 a., Brook L. 6 a., Little F. 5 a., 3 houses and gardens, schoolhouse and yard, Gate and Brook L. 11 a., Tillers M. 3 a., Far Cambrell L. 3 a., Tillers Bridge 2½ a.; total 62 a. all leased, annual value £238 6s 8d.

Income: tithe rent charge £617 11s.

Schedule of registers from 1608.

Plate: silver chalice, paten and flagon and brass alms dish.

Cressage[1]

1845. George Burd, C.

Most matters are answered under Cound.

---

[1] Cressage was a separate parish in the 12th century but in the later Middle Ages was served by the rector of Cound, and in 1545 was accepted as a chapelry of Cound. It remained a chapelry until it was made into an ecclesiastical parish in 1864: *Victoria history of Shropshire*, viii. 73. See also Cound terriers.

Part 1 (Abdon to Llanfair Waterdine)

There is no glebe house; there are two cottages and barns with small gardens.

Fees: marriage 5s, burial 6d, churching 1s 6d, headstones £1, vaults £5.

Clerk's fees as Cound.

The chancel is repaired by the rector and is in good repair.

Plate: silver chalice, 2 goblets with gilt inside, 2 patens and 2 salvers. There is an iron chest for the registers fixed to the vestry wall.

Benefactions: the interest of £50 left by W. Dutton—see Cound; 3 a. of land was left for the maintenance of the school.

1884.

Land: 26½ a. glebe leased for £68 10s p.a.

Tithe rent charge £208 15s 10d.

Schedule of registers from 1772.

Plate: 2 silver chalices, 3 silver patens, silver alms dish.

Benefactions: Dame Ann Eldred by will in 1671 left £100, the interest for the poor of Cound and Cressage (£1 p.a. for Cressage, the rest for Cound)—this is known as the Gosnell Charity.

Criftins[1]

1884*. Walter Hazlehurst, V.

House of red brick in good repair with 2 storeys, 6 chimneys, 7 bedrooms and 3 sittingrooms in 1 a. of land.

Income: tithe rent charge £74 7s 10d; grant from Eccl. Com. in 1874 of £22 10s; grants in 1881 and 1882 of £535 and £200 towards the vicarage; QAB c. £8 6s; fees average c. £2 12s p.a.

Registers from 1873.

Plate: silver chalice, 2 silver patens and brass alms dish.

The land around the church is about to be marked by a boundary to be a burial ground, but is not yet consecrated.

Benefactions: Criftins is a district separated for ecclesiastical purposes from the old parish of Dudleston and the charities have not been officially divided.

Culmington

1 Nov. 1685†. Marc. Fothergill, R; William Gough, Thomas Jones and Thomas Parrock, CWs. [6 other signatories].

House in Seifton with stable, 2 great corn barns, little barn with hay barn, backside or orchard, 2 gardens and churchyard.

House in Culmington with backside.

Land: enclosure in Plowstons 5 a., enclosure to N. of same called Little Plowstons 3 a., meadow on Corve Bank called Whittingale ½ a., Home M. enclosed 1½ a., small parcels of arable in Culmington F. and Cudney F.

---

[1] Criftins was formed into an ecclesiastical parish from parts of Dudleston and Ellesmere parishes in 1872: *P.O. directory of Shropshire* (1879), 310.

Glebe terriers of Shropshire

[bounds]; common of pasture in Seifton Forest and in the several fields of Seifton when open at harvest.

Dawley
(*and see* Dawley Parva; Malins Lee)

1612. John Davies, minister; Harry Choyse, CW.

Parsonage house of 2½ bays with little garden and court and barn 3 bays.

Land: Priests L. 6 a., Bobbins Close ½ a., Deep Lane Croft ¼ a., Leehorne Close ½ a., Horse Croft 1½ a., Portway Yate Piece ½ a., all enclosed; in the common fields 2 butts in More Fur. F. ½ a., 3 small pikes in Castle F. ½ a., 5 small butts in Reddale F. 3 a., 15 butts 2¾ a. in 7 parcels in Pool Hill F., 16 butts and 2 lands 1¾ a. in Copyed Gray F. surrounded by the land of Sir George Hayward [bounds].

Tithes in kind belong to the parsonage of Great and Little Dawley; the parsonage is impropriated; Malins Lee pays £10 p.a. in lieu of tithes.

10 Dec. 1632. Henry Choyse, Robert Taylor, Roger Roe, CWs.

Parsonage house with garden, backhouse, barn and houses of office.

The chancel is conveniently repaired.

Tithes in Great and Little Dawley are due on corn, hay, wool, lambs, pigs, geese, hemp, flax, apples and eggs; also Easter duties. Malins Lee pays £6 6s 8d for all tithes.

1682. [George Arden, C] Francis Jorden and John Haslehurst, CWs.

1 Oct. 1685. [George Arden, C] Edward Barnes and Thomas Roe, CWs.

9 Sep. 1693. [George Arden, C] Christopher Benneson and Richard Heyway.

17 Aug. 1698. [George Arden, C] William Whitehed and John Churme, CWs.

4 May 1705. George Auden, C; William Richards and John Harris, CWs.

The curate's wages are about £12 for services the whole year.

1708. [George Arden, C. No signatories].

25 July 1711. [George Arden, C] Griffith Jones and William Watkis, CWs.

Parsonage house of 2½ bays with malt house 2 bays, garden, barn 3 bays, stable, cow house 1½ bays and little fold adjoining.

Tithes: there is an ancient modus from Malins Lee; from the townships of Great and Little Dawley by ancient modus 6d is due for every calf, 1d for every new Welsh cow, 1½d for every barren cow, 1d for smoke, 1d for gardens.

Surplice fees: for reading banns 1s, marriage after banns 2s 6d, marriage with licence 5s, burials 4d, churching 4d.

The chancel is repaired by the lay impropriator.

The clerk's wages are paid by the parishioners—every living 4d, every cottage 1d.

1718. Jeremiah Tayler, C; John Pooley and Jeremiah Sambrook, CWs.

Land: Priests L. 7 a., Bobbins Croft 1 a., Horse Croft 2 a., 1 a. arable in Rednall F. now enclosed, Deep Lane croft ½ a., Goose Croft or Welch Harp ½ a., Leehorne Croft ½ a., Portway Gate Croft 1½ a., 3 a. in Copy

Part 1 (Abdon to Llanfair Waterdine)

Green F. newly enclosed and about ½ a. unenclosed, 7 a. in Pool Hill F. in several parts [bounds].
The chancel is now in good repair.

1722. [Too damaged to handle].

4 July 1726. Copy of 1722. J. Tayler, minister; John Harris and Matthew Cross, CWs.
Clerk's fees: coffin grave 1s, grave without coffin 6d, grave in church 2s 6d, ringing bell 1s, looking after the clock 10s, marriage by banns or licence 1s.
The impropriator has the modus of Malins Lee, Easter duties, surplice fees and the glebe and at present allows the curate of Malins Lee Easter duties, surplice fees and £4 10s in lieu 'as they say' of the tithe hay for Great and Little Dawley.

13 July 1730. Edward Fosbrooke, C; Edward Whitehead and Edward Whittingham, CWs.

9 Aug. 1733. Edward Fosbrooke, C; John Cuerton and Francis Pickering, CWs.
The late impropriator, John Revell, gave by will £5 to the curate of Dawley for ever; the present curate has the modus of Malins Lee, the Easter dues of Great and Little Dawley, the surplice fees and £4 10s in money and the cows and calves of Great and Little Dawley.

13 July 1736. Edward Fosbrooke, C; Richard Steventon and Lawrence Wellington, CWs.

31 Aug. 1739. Edward Fosbrooke, C; Thomas Dawes and William Keen, CWs.

17 Sep. 1742. Edward Fosbrooke, C; Melchisedec Pascall and William Whitehead, CWs.
Land: 5½ a. in Pool Hill F. now enclosed.

10 Sep. 1745. Edward Fosbrooke, C; Richard Whitehead and William Andrews, CWs.

13 Sep. 1748. Edward Fosbrooke, C; John Wyke and John Meeson, CWs.

1 Sep. 1752. Edward Fosbrooke; William Roe and John Evans, CWs.

5 Sep. 1763. Edward Fosbrooke, C; Henry Onions and Thomas Botfield, CWs.
John Revell left £5 to the curate for ever from land called Dale's tenement in Wellington; the present curate has the modus of Malins Lee, Easter dues of Great and Little Dawley, surplice fees, £4 10s in money and the cows and calves of Great and Little Dawley; Mrs Rebecca Walthall, the landlady of most of Malins Lee, left £50 to the curate for procuring QAB for the augmentation of the living, and if it could not be procured for him to have the annual interest of the £50.[1]

15 Sep. 1767. Edward Fosbrooke, C; Richard Hulet and Richard Rhodes, CWs.

---

[1] Rebecca Walthall was the daughter of Isaac Browne of Burton on Trent; she inherited Malins Lee from her father in 1713 and died in 1756: *A History of Shropshire*, xi, ed. G. C. Baugh (*The Victoria history of the counties of England*, 1985), 114.

7 Sep. 1772. Thomas Edwardson, C; William Gibbons and William Andrews, CWs.

20 Aug. 1775. James Gibbons and Thomas Lewis, CWs.

18 Oct. 1779. Roger Clayton, C; Jonah Jones and Thomas Suthons, CWs. Parsonage house is a thatched building.

3 Aug. 1783*. Roger Clayton, minister; Henry Onions and Adam Wright, CWs.

23 Oct. 1792.
Roger Clayton, minister; Thomas Suthens and Joseph Darral, CWs.

23 July 1797. Roger Clayton, minister; John Onions and Thomas Suthions, CWs.

25 Aug. 1801. Roger Clayton, minister; Thomas Southon and Jonah Jones, CWs.

1805*. Roger Clayton, minister; Jonah Jones, CW.
[Document in poor condition].

3 Sep. 1810. Roger Clayton, minister; Jonas Jones and Richard Lewis, CWs.

7 Aug. 1824. Hugo Moreton Phillips, C; William James and Richard Lewis, CWs.

12 Aug. 1828. Hugo Moreton Phillips, C; William James and Richard Lewis, CWs.
Copy of 1759.

16 Aug. 1832. John Wood, minister; William James and Adam Wright, CWs.
Copy of 1759.

7 Sep. 1836. John Wood, minister; William James, CW.
Copy of 1759.

8 Sep. 1841. John Wood, minister; R. Summers and Joseph Russell, CWs.
'. . . a good parsonage house with all necessary outbuildings'.
Vaults cost £1 10s per square yd. The chancel belongs to the impropriator and is much dilapidated as are also other parts of the church.
Plate: 1 silver cup and small plate. There is an iron chest for registers.
Benefactions: Enoch Cooper by will of 24 Feb. 1721/2 left £20 for the poor of Great Dawley; Rebecca Walthall by will Jan. 1736/7 left £40 to the CWs for the poor of Malins Lee.

13 Aug. 1845*. John Wood, minister; Joseph Russell and Thomas Summers, CWs.
Parsonage house with hall, dining room, drawing room, study, kitchen, pantry and wash house on the ground floor, 7 bedrooms upstairs, coach house, stable, pigsty, paved yard, gardens, orchard and shrubberies nearly 2 a.
2d is due from communicants not attached to the district churches of Malins Lee and Little Dawley, £5 p.a. from the rent of a cottage in Hadley, £4 10s from the patron, £6 from the Earl of Craven in lieu of tithes for his estate in Little Dawley, £26 from the Eccl. Com. in compensation for the loss of

fees to the minister of Malins Lee district church. The church of Great Dawley has more than once been augmented by parliamentary grants and QAB; the former curate received £84 17s 2d and later £4 1s 10d; no land has been purchased.

Fees: publishing banns 1s 6d, marriage by banns 3s 4d, by licence 5s, burials 1s, churching 6d, vaults £1 1s per square yd., head stones 10s 6d.

£1 p.a. is charged on a field called Castle Yard by tithe commutation for the township of Great Dawley in lieu of an ancient modus on colts, calves, milk cows, barren cows and gardens.

Clerk's fees: marriage by banns 3s, by licence 5s, burials 3s 6d, churching 6d.

The incumbent is a perpetual curate having purchased the parsonage house with the help of QAB and mortgaged to them under 'Gilbert's Act' for 30 years (7 years now expired); £19 19s 6d has been paid this year.

The repairs of the chancel belong to the lay impropriator.

Plate: silver cup dated 1746, the gift of Sarah Moreton. There is an iron chest for registers.

Benefactions: Richard Hoddens of Ludlow gave by will in 1684 £7 p.a. for poor widows; Enoch Cooper by will of 26 Feb. 1721/2 gave £20 to the poor; 'another person by the name of Cooper' gave £13 to be put out at interest; these last two were put in the hands of William James, CW, who died insolvent.

1849. John Wood, minister; E. Garbett and Robert Belshaw, CWs.

The governors of QAB paid £86 7s 2d p.a. subject to a mortgage of 1838, the last repayment being £18 5s.

Income: the impropriator pays £4 10s, Malins Lee pays a modus of £6 6s 8d; the Eccl. Com. pay £41 p.a. (£15 is unlikely to be paid to a future incumbent); Easter dues of 6d per communicant; Great Dawley pays a rent charge of £1 on Castle in lieu of cows and calves as commuted by the Tithe Commissioners.

The clerk claims 2d per cottage.

26 July 1853. William Richards, minister; Thomas Wilkes and Thomas Bray, CWs.

1884*. R. Cotterill Wanstall, V; John Thomason and Edwin Clayton, CWs.

House and land belonging to Col. Kenyon Slaney, lord of the manor, is occupied by the vicar for £1 p.a.; it has a dining room, drawing room, study, kitchen, back kitchen, 6 bedrooms, WC, stable with 2 stalls, coach house, saddle room and wash house.

The gross tithe rent charge of £165 is claimed by the impropriators, Andrew and Revell Phillips of Shifnal, solicitors; the perpetual curate's tithe is £6.

Income: £187 6s 8d from the Eccl. Com.; £95 6s 8d from QAB; fees average p.a. £10.

Schedule of registers from 1666.

Plate: 2 silver patens, silver chalice, metal flagon and brass alms basin.

Benefactions: Hoddens charity being £2 11s 4d left for the poor in 1684; interest on £200 left by Mr Lewis of Mosseygreen; one-third of the interest on £100 left by Mr Greenhalgh.

Glebe terriers of Shropshire

Dawley Parva[1]

1884*. Richard Maltby, V; James Banks and John Bradburn, CWs.
House with stable, coach house, stable, yard, lawn, shrubberies, kitchen garden and space used as a potato ground.
Income: £150 granted by the Eccl. Com. 1844; fees average p.a. £6 14s 6d.
Registers from 1846.
Plate: silver chalice and paten, glass flagon and brass alms dish.
Benefactions: £1 12s 4d from Hoddens Charity, Dawley.

Deuxhill and Glazeley

n.d. [1589].
Edward Corbett is reputed patron.
Land: 15 a. of glebe. [Details are given, but one side of the terrier is very faded].

1607. Peter Barrett, parson; William Croft and Henry Burrer, CWs.
Glazeley: house with a little garden, hemp butt, pasture W. of the house 1 a. and little pasture within the park called Parson's Close 1½ a.
Tithes of corn and hay are due and Easter duties.
Deuxhill: barn with a close adjoining 2 a., pastures called the Park 2 a. and the Pen below the Hill 3 a.; arable land in the common fields being ¼ a. in Cleeford F. at Hurden Yate, 4 a. arable in 6 pieces in Horsford F., 4½ a. in 7 pieces in Deuxhill F.
Tithe corn and all privy tithes are due.

1802. E[dward] Davenport, R; Thomas Lewis, CW.
Glazeley: parsonage house with 2 small gardens, stable and cow house to the W. of the house; little pasture called Parson's Close 1 a., churchyard 1 a.
Deuxhill: barn 4 bays, cow house, several closes round the barn bounded on the NW. by the turnpike road 16 a., churchyard ¼ a.
Corn and hay are tithable except when mowed twice or eaten off as aftermath; 5s per acre is due for flax, potatoes and turnips when drawn and sold, but nothing if they are consumed on the premises; 1d is due per cow in lieu of tithe milk, 6d per calf, 3d per lamb, ½d per barren cow in lieu of agistment, 1s per colt; wool is tithable of sheep not lambs; 6d for smoke and garden is due from communicants and 6d from a man and wife or 2d from single persons at Easter; 3 eggs are due per cock, 2 per hen and 1 per pullet at Easter; the 10th pig is due and apples and pears are due in kind.
Fees: 3s 6d per burial.

Diddlebury

n.d. [?1589]. [John Habberley, incumbent] Antony Wellence and Richard Normcott, CWs.
The canons of Hereford are patrons.

---

[1] Dawley Parva was formed into an ecclesiastical parish from part of Dawley parish in 1844: *Victoria history of Shropshire*, xi. 128.

House with barn and stable 8 to 10 bays, garden, orchard and ½ a. enclosed meadow; house in Diddlebury 3 bays.

Land: common pasture in the Long Forest and in Corfton F.

Tithes are due from Corfton and Sparchford.

22 Apr. 1637*.[1] [Hereford copy allmost illegible; 2 copies in SRRC undated]. Thomas Habberley, incumbent; William Wigley and William Tyler, CWs.

Meres and bounds of the parish: from Dinchope to Eaton, Munslow, Ditton, Clee, Cold Weston, Stanton Lacy, Culmington and Dinchope.

Corfton: house, stable and barn 10 bays, 2 gardens, 2 orchards, chapel yard.

Diddlebury: house, barn of 4 bays and garden.

Land in Corfton: meadow ½ a. on Corve Bank, common of pasture in Corfton Wood in the Long Forest and in the fields of Corfton; common of estover in Corfton Wood.

Tithes of corn and grain are due in Corfton, Sparchford and the home closes in the other parts of the parish (unless money is paid); payments are made in lieu for milk, dove houses and hay; 2 ancient dove houses in Diddlebury pay 2d p.a. each; Bach Mill pays 2s, the mill in Moore 1s; the tenants of Edward Bawdewin in Diddlebury [names given] pay 3s for tithe hay, those of Gertrude Bawdewin 1s, other tenants [names given] make small payments; similar small payments are made in Corfton, Aston, Sparchford, Westhope, Middlehope, Peaton, Broncroft, Great Poston, Clee St Margaret, Great Sutton and Little Sutton with Lawton; Earnstrey Park pays in kind; small tithes of wool, lambs, apples, pears, geese, pigs, hemp and flax are due; also 2 eggs per hen at Easter and 3 per cock; 1d is due for a garden, 1d for wood and fuel burnt; for every communicant servant, tradesman, or artificer one-tenth of his clear gain after charges are deducted; other communicants pay 2d; one-tenth of the yearly value of the pasture of barren cattle is due; ½d is due for each sheep sold.

There is a convenient seat in the chancel for the vicar and his assistant adjoining the reading place and free egress and regress to the chancel for the administration of the sacrament etc. and for receiving money in lieu of tithes, putting on robes and a chest for the same.

Fees: marriages 1s 8d if married in the parish, and also if of the parish but married elsewhere, burials 6d, churching 6d; mortuaries according to statute.

Ditton Priors

1589. [Signatories worn].

Humphrey Packington of Chaddesley Corbett is patron.

House with barn and hay house.

Land: 19 butts arable on both sides of Mill Croft L., parcels of 3 butts, 5 butts and 11 butts in the common field on the way to Ruthall, 1 a. of

---

[1] See also E. H. Martin, 'Terrier of the parish of Diddlebury 1637', *Trans. Shropshire Archaeol. Soc.* 3rd ser. vii (1907), 139–49.

meadow in Ruthallsitch, 5 lands in other men's land; pikes in Middleton. 8 parcels in Denway F., butts in Bradbridge F. and Over F. [bounds].

12 Dec. 1604. William Hotchkis and John Reignoldes.
House of 2 bays with 2 cross chambers at the end, barn 3 bays and a stable at the end, hay house 1 bay, 2 gardens and little orchard.

20 Mar. 1607/8. William Warde, V; John Reignoldes, John Blakeway, William Hassall.
House with chamber and cross end, barn and stables, little hay barn and 2 yards with 3 apple trees.
Land: arable in Wyldyche F. and Over F. [many dispersed parcels]; meadow and pasture [bounds].

2 May 1625. Thomas Jenks, V.
House with barn, stables, cow house and 2 gardens.
Land: furlong of 11 ridges and 1 a. of 6 ridges in Brodbridge F., little meadow in Rea M., small yard, parcel of meadow in Ruthallsitch, furlong and 1 a. of arable in Ruthall F., pastures called Milcroft and New L. [bounds.
Tithes of corn are due in Further Middleton, some lands in Hither Middleton [specified] pay 12s p.a.; tithe of corn and hay is due from the home closes in the whole parish except for the manor house; tithe is due on wool, lambs, calves, herbage, apples, pigs, geese, hemp, flax and all other duties 'ordinarily belonging or of right appertaining unto other our neighbour churches and Ecclesiasticall liveings' throughout the parish. Mortuaries are due.

Dodington[1]

13 Aug. 1841. Charles Long, minister; Henry Corser and John Ravenshaw, CWs.
There is no house or land.
The minister has dividends on £2,000 stock in 3% consols; he has no fees.
Clerk's salary is paid voluntarily by the minister.
Plate: paten, flagon and cup of silver.
There are no benefactions for the minister or the poor.

23 Oct. 1849. H. Egerton, minister; Henry Corser and William Darlington, CWs.

Donington

22 Oct. 1612. John Chapman, minister; John Whystons and Thomas Perst, CWs.
House with kitchen, stable, cow house, barn, cote, dove house, orchard, gardens and little yard adjoining 1 a.

---

[1] Dodington chapel was built as a chapel of ease for Whitchurch in 1836: *Kelly's directory of Shropshire* (1895), 263. See also Whitchurch terrier of 1857.

Part 1 (Abdon to Llanfair Waterdine)

Land: 1 close bounding on Albrighton Park 2 a., 4 closes bounding on Sir Vincent Corbett's land 9 a., 2 closes bounding on the land of Humphrey Lee Esq. 4 a., 3 selions or butts in a close amongst Corbett's land 1 a., cottage and 2 a. of land, 4 a. arable land in Middlecroft F., 3 a. in Porrow F., day's math in Harggur M. [bounds].

Tithes are due on corn, hay, hemp and flax, wool, lambs, pigs, geese and fruit; 6s 8d for Mrs Gifford's custom, 1s 4d custom for a cottage on Gifford's land, 2s custom for a mill in Shackerley.

Oblations: 2d for every married person, 1d for every single person born in the parish.

1681. John Fisher, R; John Bishton and Thomas Johns, CWs.

Garden, orchard and dove house yard 1 a.

Land: Millcroft 4 a., Gods Croft adjoining the churchyard 3 a., Walnut Tree L. E. of the church 4 a., Lambs L. butting to Albrighton Pool 4 a., Carecroft 3 a., Long L. 5 a., Long Croft 5 a., Shacroft Stile L. 7 a., Landers Croft ½ a., Harbour M. 1½ a., 4½ a. in 3 yards in Little F., 1 land in Clock F. 1 a., 2 lands in Parrow F. 1 a.; field land being 5½ a. in Clock F. 5½ a., 6 a. in Middle Croft F., 10½ a. in Parra F. [bounds].

27 Sep. 1693. George Plaxton, R; John Bishton and Joseph Yates, CWs.

Parsonage house of 4 bays, very large and old built with kitchen, malt house of brick and new malt kiln 3 bays, new built dove house 1 large bay, stable, cow house, ox house with 2 large bings for fodder and straw 4 bays, newly repaired tithe barn 3 bays, long barn 7 bays with hay house at the end, sheepcote 3 small bays, draw well, large fold or orchard, large garden lately planted with apple trees and yard with a long pool to S. belonging to the rector and the Earl of Shrewsbury, the stream being the boundary with Albrighton; the rectors have anciently received part of the fishing.

Land: Gods Croft 4 a., Mill Croft 1½ a., meadow 1 a., Walnut Tree L. 5½ a., Pool L. 4 a., Care Croft 4 a., leasow leading towards Humphreston 7 a., Littlefords Yard 4 a., Long Croft 6 a., Shawcroft Stile 9 a. with a small meadow, Harbour M. 1 a.; field land: being 13½ a. in Clock F., 14 a. in Middle Croft F., 11 a. in Porrow F. [bounds]; the rector has commoning on all heaths and common fields.

Tithes of hay, clover, corn, pulse, lambs, wool, calves, pigs, geese, apples, pears and eggs are due; 6d per colt, offerings of 6d per house, 3d per stall of bees, 3d per artificer, 3d per servant; 2s custom for Shackerley Mill, 1s 4d for Widow Fletcher's tenement in Shackerley, 6s 8d for White Ladies and Boscobel. 300 a. belonging to Cosford Grange used to pay in kind and the present rector brought a suit in the Exchequer to recover them; the rector pays a pension of 6s 8d to the king as fee farm rent.

Fees: burials 1s, marriages 5s, churching 4d.

The parish consists of Donington, Humphreston, Kilsall, Shackerley, Neachley, Dairy House, White Ladies and Boscobel. White Ladies and Boscobel formerly had baptisms and burials at Donington but they are all papists now and have a burial place of their own.

79

24 July 1718. W. Cradock, R; Joseph Yates, Jeffery Tildesley and Dositheus Twigg.

1722. W. Cradock, R; Joseph Yates and Richard Wall, CWs.
[2 copies, 1 parchment, 1 paper].

1726. W. Cradock, R; Joseph Bridgin and John Crutchley, CWs.
Land: large garden lately paled; the *sylva cedua*[1] is particularly accounted for when cut down and corded and attested by public notary, a copy is in the rector's hand.
The tithes of Cosford Grange, 300 a. lying within the parish, have been received by decree in the Exchequer since the present rector came paid in kind or annual composition; there were formerly houses in Cosford from which the rector received the usual offerings, but they have now been demolished.

1730. W. Cradock, R; William Bishton and Dositheus Twigg, CWs.
Land is as in the 1693 terrier; a copy was attested by public notary and kept in the rector's house.

1733. W. Cradock, R; William Whiston and William Perry, CWs.

1736. W. Cradock, R; William Smith and Jonathan Dudley, CWs.

1739. William Sheinton, C; Dositheus Twigg and Thomas Ellis, CWs.

1742. William Sheinton, C; William Bishton and John Crutchley, CWs.

1745. William Sheinton, C; Thomas Jellicorse and William Yates, CWs.

1748. W. Sheinton, C; William Smith and . . . [faded], CWs.

1751. W. Sheinton, C; William Bishton and Jonathan Dudley, CWs.

1756. W. Sheinton, C; Thomas Jellicorse and William Yates, CWs.

1759. William Sheinton, C; John Smith and John Elliotts, CWs and John Dudley, late CW.

1763. Samuel Dickenson, C; William Bishton jr. and John Olwen, CWs.

1767. John Browne, C; William Yate and William Cheatham, CWs.

1775*. John Chappel Woodhouse, R; William Yates, CW.
Parsonage house old, but repaired by the present rector, John Chappel Woodhouse, with new piece of building adjoining built by the present rector, old kitchen or malt house of brick, new coach house and stable, cow house and bing for fodder lately rebuilt, old tithe barn 3 bays, fold yard adjoining lately fenced with a brick wall by the present rector, draw well and pump and large garden adjoining the coach house.
Land: Mill Croft and pool, Church L., Church Lane Flatts and Cote L. now all called Clock Mill L. 33 a.; new messuage in the field lately called Clock F. now Chapel House being a large piece of building with barn, stable, cow house, bing for fodder, cart house, granary over, fold yard, rick

---

[1] '*Sylva cedua*' refers to the tithe on coppice wood when felled: Burn, *Ecclesiastical law*, ed. Fraser, iii. 411, 479.

yard and garden E. of the road leading from Albrighton to Tong and more land W. of the road between it and the turnpike road from Bowling Green to Kilsall, Hempole L., Common L., Black Close, 2 new enclosures W. of the turnpike, Rough Common L. and Cosford Corner; 159 a. in total, lately part of the common fields called Middle Croft F., Clock F. and a common called Kilsall Heath.

Tithes: by act of 1771 the tithes and customary payments were ended on certain lands; White Ladies and Boscobel still pay 6s 8d at Easter and Thomas Fitzherbert Esq. of Neachley pays 6d for a meadow.

1779. John Chappel Woodhouse, R; William Jellicorse and John Elliots, CWs.

Parsonage house is an old building lately repaired by the present rector with new piece of building adjoining, old kitchen or malthouse, new coach house and stable and old stable.

Land: Gods Croft, Lawn and Highway Piece 40 a. lying together with Albrighton Pool to S., Fold Piece or Mill Croft, Church L., Church Lane Flatts, Cote L. and 3 pieces called Clock Mill L. lying together with the road from Albrighton to Donington to E. and a lane from Wolverhampton to Newport to W. 33 a., large building with barn, stable, cow house, bing, cart house, granary, fold yard, rick yard and garden, 2 pieces called Little Middle Croft, several pieces to W. of the road from Albrighton to Tong called Crabtree L., Yewtree L., Lambs Yard, Colts Croft, Dockey L., Little Clock F., Great Clock F., Hemphole L., Common L., Black Close and 2 new enclosures on the W. of the turnpike from Bowling Green to Kilsall called Rough Common L. and Cosford Corner lately part of the common fields enclosed by act of parliament 1772 and allotted to Revd George Butt, then rector; total 159 a. lying contiguous.

Tithes are due on all lands in the parish not exonerated by the enclosure act, i.e. Cosford, the land of William Yates (excepting his allotment on Kilsall Heath), the land of William Jellicorse called Dairy House Farm, the land of Thomas Jellicoe (excepting his allotment on Kilsall Heath); tithes are due on hay, clover, corn, pulse, lambs, wool, calves, pigs, geese, apples, pears; eggs, cows and calves are paid in the usual way being 1½d for a cow and calf and 1d for a barren cow except Dairy House Farm and Thomas Jellicoe who pay 1s 8d at Easter; 6d is due on colts, 6d per house, 3d per stall of bees put down for honey, 3d for artificers, 3d for servants; the customary tithing of White Ladies and Boscobel is 6s 8d.

The rector pays a pension of 6s 8d to the king as fee farm.

Fees: burials 1s, marriage with licence 5s, with banns 2s 6d, churching 4d.

1783*. J. C. Woodhouse, R; James Boulton, CW.

Messuage built by the present rector in the late Clock F. and known as Chappel House with fold, yard, rick yard and garden.

1792*. J. C. Woodhouse, R; John Bishton jr. and James Boulton, CWs.

Schedule of lands still tithable with field names and acreages, total 555 a.

1797*. J. C. Woodhouse, R; John Bishton and James Boulton, CWs.

Glebe terriers of Shropshire

1801. J. C. Woodhouse, R; John Bishton and James Boulton, CWs.

1805. J. C. Woodhouse, R; John Bishton and James Boulton, CWs.
The rectory house and garden is surrounded by a brick wall built by the present rector.

1810. J. C. Woodhouse, R; John Boulton, CW.
[Document very damaged].

1824. J. C. Woodhouse, R; Thomas Pearce and John Boulton, CWs.
The land is held by William Picken except the rectory house with outbuildings and garden; Gods Croft and a small meadow are occupied by Revd Joseph Dale, curate, a strip of land, 5 a., was sold in 1810 to Thomas Bishton under the Land Tax Redemption Act to to redeem the land tax chargeable on the rectory.

1828. Thomas Pearce, CW.

1832. Thomas Bishton and Thomas Pearce, CWs.

1836. Henry Howard, R; Thomas Pearce and John Boulton, CWs.
House in 2 parts, one built by the last rector and one by the present rector to replace an old building with stables, cow house, binn for fodder, old barn commonly called tithe barn 3 bays, large garden adjoining and coach house.

1841. Henry Howard, R; John Boulton and Thomas Pearce, CWs.
Communion plate: cup, flagon and paten of silver. There is an iron chest for registers.
Benefactions: Revd W. Chapman rector of Donington in 1746 bequeathed an estate in Donington worth 10s p.a. due on St Thomas's Day; Sarah, wife of Humphrey Manning alias James Steward, bequeathed 2s p.a. out of real estate in Shackerley payable by Thomas Jellicorse and Jonathan Ruston, first paid in 1745; these bequests are on a board in the church.
Clerk's fees: marriage 2s, churching 4d, digging a grave and tolling the bell 2 hours 3s 6d for a child under 8 years, others 5s and double if not parishioners; clerk's wages are £3 12s p.a. paid by the parish.
The chancel is repaired by the rector and is in a good state.

1845*. Henry Howard, R; Thomas Pearce and John Boulton, CWs.
The tithes are now agreed to be commuted for a rent charge of £200 p.a.

1853*. Henry Howard, R; John Jellicorse and John Sherratt, CWs.
[Tithes due are restated, though commuted according to deeds of apportionment kept in the parish chest].

1884*. H. G. de Bunsen, R.
House with stable, yard, garden, old tithe barn and former fold yard 3½ a.
Land: plantation, grounds, new foal yard and fowl house 3 a., Chappel House Farm with house and farm buildings 240 a. of land leased at £480 p.a.
Income: the yearly interest on £1,402 14s being £42 1s 6d is paid to the rector by the accountant-general every half year; this sum was acquired by the sale of 7 a. of glebe in 1845 to the Shrewsbury and Birmingham Railway (since incorporated into G.W.R.); tithe rent charge by apportionment

3 Apr. 1843 is £250 gross on 1,217 a.; Chappel House farm rent is £540, but since 1878 £60 has been returned to him for each of the last 5 years because of the bad times and whether the full rent can be paid again remains to be seen; Boscobel modus by appointment 12 Sep. 1845 was fixed at 6s 8d in lieu of tithes on extra-parochial land, Barn Piece, 19 a.; average fees p.a. £1 17s 10d.

A Crown rent of 7s 6d is payable, £1 7s 2d tenths are payable to QAB and 14s for procurations and synodals.

Schedule of registers from 1556.

Plate: silver chalice, paten and flagon and carved walnut alms dish.

Benefactions: 10s p.a. rent charge from Shackerley was given by George Jones of Shackerley Hall, 10s p.a. rent charge on the land of Francis Yates.

Donnington Wood[1]

1884*. Thomas O'Regan, V.

There is no house or land.

Income: tithe rent charge £9; Eccl. Com. grant £96 16s; QAB £74 14s.

Registers date from 1850.

Plate: silver chalice and paten.

Dorrington[2]

1884. Thomas Finch, V.

House of brick and slate with entrance hall, 3 sitting rooms, 7 bedrooms, kitchen, 3-stalled stable, coach house with 2 rooms and hay loft over, 2 sheds, coal shed, stable yard, flower garden and kitchen garden, 1 a.

Land: meadow of 2¾ a, adjoining the garden to the S.

Income: QAB £127 7s 8d; £20 pew rents; fees £1 10s p.a. average.

Schedule of registers from 1845.

Plate: silver chalice, paten and flagon.

Benefactions: £121 10s 4d invested for church expenses and the surplus for repairs; £3 9s p.a. from Pryce's Charity for the C. of E. school and a like sum for the school attached to the Congregational chapel; £5 p.a. from Pryce's Charity for bread for the poor on St Thomas's Day; £5 from Hayward's Charity in February.

Dowles[3]

1589. Thomas Warter, R.

Francis Newport and Humphrey Hill are patrons.

---

[1] Donnington Wood was formed into an district chapelry from part of Lilleshall parish in 1850: *Victoria history of Shropshire*, xi. 172. See also Lilleshall terriers for 1841 and 1844.

[2] Dorrington township was formed into an ecclesiastical parish from Condover in 1845: *Victoria history of Shropshire*, viii. 53.

[3] Dowles was transferred to Worcestershire in 1895: *Victoria history of Shropshire*, ii. 215.

House of 1½ bays with small garden and 2 a. of pasture adjoining the churchyard.
Land: no arable or commons, only a small piece of coppice.
Herbage is worth *c*. £4 p.a., the Easter book *c*. 12s; tithe wool, lambs, pigs and geese *c*. 5s; wood over 20 years was worth £20.

9 May 1698. Nathaniel Williams, R; Francis Radnall, CW [signatures of 4 sidesmen].
House with 3 little ground rooms, 2 chambers and little garden.
Land: small parcel a little W. of the churchyard, small parcel of meadow with the highway on the W. and Dowles Brook on the N. and E.
There is no modus for any tithes, but all ought to be paid in kind, 'only in as much as there is noe Barn belonging to the Rectory and the parish lying on both sides Seaverne the gathering Tythes in kind would be very troublesome'; there are therefore usually compositions, but not to bind future rectors.

Dudleston[1]
(*and see* Criftins)

1693. Edward Prichard, CW; the fellow warden, Mr Nickson is removed out of the diocese.
'In obedience to your summons . . . I assure you that I know not what profit the minister makes of his services and pains for it Consistts wholly upon the Distribution of the township and what the whole may be is altogether uncertaine'.

n.d. J. Ottiwell, minister; Thomas Langford and Richard Hughes, chapelwardens.
Benefactions: Madam Edwards of Kilhendre gave £2 p.a., the executors of John Jennings 12s p.a., Roger Jennings 6s p.a., Robert Longford 12s p.a. for a sermon on New Year's Day, Thomas Hughes 6s 8d p.a.

1701. J. Ottiwell, C; John Edwards and Edward Powell, chapelwardens.
The inhabitants of the chapelry, not the incumbent pay the curate and he usually has £20 p.a. from the gentlemen, freeholders and inhabitants.
The curate has never had any tithes.
There are no written settlements extant for the benefactions.

2 May 1705. J. Ottiwell, minister; Edward Morrall and Thomas Vaughan, chapelwardens.

23 Oct. 1718. John Sherratt reports that the cure of the chapel of ease to Ellesmere is maintained by 'precarious subscriptions. I have nothing to make a terrier of. Till the late Queen's Bounty with other Gentlemens Charity be laid upon lands or Tythes which I hope in short time will be happily perfected my Ld. Bishop att Ellesmere lately has promised me his good services'.

---

[1] Dudleston was a chapelry of Ellesmere: see the Ellesmere terrier for 1841.

Part 1 (Abdon to Llanfair Waterdine)

18 Oct. 1726. John Sherratt, C; Richard Kyffin and Robert Fernall, chapelwardens.

A tenement of 29 a. has been purchased in Ifton township, Oswestry.

Surplice fees: churching 1s, burial 1s, marriage by banns 2s 6d, by licence 5s.

Benefactions: the interest of £60 being £20 from Edward Morral, £10 from John Jennings, £10 from Robert Langford, £10 from Widow Jennings and £10 from Edward Richards is distributed on St Thomas's Day.

28 Aug. 1730. John Sherratt, C; John Richards and Randle Groom, chapelwardens.

7 Aug. 1733. John Sherratt, C; John Owens and Richard Marsh, chapelwardens.

Since the last terrier a charity school has been founded and endowed by Frances Edwards late of Kilhendre for 24 poor children including £4 10s for the salary of a school dame, besides house and garden and 10s for books, £3 p.a. for setting out apprentices, £2 p.a. for bread and flannel for the poor.

17 July 1736. John Sherratt, C; John Jones and Walter Thomas, chapelwardens.

1739. William Rogers, C; Daniel Burrough and William Rogers, chapelwarden.

18 Sep. 1742. John Sherratt, C; John Richards and John Hodges, chapelwardens.

27 Aug. 1745. John Sherratt, C; William Griffiths and Edward Hatton, chapelwardens.

£500 is in the hands of the governors of QAB for augmentation of the living.

14 Sep. 1748. John Sherratt, C; Edward Griffiths and Richard Reynolds, chapelwardens.

1752. William Tomkiss, minister; John George and John Crump, chapelwardens.

The tenement near Oswestry is let for £23 p.a.; the corn tithes of Little Ness have been purchased for £19 3s.

1756. William Tomkiss, C; Thomas Newnes and David Strange, chapelwardens.

1759. William Tomkiss, C; David Evans and William Carier, chapelwardens.

The land near Oswestry is leased for £29 and the corn tithes of Little Ness for £17.

1810. E. Evans, minister; John Wall, chapelwarden.

1824. Richard Hilton, minister; Arthur Shone and John Reynolds, chapelwardens.

12 Aug. 1828. Richard Hilton, minister; John Barlow and John Jones, chapelwardens.

10 Aug. 1832. Richard Hilton, minister; John Woodvill, chapelwarden.

Glebe terriers of Shropshire

14 Aug. 1845*. David Birds, minister; William Dickin and Arthur Hughes, chapelwardens.

Subscriptions for enlarging the chapel: Josiah Boydell £25 for an altar piece, Capt. Morrall the stained glass, Revd E. Evans the font in memory of 50 year's service.

In 1819 the Society for Promoting the Enlargement of Churches and Chapels in London gave £200 for 14 benches for free sittings on the N. side of the chapel; with other donations total £431 15s.

Benefactions: Philip Jennings silver cup, Ann Edwards silver chalice and table cloth, Frances Edwards silver chalice, linen cloth for the altar and 3 books, Edward Jennings of Dudleston Hall a small press of books from the Society for the Propagation of the Christian Gospel, Philip Kinnersley pulpit cloth, Thomas Kynaston bible and prayer book, in 1745 Philip Jennings gave the communion rails and beautified the altar and built the vestry, in 1838 Miss Longford late of Whitchurch gave £10 for the Dudleston Clothing Club, in 1841 Revd David Birds gave £25 towards painting the chapel.

Surplice fees are double for illegitimate.

The repairs of the chancel belong to the lay rectors and it is in a good state.

The farm near Oswestry is worth £80 p.a.

The tithes of Little Ness have been commuted for £151 p.a.

Clerk's salary: £10 p.a.

[Long] list of legacies to the poor and benefactors to both grants from QAB; in 1719 Mrs Edwards of Kilhendre endowed a school for 12 boys and 12 girls; in 1730 a small farm was purchased in Dudleston.

24 July 1849. David Birds, minister; John Hampson, chapelwarden.

1884*.

Square brick built parsonage house built in 1880 with 3 sitting rooms, 7 bedrooms and suitable offices, stabling for 5 horses and garden.

Income: 21 a. pasture at Oswestry with a brick building on it for 12 cows built in 1879 leased for £73 10s p.a.; the incumbent has the interest on £210 for land originally part of the glebe bought by the Cambrian Railway; tithe rent charge £147 10s.

Schedule of registers from 1693.

Easthope[1]

n.d. [?1589]. [William Benbow, parson] Thomas Geirie and Nicholas Geirie, CWs.

Moris Ludgecote is patron.

House.

Land: 25 a. all enclosed by exchange with Richard Blakeway, 3 little commons—Natle, Southwood and Easthope Wood [bounds].

Tithes are due throughout the parish.

[1] Easthope is also included in the Cound terrier for 1705.

86

Part 1 (Abdon to Llanfair Waterdine)

9 May 1607. William Benbow, parson; Thomas Ball and Edward Fewtrell, CWs.

House with barn and small orchard standing in 3 a. divided into 2 parcels.

Land: 3 a. on the E. of the township being barren land, little parcel of meadow, all enclosed and butting on to Natle Common, 5 a. in 2 parcels on the other side of the township butting on Southwood Common.

Tithes are due on 1 parcel in Hughley lordship.

23 Sep. 1625. [Richard Wrednall, parson] John Lowe, CW.

Nicholas Croswaite, citizen and pewterer of London, and his wife Frances sold to Richard Lutwich their tenement and 4 parcels of common, Nether Wood, Edge, Natle and Southwood to be measured and allocated and sold the advowson to Thomas Ludlow of Morehouse reserving 2 parcels of common; George Ludlow of Morehouse is now patron. The parson for the time being has had wood cut on the 2 parcels of common.

Eaton Constantine[1]

2 Sep. 1682. Daniel Piper, minister; Thomas Dossett, CW.

Dwelling house S. of the church of 1½ bays with barn, cow house and other outbuildings of 5 bays, orchard and hemp yard of 1½ a.

Land: 2 pieces of land W. of the church adjoining Longwood 6 a., part of a cottage, piece adjoining Longwood 1½ a., 1 a. in Stanilye F., 2 pieces S. of the church called Wyarswood 7 a., Wett Reans 2 a., ½ a. at the W. end of Hook F. leading to the R. Severn, piece called Meer Oaks 2 a., 2 pieces E. of the church called Muckalls M. 3 a.

n.d. Thomas Langley, CW; Thomas Dossett, overseer.

Land: Muckalls M. 2 a., Eye Rean 2 a., Wett Rean 3 a., 1 butt of ½ a. in Hook F., Two Wares Wood 8 a., 3 butts in Stannill Pit F. 1 a., Owens Corner joining Long Wood 2 a., Two Wood L. 6 a.

6 Sep. 1693. John Sweynsen, R.

16 Aug. 1698. [No signatories].

House of 2 bays with barn 2 bays with threshing floor in good repair, stable and cart house, hay bay and cow house under 1 roof and little house for geese, all in good repair; orchard, hemp butt and fold yard 1 a.

Land: 2 pieces called Wasewood 8 a., 2 pieces called Parkers Pieces 6 a., Eye Reans 2 a., Owens Corner 2 a., Muckalls M. 2 a., Nanhill Pitt 1 a., ½ a. in Hook F., Wett Reans 2 a.

Tithes of corn and hay are due in kind; 1 pig or goose is due at 7 without allowance; 1 lamb is due at 7 according to the discretion and choice of the rector, but he must allow 3d each for odd lambs and so proportionably if he takes a lamb at 8 or 9, but if there are under 7 the custom is to reckon them on to the next year or pay 3d each.

Offerings: all communicants pay 2d, 1d per orchards, 1d for smoke and garden, 1½d for a cow and calf, 1d for a barren cow, 4d for a colt.

[1] Eaton Constantine is also included in the Leighton terrier for 1612.

Glebe terriers of Shropshire

21 Oct. 1701. John Warham, R; Henry Langley, CW.
Land: Great Wasewood 6 a., Long Wasewood 3 a., Little Wasewood ½ a., Owens Corner 1 a., Parkers L. 7 a., Muckalls M. 3 a., Eye Rean 3½ a., Wett Reans 2 a.
All tithes are paid in kind, but the vicar of Leighton has one-third of all tithes according to a custom of time out of mind.
Clerk's wages are customary and paid from house to house.

2 May 1705. John Warham, R; Thomas Brian, CW.
The glebe is valued at £12 p.a. and the tithes at £18 p.a., but one-third belongs to the vicarage of Leighton, the total value of Eaton Constantine being £24 p.a.

n.d. [?1718]. John Warham, R; Henry Langley, CW.

1722. John Warham, R; Thomas Wethersby, CW.
Tithes: two-thirds of all tithes are due in kind except on apples for which there is a modus of 1d per orchard p.a.
£10 p.a. is given to the rector by the Earl of Bradford from lands at Wilcott, Shrawardine parish.

7 July 1726. John Warham, R; Edward Dorsett, CW.
The vicar of Leighton claims one-third of the tithes because of the interpretation of the phrase, 'Et percipiet vicarius de Leighton tertiam decimam decimarum garbarum villae de Eaton', and receives £6 p.a.

28 Aug. 1730. John Warham, R; Richard Langley.

7 Aug. 1733. John Warham, R; William Stockings, CW.
Land is worth £14 p.a.

16 July 1736. John Warham, R; John Pearson, CW.

1739. Edward Tipton, R; John Ward, CW.
Copy of 29 Oct. 1701.

1742. Edward Tipton, R; Thomas Stockin, CW.

7 Nov. 1748. Edward Tipton, R; George Warham, CW.

1756. James Dewhurst, R.

20 Sep. 1759. James Dewhurst, R; Davie Davis, CW.

1763. James Dewhurst, R; Thomas Wethersby, CW.

1767. James Dewhurst, R; Thomas Rogers, CWs.

8 Sep. 1772. James Dewhurst, R; Andrew Langley, CW.

Aug. 1775. James Dewhurst, R; Francis Parbutt, CW.

5 Aug. 1783. Edmund Dana, R; Richard Mann, CW.

1787. [Edmund Dana, R] Thomas Smith, CW.

29 June 1805. [Edmund Dana, R] Francis Parbutt, CW.

27 Oct. 1810. [Edmund Dana, R] Samuel Langley, CW.

10 Aug. 1824. Samuel Sheppard, R; John Mann, CW.

Part 1 (Abdon to Llanfair Waterdine)

13 Aug. 1828. Samuel Sheppard, R; Samuel Langley, CW.

n.d.[1] Henry Beckwith, incumbent; Zachariah Smith, CW.

7 Sep. 1841. Henry Beckwith, minister; Thomas Clud, CW.
House is a suitable and substantial building with 3 sitting rooms, 2 kitchens, butler's pantry, brew house on the ground floor, 2 stables, 2 coach houses, saddle room, hovel, cow house and pigsty all recently erected.
Land: garden and shrubbery 1 a., meadow 3½ a., High Reans 3 a., part Cow Pasture 3 a., Wet Reans 5 a., Barley Croft 10 a., churchyard ½ a.
The tithes have been commuted for a rent charge of £130 and £46 6s for the vicar of Leighton.
Surplice fees: marriage by banns 5s, churching 1s.
Parish clerk's fees: marriage 2s 6d, churching 6d.
The profits of the living are mortgaged to the governors of QAB in the sum of £567 12s by deed of 16 Apr. 1839.
The incumbent repairs the chancel and it is in good repair.
Plate: 1 silver cup, pewter tankard and pewter plate. There is an iron chest for the registers.
Benefactions: £20 in stock of unknown origin is now in the Salop Co. Savings Bank; William Warham left £100 by his will of 1816 to take effect after the death of his wife (who died in 1826), the interest to be given to the 5 poorest men of the parish on Candlemas Day.

14 Aug. 1845. Henry Beckwith, perpetual curate; William Vickers, CW.
House built of bricks and slate with a large portico recently erected.
The clerk is paid £ 10s from the church rates.

1884*. Henry Beckwith, incumbent.
House with 3 dwelling rooms, entrance hall, 9 bedrooms, 2-stalled stable, coach house and loft, another building with saddle room, coach house and 2-stalled stable with loft, garden and shrubbery 2 a.
Land: 3 meadows of 11 a., 3 a. and 3 a. and 2 arable fields of 3 a. and 4 a.; *c.* 45–47 years ago inferior glebe was exchanged with the Duke of Cleveland for better land adjoining the rectory house.
Income: £10 p.a. given by Francis, Earl of Bradford from rents of a farm in Shrawardine; tithe rent charge £130; fees average p.a. 15s 6d.
Schedule of registers from 1684.
Plate: silver chalice and paten and pewter paten and flagon.
Benefactions: money left by Mr Warham yields £3 8s 4d given to 5 of the most needy men on Candlemas Day; £20 produces 11s given to poor widows.

Eaton under Heywood

n.d. [?1589]. Richard Clarke, V; Edward Haberley and Thomas [?]Oxenbold, CWs.

---

[1] This terrier was probably drawn up in 1832 or 1836; Henry Beckwith was rector of Eaton Constantine 1832–89.

Francis Jenkes is patron.
House with barn, kitchen and stable, orchard and close.
Land: 10 a. arable, Ventnalls M. 2 a., pasture adjoining called Twentie
    Ridges, Ottersole M., pastures called Long Lands, Fennyford and
    Knightley Coppie, dole in Hither Howe M., 6 ridges of arable adjoining
    Eaton Edge, Balstons meadow (leased).

8 June 1607. Richard Clarke, V; John Clarke, Richard Haberley, William
Taylor, Thomas Clarke.

1 Mar. 1619. Ambrose Phillips, V; William English and Thomas Dyke, CWs.
House covered with tile of 2 bays with barn 2 bays and house for cattle 1½ bays.
Land: Ventnalls M. 2 a., Twenty Ridges L. 3 a., Ottersole M. 1½ a., Long
    Lands L. 2 a., Knightley Copp L. 6 a., dole of meadow in Nether Howe M.
    1 a., 6 ridges of arable 1 a., close adjoining the house ½ a., orchard 1 a.,
    churchyard.

Edgmond[1]
(*and see* Church Aston; Sambrook; Tibberton)

1682. John Holbrooke, R. [11 other signatories].
House with 2 barns, cart house, stable, dove house, garden and 4 crofts near
    the house.
Land in Edgmond: 10 butts in Moor F., 8 butts in Waterstead F., 44 butts in
    Park F., 58 butts in Hill F., 2 meadows called Red Lake and Parrock.
Land in Tibberton: 1 house, 7 butts in Awfield, 12 butts in Cawdy F., 11
    butts in Bobberson F., 4 butts in Tunstall F.
Land in Church Aston and Chetwynd Aston: Priest Croft, 23 butts in
    Moor F., 6 butts in Windmill F., 29 butts in Hill F., 12 butts in Port F.

26 Apr. 1694. John Holbrooke, R; Richard Taylor, CW of Edgmond, and John
Shelton, CW of Aston.
Land in Tibberton: 7 butts in Awfield, 7 butts in Caudwell F., enclosures
    called Drymore and Hodghay Corner, 2 enclosures in Bobberson F.
Tithes in Edgmond, Cherrington and Caynton: corn, a composition for hay
    according to days' math when mowed and all other tithes in kind.
Tithes in Calvington, Tibberton and Pickstock: a modus for hay and all else
    as Edgmond. Tithes in Adeney: a composition for hay of 8 loads of hay one
    year and 7 the next, the rest as Edgmond.
Tithes in Church Aston and Chetwynd Aston: corn and hay in kind and the
    rest as Edgmond; Buttery Farm pays 2 loads of hay and the rest as
    Edgmond.
Offerings: 2d for man and wife, 2d for servants, ½d for a child, 1d per stall
    of bees, 3d per pigeon house, 1d per smoke, 1d per garden.
Fees: burial 5s, church 4d, grave in chancel 10s, funeral sermon 10s, wed-
    ding after banns 1s 2d, banns 6d, wedding by licence £2 (more or less
    depending on the quality of those named).

[1] Edgmond is also mentioned in the Tibberton terriers for 1701, 1845 and 1849.

Part 1 (Abdon to Llanfair Waterdine)

17 Aug. 1698. John Holbrooke, R; Richard Renalds, CW.

Land in Edgmond: Parrock M., Red Lake M., Marl Hillock pasture, 4 flats, 25 butts and a stone quarry in Hill F., a hemp butt and new orchard adjoining the parsonage house, butts in Park F., Moor F. and Waterstead F.

Land in Tibberton: cottage and yard, Drymore Piece, Hodge Corner Piece, butts in Awfield, Caldwell F., Bobberson F. and Tunstall F., commoning for sheep on Tibberton Moor without stint.

Land in Chetwynd Aston: butts in Hill F. and Port F.

Land in Little Aston: butts in Moor F., Windmill F. and Hill F.

1701. Dryden Pigott, R; Francis Adams and William Jenens, CWs.

4 May 1705. Dryden Pigott, R; Michael Orme and John Skitt, CWs.

Land [in Edgmond only]: butts in Hill F., Waterstead F., Park F. and Moor F.

3 Oct. 1718*. Dryden Pigott, R; Francis Adams and William Carter, CWs.

House of 4 bays with 2 barns 4 bays, garden, orchard and fold.

Land in Edgmond: Dovehouse Yard 2 a., Paddock 4 a., Red Lake 4 a., Lower Marl Hillock 8 a., Upper Marl Hillock 10 a., Foxhole 7 a., Hill Piece 14 a., Broomditch 13 a., Banlands Flat 2 a., all enclosed and a dole in common called Queer 1 a.

Tithes: all are due in kind except a modus for the meadows of Adeney and Buttery, Adeney paying 10s per living or 1 load of hay and Buttery 13s 4d or 2 loads; tithes are due on calves, lambs or pigs over the number of 7, or 1½d each under 7.

Fees: burials 6d, churching 4d, marriage with licence 5s, banns and marriage 4s.

The clerk's wages are £2 5s. paid by the CWs.

The minister has no right to any seats or burial places in the church, but has had 3 seats in the chancel for time out of mind; he does no repairs of the church or churchyard, only the chancel.

2 July 1722. Dryden Pigott, R; Robert Mansell and John James, CWS.

4 July 1726. Dryden Pigott, R; Thomas Vernall and Thomas Davis, CWs.

29 Aug. 1730. Dryden Pigott, R; Thomas Orme and Richard Bayley, CWs.

10 Nov. 1733. Dryden Pigott, R; John Orme and Richard Bayley, CWs.

1736. James Onions, C; Robert Bailey and Thomas Adams, CWs.

27 Aug. 1742. William Pigott, R; William Holmes, CW.

[Register of baptisms, burials and marriages 1739–42].

1745. William Pigott, R; John Orme, John James and Thomas Beetenson, CWs.

29 Aug. 1748. William Pigott, R; John Orme and Thomas Chaliner, CWs.

1752. [William Pigott, R. No signatories].

[Register of baptisms, burials and marriages 1748–52].

1756. [William Pigott, R. No signatories].

1767. R. Acton, C; John Beetenson, CW.

Glebe terriers of Shropshire

1775. Benjamin Reynolds, C; John Bayley and John Arkinstall, CWs.

18 Nov. 1779. William Pigott, R; John Bayley, CW.

n.d. Benjamin Reynolds, C; John Bayley and William Rose, CWs.

18 Nov. 1797*. William Pigott, R; Richard Bayley of Edgmond and William Briscoe of Caynton, CWs.
Clerk's wages are now £5 5s.

24 Aug. 1801. William Pigott, R; Richard Bayley and Thomas Liversage, CWs.

29 June 1805*. William Pigott, R; William Briscoe and Richard Bayley, CWs.

1824. John Dryden Pigott, R; John Bayley of Bridge and John Bayley of Summer Hill House, CWs.
Copy of 1797.

11 Aug. 1828. John Dryden Pigott, R; John Bayley and James Wright, CWs.
Copy of 1797.

16 Sep. 1832. John Dryden Pigott, R; John Bayley, CW.
Copy of 1797.

9 Sep. 1841. John Dryden Pigott, R; John Cooke Hill, CW.
Fees: vaults at the rector's option, headstones £1.
Clerk's fees: marriage 2s 6d, burials 1s, churching nothing; salary: £5 5s.
Tithes are valued at £2,400.
The chancel is in a good state.
Plate: silver salver, chalice and flagon. There is an iron chest for the registers.
Benefactions: Mrs Elizabeth Watson of Aston £10; Thomas Pigott of Chetwynd £5; Martha widow of John Hill, rector, £10; Walter Pigott of Chetwynd £10; Richard Sneyd plate for communion bread; John Holbrook, rector, £10; Roger Adams of Long Lane £10; John Carter of Adeney £5; Abdias Adams £5; Philip Yonge of Caynton £5; John Moreton £26; John Wooton of Adeney £5; R. Pidgeon of Edgmond £200; William Ore of Chetwynd £5; John Bayley £5; Richard Lineal £5; Anne Pigott, daughter of John Dryden Pigott, wife of Walter Pigott pulpit cloth and cushion; Dryden Pigott, rector, communion plate; David Owen £30 to the poor of Edgmond; Revd Dryden Pigott £200, the interest to go to clothing poor boys; John Smith £100, the interest for the poor on St John's Day; Robert Pigott in 1746 gave £50 to the poor.

13 Aug. 1845. John Dryden Pigott, R; John Cooke Hill, CW.
The parsonage house is 'tolerably large' and in good repair with 4 rooms and kitchen on the ground floor, 7 rooms on the first floor and garden 4 a.
No Easter roll or mortuaries.
The chapelry of Aston has no parsonage house, but has 24 a. of glebe in 6 fields leased; there is no separate terrier for the chapelry.
The clerk's wages are £6 p.a.
The rector is responsible for repairs to the chancel; it is in a good state.
Plate: silver salver, chalice and flagon. There is an iron chest for the registers.
[There is a copy of the 1797 terrier on the dorse of this terrier and the 1845 glebe is said to be the same].

Part 1 (Abdon to Llanfair Waterdine)

23 July 1849. John Dryden Pigott, R; John Hill and Richard Asterley, CWs.
Copy of 1805.

1884*. C[harles] F. C. Pigott, R.
Fees amount to *c*. £3 p.a.
Schedule of registers from 1668.
Plate: 2 silver chalices, 3 silver patens, glass and silver flagon, 1 silver and 1 brass alms dish.
Benefactions: [in addition to those in the 1841 terrier] Elizabeth Watson of Aston £10; Elizabeth Butler £10; Margaret Roberts £5; Edward Banton of Standford Hall in 1856 £100 18s, the interest to poor widows.
[A plan of the property belonging to the poor and a plan of the churchyard and rectory are included with the Lichfield copy of the terrier].

Edgton

n.d. [?1589]. Roger Birde and Humphrey Turner, CWs.
Thomas Harley is farmer.
'Bilding ther is none nor hever was as we can learne'.
Land: 43½ a. arable, 1½ a. meadow; there is no enclosed pasture, and 'What common we know not'.
Tithe corn and oats and all other tithes ar due.

Edstaston[1]

1884*. Francis Talbot Purcell, minister.
There is no house or land.
Fees: churching formerly 1s regarded as a payment, now a thanksgiving and usually 1–2s with an average of 8 over the last 3 years, 12s; banns 1s, marriage 2s 6d, an average of 6 over the last 3 years; burials 1s 6d, average in the last 3 years 6.
Schedule of registers from 1727.
Plate: silver chalice and paten, glass and silver flagon and brass alms basin.
Benefactions: Noneley's Charity pays £4 8s 2d p.a. to the school; Took Charity £2 15s 10d; Mrs Hankey's charity 10s p.a.; the late Lord Hill's legacy £1 p.a; £1 10s p.a. from lands in Whixall held by Sir William Honyman.

Ellesmere
(*and see* Cockshutt; Criftins; Dudleston; Lyneal cum Colemere)

Oct. 1612. Humphrey Kynaston, Edward Philips and John Paterson, CWs.
House with barn, orchard and yard adjoining the lands of Sir Robert Vernon.
All tithes, offerings and oblations are due to the vicar except corn and hay.

---

[1] Edstaston was an ancient chapelry in Wem parish; the parish was formed from Edstaston and Coton townships in Wem parish in 1850: *P.O. directory of Shropshire* (1879), 317. See also the Wem terriers for 1696 and 1718.

n.d. John Sans and Edward Alin.

House of 5 bays with barn and stable bays, turf house 2 bays, orchard, garden and yard ½ a.

1682. John Whildon and Richard Warbaton.

26 Nov. 1693. Joseph Ottiwell, V; Thomas Husband and John Vaughan, CWs.

A legacy of £24 p.a. was left to the vicar by James Phillips, once sheriff of London, but his family suffered misfortune, and the legacy is now worth only £6.

1 Oct. 1694. Joseph Ottiwell, V; Thomas Husband and John Vaughan, CWs.

'. . . there is noe other Account can be given by us the wardens of Ellesmere but this'.

House in good repair with orchard, garden ½ a., turf house 2 bays.

John Phillips Esq. of London gave 10s for a lecture every Thursday, but the buildings to pay it were consumed by fire and now only pay for a lecture on the last Thursday of the month.

Surplice fees: burials 1s, baptism and churching 10d, marriage 2s 6d.

Parish clerk's fees: marriage 2d, burial 4d, baptism 4d.

16 Aug. 1698. James Ottiwell, V; Thomas Studley, George Betton, Thomas Richards and John Brook, CWs.

House of 5 bays with little buttery adjoining, barn and stable 2½ bays and turf house 2 bays.

Tithes: the farm of Crickett is exempt from the great tithe; 1 lamb is due at 7 and 3d at 6, half a lamb at 5; at Easter 1½d is due for a cow and calf, ½d for a cow, 4d for a colt and 4d for tradesmen.

Surplice fees: burial 1s, registering it 4d (the town of Ellesmere 10d), baptism and churching 1s and 4d registering (Ellesmere 10d), marriage by licence 5s, by banns 3s 6d.

Clerk's fees: marriage 1s, baptism 4d; wages: 4d per tenement and 2d per cottage at Easter (except from those in the poor book).

The curates are paid by the inhabitants of the chapelries.

23 Nov. 1701. James Ottiwell, V; Thomas Tydder, Thomas Sparrow, Robert Fluck and Richard Moody, CWs.

2 May 1705. Thomas King, V; Edward Kynaston, William Salisbury, Edward Morrall and Richard Mathews.

Tithes: wool is due in kind, hemp and flax are due in kind or 1s per measure sowing at the option of the vicar; goslings are due in kind as lambs or pigs; every house out of the liberty of the town pays 1d for smoke or garden; tithes are due on the fruit of all orchards within the liberty.

Fees: if a man of this parish marries a woman of another by licence the fee is 5s, by banns 2s 4d and the banns 1s; burials of everyone out of the liberty pay 1s for registering and 4d within.

Offerings: 3 eggs are due per cock and 2 per hen (ducks and drakes likewise) on the Sunday in mid-Lent. Mortuaries are due according to statute.

17 Apr. 1723. Ri. Deane, V; John Hatton and John Evans.

Part 1 *(Abdon to Llanfair Waterdine)*

House of 4 rooms per floor with one garden to E. and one to W., a fold yard to N., barn, stable, small pigsty adjoining, turf house 6 yd. × 3 yd.

7 July 1726. Ric. Deane, V; John Fewtrell, Thomas Edwards, Richard Thomas and John Jones, CWs.

Tithes: bees 1d per hive or 4d per swarm; potatoes, carrots and garden stuff are due in kind or paid for.

Offerings: 2d for all over 16.

The chancel is repaired by the impropriator.

Clerk's fees: churching 4d, marriage by licence 1s 6d, by banns 1s, burial 4d; wages: 4d per ploughland, 2d per cottage due at Easter. William Gough, clerk.

[This clerk's terrier is on a separate sheet of parchment. From this date details of the clerk's fees and dues are on the same document but separately signed].

31 Oct. 1734. Samuel Jenks, V; Thomas Higginson and John Hughes, CWs.
The stable will hold 3 horses.

16 July 1736. Samuel Jenks, V; John Price, William Dickin, Philip Phillips and William Edwards, CWs.

11 Apr. 1740. Samuel Jenks, V; William Lea, John Prichard and John Stoaks.

18 Sep. 1742. Samuel Jenks, V; Robert Perrott and Edward Bartley, CWs.

1745. Samuel Jenks, V; William Challinor, John Edwards and Roger Kynaston, CWs.

10 Sep. 1748. Samuel Jenks, V; Thomas Tomkiss, R. Acherley, John Wynn and Richard Jacks.

1752. Samuel Jenks, V; Henry Kynaston, Thomas Hickson and John Edwards, CWs.

14 Sep. 1756. John Lee, Thomas Taylor and William Griffiths, CWs.

21 Sep. 1759. Samuel Jenks, V; John Price, William Dod and John Evans, CWs.

14 Sep. 1767. Joseph Adams, V; Thomas Gough, Edward Furniston, David Marsh and Samuel Bickley, CWs.

1772. Joseph Adams, V; Thomas Griffiths and James Butler, CWs.

22 Aug. 1775. Joseph Adams, V; John Fallows and Philip Jones, CWs.

23 Oct. 1792. T. Hough, John Sadler and Edward Morris, CWs.

27 Aug. 1836. Richard Hilton, incumbent; Joseph Booth and John Basnett, CWs.
Land: 23 a. of land in Oswestry parish.
Tithes: the great tithes of Great Ness, Baschurch parish are due.

7 Sep. 1841. Joseph Almick Cotton, V; John Owens and William Taylor, CWs.

House of 5 rooms per floor, part old and part modern with 3-stalled stable, saddle room, cow house, pigsty, carriage house, thatched garden house, boarded hovel, garden and land 3 a., churchyard with thatched building in it, thatched cottage adjoining the vicarage leased.

Tithes of the Shropshire part of the parish have been agreed, though not yet commuted, at £430 and of Penley township, Flintshire at £25.

The chancel is in a good state.

Plate: 2 flagons, 2 chalices, large paten, small paten and plate for the offertory, all of silver. There is an iron chest for the registers and another for the plate.

Benefactions [on a separate sheet]: in 1730 several small benefactions amounting to £308 were laid out on 22 a. in Prees with 1½ acre allotment of common; Edward Jeffreys in 1687 left the rent of a tenement of Osbaston, Oswestry for the poor; James Phillips of London left ¼ of the produce of an estate in Southwark for a lecture every Thursday and clothes for the poor; William Wenlock in 1691 left £3 p.a. charge on a tenement in Northop, Flint for bibles; Jane Higginson in 1708 £6 on an estate in Malpas for the poor; Ruth Davies £10, the interest being for bread in Lent; John Higginson in 1774 left £20 with the interest for the poor and £20 for the organist; Sir Richard Oulton £100 with the interest for coals for the poor; John Whettall of Greenwich in 1799 £200 with the interest for 10 poor people; Penelope Vaughan of Oteley Park in 1806 £100 with the interest for the poor; Richard Wynn of Crickett in 1824 £100 with the interest for poor widows and widowers; John Hinkesman in 1832 £50 with the interest for bread for the poor (the executors have only been able to pay £25); William Hawkins in 1834 £200 with the interest for the poor on St Thomas's Day; Elizabeth Gough in 1836 1 pew and 2 sittings in the N. gallery, the rent to be used for the school; Mary Hatchett in 1837 £200 with the interest for poor children in Lee and Ellesmere and the Ellesmere Madras School and £1 1s for the Dudleston Madras School;[1] Edward Edwards in 1840 £300 with the interest for 12 decayed persons in Ellesmere and Lower Ridge on St Thomas's Day.

2 Oct. 1849. John Day, V; Edward Edwards and Thomas Riden, CWs. Copy of 1712.

Eyton upon the Weald Moors[2]
(and see Wrockwardine Wood)

1635. Christopher Luellin minister during a vacancy. [5 other signatories]. There is no house for the parson, 'nor ever was'

---

[1] Madras schools used the monitorial system of education devised by Dr Andrew Bell, an Anglican clergyman in the Indian army, which he published in 1797. He had little influence until his ideas were taken up by Joseph Lancaster and became better known as the Lancasterian system: W. H. G. Armytage, *400 Years of English education* (1970), 90.

[2] Eyton upon the Weald Moors is also included in the Wellington terrier for 1884.

Land: croft called Parsons Yard 1 a., piece of meadow in Mill F. near the mill brook which will bear about half a load of hay, butts of arable containing about 6 strike sowing in each in the 3 leet fields; 5 cottages in Eyton belong to the parish, they have no team and some have no cow, only a house; at Hortonwood there are 4 cottagers [named] who keep no teams and 2 have no cows' grass belonging to them; Sir Philip Eyton keeps the only team in the parish; he pays tithes part to Eyton and a third to Wellington; in Hortonwood there are 10 men who all 'have iiii^{or} Acres of land layd to their howses which weare before all Cottages & and for the Tith parte hath bene gathered for Eyton parish & part hath bene gathered by Mr Charlton that maketh a title thereunto for the parish of wellington this yeare & a suite is to beginn for the trial of the tith to know to whose parish the Tith doth belong unto, for these tithes have bene formerly paid & all other duties to the parish of Eyton but now they Challeng them to belong to the parish of wellington And all these people of Hortons wood before named have ever & still doe receave the Communion in Eyton & pay there their duties but they Christen & bury at wellington.

'David Roe of Eyton hath formerley houlden all this glibe land & the Tithes & proffittes in the tyme of Mr Manninge parson of Eyton for the space of eight yeares togeather at the rate of Seaven powndes thirteene shillinges & Fower pence a yeare'.

10 Oct. 1694. John Eyton, R; Francis Bradley, CW; John Jones, Sowdley Eyton, Thomas Bickley.
Land: New Inclosure 6 a. lately exchanged 'for the benefit of the rector' for butts in Dossett F. and Little F., Calves Croft 7 a. exchanged for Mill F. 6 a., Parson's Orchard 2½ a., butts of arable in Holt F. 2½ a., 1 a. in Dossett F. [bounds]; 3 cottages in Eyton belong to the rectory.

10 Aug. 1698. John Eyton, R; John Oliver alias Symon and Sowdley Eyton, CWs.
Land: New Enclosure 6 a., Calves Croft 7 a., 1 cottage.
Tithes: Eyton pays tithe hay in kind but those holding land below the mill pay individual moduses; at Easter 1d is due per stall of bees put down in lieu of tithe honey, 1d per colt, 2 eggs for every hen or duck, 1 egg or every cock or drake; the Uplands belonging to the whole town pay in kind; hemp and flax pay in kind 'only now restrained by Act of Parliament';[1] tithe hops and pigeons pay in kind; every pig, calf and goose, wool and lambs 'pays at the tenth but in case the Lambes amount but to Seaven then the Rector pays to the owner nyne pence & if Eight hee pays six pence & if nyne three pence and tythe att Seaven And soe after the same maner for wooll but in case there is but Eight single pounds then the Rector pays the owner three half pence in case nyne three pence And soe Tythes att Seaven But in case

---

[1] 11 & 12 William III, cap. 16; the sowing of hemp and flax was encouraged as beneficial to the economy, but as it was recognised that tithing it was difficult, the Act said that it could, therefore, be tithed in money at the rate of 5s per acre: Burn, *Ecclesiastical law*, ed. Fraser, iii. 496.

they be double pounds or two waxweights if there bee eight hee pays to the owner three pence & if nyne hee pays six pence & Tythes att Seaven'.

Surplice fees: marriage by licence 5s, by banns 2s 6d, churching 1s, burial in the churchyard, in the church 1s.

Clerk's fees: 1 egg from every communicant at Easter, marriage by licence 1s 6d, by banns 1s, churching 1s, burial in the church 1s, in the churchyard and ringing the bell 8d.; salary: £1 10s p.a. paid by the CWs for sweeping the church and looking after the clock.

[2 copies].

14 Oct. 1701. John Eyton, R; John Jones and William Reynoldes, CWs.

Tithes: wool and lambs pay in kind; no tithe of calves only 1d per cow; tithe hay is paid in kind in the upland part of the parish but 9 tenements [named] below the mill pay moduses of 6d–2s 6d.

4 May 1705. John Eyton, R; Richard Key, CW.

23 July 1718. Robert Eyton, R; John Jones, CW.

6 July 1722. Vincent Corbet, R; John Cooper, CW.

6 July 1726. Vincent Corbet, R; Pelham Reynolds, CW.

14 Oct. 1730. Richard Tourneor, C; William Begshaw, CW.
Copy of 1701.

1733. R. Tourneor, C; Thomas Randall, CW.

1736. Richard Tourneor, C; Richard Watkys, CW.
Copy of 1701.

1739. Richard Tourneor, C; Richard Johnson, CW.

Tithes: demesne lands pay tithes of corn and hay in kind; there are individual moduses for hay in the rest of Eyton, i.e. Ross Farm, Blests Land, Twomleys, Bagshaw and Newns 8d, Lidgleys Farm 2s 6d and Machams 6d; in Bratton township Thomas Blest pays 6d, John Johnson 5d and Roger Cooper 4d; three pieces of land belonging to Shawbirch pay a modus of 6d; the rector pays John Charlton Esq. £5 14s p.a. for the tithes of Eyton belonging to Wellington parish; wool and lambs are paid in kind, a lamb at 7 and 2 at 17, for every lamb under a tithable number the parishioner allows the rector 3d and wool is the same; at Easter the tithe on poulty is due throughout the parish and also 1½d is due per cow and calf, 1d per barren cow and 4d per colt.

Offerings: 2d for smoke and garden, 2d for each communicant.

16 Sep. 1742. Henry Wood, minister; Thomas Reynolds, CW.

25 Aug. 1745. William Corbet, R; William Massey and Thomas Reynolds, CWs.

1748. Richard Smith, C; John Kinsole, CW.
Copy of 1701.
[Register for Sep. 1745–Jul. 1748].

1 Aug. 1752. Edmund Pryce, C; James Johnson, CW.

16 Sep. 1756. John F.house, R; John Jones, CW.

Part 1 (Abdon to Llanfair Waterdine)

19 Sep. 1759. Stephen Panting, C; John Jones, CW.

3 Sep. 1763. Richard Smith, R; Richard Low, CW.

14 Sep. 1767. Richard Smith, R; John Armeson and Joseph Beddow, CWs.

1772. Richard Smith, R; Richard Low, CW.

1775. H. Kyffin, C; Joseph Beddow, CW.
Copy of 1756.

1779. Stephen Panting, R; Richard Belliss, CW.
Copy of 1756.

1783. John Rocke, R; John Bladen, CW.
Copy of 1756.

1787. John Rocke, R; Richard Boothby, CW.
Copy of 1756.

1792. John Rocke, R; John Cooke, CW.

1797. Thomas Oliver, C; John Cooke, CW.

14 Oct. 1801. Thomas Oliver, C; William Bellis, CW.
Copy of 1756.

20 June 1805. Thomas Oliver, C; John Armeson, CW.
Copy of 1756.

10 Aug. 1828. Thomas Riddell, curate of Wellington; William Bellis, CW.
Copy of 1756.

1832. Edward Pryce Owen, R; John Cooke, CW.
Copy of 1756.

Fauls[1]

13 Apr. 1861. Henry Meynell, incumbent; John Dickin and John Maddocks, CWs.
House adjoining the church built in 1858 at the expense of Viscount Hill aided by a grant of £200 from the Lichfield Diocesan Church Extension Society with small stable and other outbuildings, also garden and orchard c. 1½ a, the gift of Viscount Hill.
Land: 6 a. of land on rising ground E. of the church was alienated from Prees glebe as part of the endowment of the perpetual curacy of Fauls, originally allotted to Prees church on the enclosure of Fauls Green.
Income: the minister is endowed with £46 p.a. from the vicar of Prees; £100 was received from QAB in 1857 yielding £2 17s 6d p.a.
Fees: publishing banns 1s, marriage by banns 5s, marriage by licence 10s, burial 1s 4d, headstone 10s, flat stone £1, tomb or brick grave £2.
Clerk's fees: marriage by banns 1s, marriage by licence 1s 6d, burial 3s 2d.

---

[1] Fauls was formed into an ecclesiastical parish from part of Prees parish in 1856: *P.O. directory of Shropshire* (1879), 385.

Plate: chalice, paten and flagon of silver gilt, credence paten of metal gilt and offertory basin of brass all in an oak chest, 2 altar candlesticks, 2 candle corona of worked brass, porch lantern. There is an iron chest for the registers.

Benefactions: in 1807 Arthur Harper gave £40 to Prees for 'poor industrious Householders belonging to the township of Darliston as are not chargeable to any parish'.

1884*. Harold Burton, V.

House erected 1855–6, well built, with 6 bedrooms, 3 sitting rooms, pantries, kitchens, stable, coach house, wash house, saddle room, *c.* 1½ a. gardens and paddocks.

Land: 6 a. pasture, 3 a. of which is occupied by the vicar.

Income: tithe rent charge £40 charged on Prees; Eccl. Com. £249 p.a. in 1874; interest on a benefaction of £100 from QAB.

Registers from 1856.

Plate: silver gilt chalice, paten and flagon and brass alms dish.

Benefactions: Harper's Charity being the interest of £400 for Darliston township, Fauls.

Fitz[1]
(*and see* Leaton)

23 Oct. 1612, Gedeon Hancocks, R; Andrew Weston and William Paine, CWs.

Parsonage house with 2 barns, orchard and garden adjoining and home close adjoining the orchard.

Land in Fitz: Wall Croft and Wood L.

Land in Grafton: Grafton L. and Hengreave, all closes [bounds].

Tithes: one-third of the tithes of the farm of Fitz are due and all the tithes of the rest of the township and all of Mytton; ¾ of tithe corn and small tithes of Grafton are due and 3s 4d for tithe hay.

1682. Ja[mes] Clerke, R; H. Waring and J. Vaughan, CWs.

House of 2 bays W. of the church with backside, beast houses 4 bays, garden, orchard and hemp yard, 3 a.

Land in Fitz: Spring Croft 2 a., Well Croft 2 a.

Land in Grafton: Hengreave 1 a., Parsons Croft 1 a.

8 May 1694. Ja[mes] Clerke, R; Richard Greenhouse and John Clarke, CWs.

House of 2 bays with barn 3 bays, stable for 2 horses, cow house for 6 cows, garden, orchard and Parson's Croft adjoining 7 a., valued at £3 p.a.

Land: Spring Close 5 a. with some coppice wood is let for £2 10s, Well Croft 6 a. for £3, Hengreave 1 a. for 6s, Grafton Croft 3 a. for 13s 4d.

Small tithes: 1d for a cow, ½d for a calf; wool and lambs are due in kind, but no tithe apples.

n.d. [?1700]. Ja[mes] Clerke, R; William Farrington and Henry Rogers, CWs.

---

[1] Fitz is also included in the Baschurch terrier of 1698.

Part 1 (Abdon to Llanfair Waterdine)

21 Oct. 1701. Ja[mes] Clerke, R; Thomas Farrington and Richard Higgs, CWs.

The farm of Fitz has 2 parts of the impropriate tithe; Grafton only pays a modus for hay.

2 May 1704 [Labelled 1705]. Thomas Clerke, R; William Farrington and Thomas Farrington, CWs.

Surplice fees: burial 6d, baptism 6d, marriage 2s 6d.

Easter dues: 2d offerings, cow 1d, calf ½d, colts 4d, stall of bees 1d.

The total profits of the living amount to £50 p.a.

1712†. Thomas Clerke, R; Richard Higgs, Thomas Farrington, CWs.

House of 4 bays with barn 3 bays with a threshing floor, stable, cow house and bing 2 bays, garden, orchard and hemp butt.

Land in Fitz: Yards 6 a., Well Croft 5 a., Spring Coppy 7 a.

Land in Grafton: Hengreave Croft 1½ a., Heath Croft 3 a.

Tithes are due in kind except from the manor house and all the demesne where only one-thirtieth is due except for 1 meadow which is due at one-tenth; Grafton pays a modus for hay of 4s 4d; the tenants of John Rogers and Steven Denston in Grafton pay half their white tithes to the parish of Baschurch; Eaton in Baschurch pays tithes of best lamb and wool to the parson of Fitz; Allen's Tenement, Yagdon Lane pays 6d to Fitz; dovecotes pay 4d, gardens 1d, smoke 1d, 1d for each hive of bees put down; every sow that pigs 7 or upward is due for tithe; mills pay 3s 4d each and 3s 4d for the weir.

Fees: baptism and churching 1s, burial 1s, marriage with banns 3s 6d, marriage with licence 5s.

Clerk's wages: 6d and 1d worth of eggs from each tenement.

Copy of a terrier of 1704.

Thomas Clerke, R; William Farrington and Thomas Farrington, CWs.

As above except for tithing customs: the customary tithing for corn is the 10th sheaf, for hay the 10th cock, for wool the 10th fleece with 1½d for odd ones, for lambs the 10th with ½d for odd ones.

The profits of the rectory amount to £50 p.a.

23 July 1718. Thomas Clerke, R; Thomas Farrington and Edward Barrett, CWs.

The rector has the tithe of corn and hay except for Grafton where they pay 1s per house.

There are 3 seats in the chancel, 1 belongs to the minister.

3 July 1722.[1] Thomas Clerke, R; Richard Higgs and Thomas Farrington, CWs.

7 July 1726. Thomas Clerke, R; John Rogers and Edward Edwards, CWs.

21 Aug. 1730. Thomas Clerke, R; Humphrey Waring and Edward Edwards, CWs.

Clerk's wages: 6d per tenement and 1d in eggs.

---

[1] The 1722 terrier for Fitz is included in the printed parish register (Shropshire Parish Register Soc. 1903), 71–2.

7 Aug. 1733. Adam Newling, R; Robert Wood and John Rogers, CWs.

16 July 1736. Adam Newling, R; Thomas Jones and Evan Evans, CWs.

3 Sep. 1739. Adam Newling, R; Edward Edwards and Samuel Blease, CWs.

18 Sep. 1742. Adam Newling, R; Edward Eddowes and Robert Brockfield, CWs.

11 Sep. 1745. Adam Newling, R; John Blakeway and Peter Jones, CWs.

1748. James Ralph, R; Stephen Denston and Thomas Eddows, CWs.

1752. William Powell, C; John Jones and Stephen Denston, CWs.
Copy of 1722.

10 Aug. 1756. W. Powell, C; Thomas Evans and Robert Blease, CWs.
Copy of 1722.

16 Aug. 1759. William Powell, C; Thomas Mathias and John Brookfield, CWs.

6 Sep. 1763. William Powell, C; Stephen Denston and ... [faded] Humphreys, CWs.
Copy of 1722.

13 Sep. 1767. Thomas Amler, C; Harlett Lloyd and John Jones, CWs.
Copy of 1722.

1775. William Hopkins, R; Thomas Evans and Robert Blease, CWs.

30 Sep. 1779. William Hopkins, R; John Davies and Thomas Matthews, CWs.

26 Oct. 1787*. William Hopkins, R; John Evans and William Billington, CWs.

25 Oct. 1792. William Hopkins, R; Samuel Vaughan and William Kent, CWs.

1797. William Hopkins, R; John Davis and Benjamin Edwards, CWs.

24 Aug. 1801. William Hopkins, R; William Lloyd Bayley, CW; John Blease, overseer.

1805. William Hopkins, R; Thomas Vaughan and John Kent, CWs.

27 Oct. 1810. William Hopkins, R; Benjamin Edwards and Henry Kent, CWs.

5 Aug. 1824. William Hopkins, R; William Lloyd Bayley and Thomas Vaughan, CWs.

12 Aug. 1828. William Hopkins, R; William Maddocks, CW.
Parsonage house with coach house with granary over, barn, stables, cow house, pigsties, shed and cart house.
Land in Fitz: Yards 7 a., Well Croft 5 a. and Springs 7 a.
Land in Grafton: Heath Croft 4 a. and Hengreave Croft 2 a.; 2½ a. allotted from the enclosure of Forton Heath and 1 a. from the enclosure of Fitz Common.

Aug. 1832. William Hopkins, R; Thomas Evans and Edward Kent, CWs.

31 Aug. 1836. William Hopkins, R; Richard Vaughan, CW.

Part 1 (Abdon to Llanfair Waterdine)

7 Sep. 1841*. William Hopkins, R; Sampson Morris and Richard Pugh, CWs.
House 'fully sufficient for the residence of the incumbent', with outbuildings, yards etc. 1 a.
Land: Mockhall F. 4 a., Upper Common L. 2 a., Lower Common L. 2 a., Hengreave 1½ a., F. by the house 3 a., M. 4½ a., Well croft 6 a., Near Springs 3 a., Far Springs 4 a., coppice 2½ a., allotment from Fitz Common ½ a.
Tithes have been commuted for £266.
Clerk's wages are £3 p.a. with 10s as a share of the money for the singers.
The repair of the chancel belongs to the rector and is perfect.
Plate: salver, a large cup the gift of Revd William Hopkins, father of the present incumbent, and a small cup, all of silver.
There are no benefactions.

7 Sep. 1841. Daniel Nihil, C; R. Middleton and J. Vaughan, CWs.

14 Aug. 1845. William Hopkins, R; Sampson Morris, CW.

26 July 1849. Daniel Nihil, R; R. Middleton and Samuel Onions, CWs.
An exchange is in progress of Near Springs, Far Springs, Coppice and the allotment from Fitz Common with J. Arthur Lloyd.

27 July 1853*. Daniel Nihil, R; W. Rowlands and R. Middleton, CWs.
Banky L. 1½ a. and Gravelly Croft 5½ a. gained by exchange.

5 Aug. 1857. Daniel Nihil, R; R. Middleton, CW.

1884*. William Parry, R.
House fully sufficient for the incumbent with outbuildings, garden, yard and folds 1 a.
Land: 8 fields 30 a. all leased.
Tithe rent charge £266; fees average 4–5s p.a.
Plate: 3 silver chalices, 2 silver patens and pewter flagon.

Frodesley[1]

1635. Nicholas Keysell, R; Robert Burton and Edward Screven, CWs.
House of 2 bays with barn 3 bays, cow house and sheep cote adjoining, small garden and orchard.
Land: Parsons Close 1½ a., Hornepit L. 17 a., Parsons Wett M. 2 a., Parsons Rowe L. 3 a. [bounds].

26 Sep. 1673. John Wilkes, rector of Pitchford; John Pursell and Thomas Wall, CWs.

29 Sep. 1682. John Wilkes, R; Thomas Jones and John Purcel, CWs.
Land now includes 3 hemp butts.

16 Sep. 1685. John Wilkes, R; Griffith Gough and Thomas Screven, CWs.

21 July 1693. John Wilkes, R; John Richards and John Butcher, CWs.

---

[1] Frodesley is included in the Condover terriers for 1701 and 1705.

16 Aug. 1698. John Wilkes, R; Richard Langford and Thomas Campian, CWs.

House of 2 bays with barn, cow house and stable 3 bays, garden and close.

Land: meadow rented at £1 8s p.a., Row L., Horning Pit L., 4 pieces of arable at the town's end, hemp butt by the churchyard, parcel at the town's end leased.

Tithes are due in kind; lambs are due at 7, allowing lambs to the next year; if under 7 reckoning on till they come to that number.

Offerings: at Easter 2d is due from every communicant, 1d per cow, ½d per calf, 1d per garden, 1d per house, ½d per sheep sold, 4d per stall of bees or one-tenth of the honey, 4d per colt.

Fees: marriage by banns 2s 6d, by licence 5s, baptisms 6d.

21 Oct. 1701. John Wilkes, R; Thomas Clutton and Richard Hickman, CWs.

2 May 1705. John Wilkes, R; Joseph Bollin and Richard Langford, CWs.

1718. William Roe, R; Richard Jones and Arthur Soley, CWs.

Surplice fees: marriage by banns 2s 6d, marriage by licence 5s, churching 4d.

Clerk's fees: marriage by banns 1s, marriage by licence 2s, churching 6d; wages: £1 p.a. paid by the CWs out of the lewn.

5 July 1722. William Roe, R; Alexander Hickman and William Yeates, CWs.

Great and small tithes are due except from 4 parcels of land [named] which pay only half the tithes of cock and sheaf.

Burials pay 10d to the vicar of Condover where the inhabitants of Frodesley have the right to bury.

7 July 1726. William Roe, R; Samuel Fewtrell and Rowland Hodge, CWs.

4 seats were erected in the chancel (though not within living memory) belonging to Godolphin Edwards of Frodesley Hall, for which privilege he repairs the chancel.

28 Aug. 1730. William Roe, R; Richard Baxter and Richard Lee, CWs.

7 Aug. 1733. William Roe, R; Richard Lee and Richard Diganay, CWs.

16 July 1736. William Roe, R; Alexander Hickman and Richard . . . [faded], CWs.

1 Sep. 1739. William Roe, R; Alexander Hickman and William Yeats, CWs.

Easter offerings: 3 eggs per cock and 2 per hen to the rector; 2 per cock and 1 per hen to the clerk.

1742. Samuel Jones, R; Daniel Lowe and Richard Roberts, CWs.

Rectory house built by Samuel Jones of 2 storeys.with 3 rooms per floor.

1745. Samuel Jones, R; John Bromley and Francis [?]Jenness, CWs.

There are 2 seats in the church for the rector's family, 1 on the S. side under the pulpit and the other opposite.

30 Aug. 1748*. Samuel Jones, R; Thomas Yates and Samuel Thomas, CWs.

Rectory house built in 1742 by the present rector with 3 rooms per floor plus closets and 3 storeys excluding cellars; barn, cow house, binn and cart house of 6 bays built by William Roe in 1714.

Part 1 (Abdon to Llanfair Waterdine)

30 Aug. 1752. Samuel Jones, R; John Wilcox and Rowland Hodges, CWs.

12 Sep. 1756. Samuel Jones, R; Daniel Lowe and Richard Baxter, CWs.

18 Sep. 1759*. Samuel Jones, R; John Wilcox and William Parton, CWs.

7 Sep. 1763. Francis Edwardes, R; William Rubbathan and Samuel Thomas, CWs.

1 Oct. 1801. John Edwardes, R; John Bowen and William Heighway, CWs.
Slated house with barn, 2 stables, cowhouse, granary with dairy under, garden adjoining and barn yard open to the lawn.
Land: Townsend M., Rail F. M., Hovel F. M., Horny Pitt M., garden platt at Cross Way, some land in a meadow by wet lake; Row F. was exchanged by the late rector, Sir Thomas Edwards with Sir Edward Smythe for land surrounding the rectory.

12 June 1805. J[ohn] Edwardes, R; John Bowen and Martin Millington, CWs.

26 Sep. 1810. John Edwardes, R.
Land: lawn before the house, Townsend Piece, Rail F., Hovel Piece, Brickkiln F., all meadows.

10 Aug. 1824. John Hawkins, C; Richard . . . and Edward Hudson, CWs.
House with barn, 2 stables, cow house, coach house, garden, shrubbery, orchard and lawn.
Formerly there were 2 pews in the chancel for the rector and 1 in the church, but since the rebuilding of the church in 1809 there are only 2 pews in the chancel.

13 Aug. 1828. Thomas Gleadowe, R; Richard Wood, CW.

5 Sep. 1836. Thomas Gleadowe, R; Francis Scott, CW.

7 Sep. 1841*. Thomas Gleadowe, R; Richard Wood and William Hughes, CWs.
House with 5 rooms on the ground floor, 6 chambers and 4 garrets above, yard and out offices, barn, 2 stables, coach house, cow house, pigsty, garden, shrubbery, orchard, plantation and lawn, in all 7 a.
Land: Townsend Piece 4½ a., Rail M. 2½ a., Hovel Piece 3 a. and Hornet Pit 6 a.; other detached pieces mentioned in earlier terriers were *c.* 1784 exchanged for land nearer the house.
Lands only paying half tithe amount to 63 a.
The churchyard was not consecrated until 1781 and burials had to take place at Condover.
Tithes were commuted 14 July 1841, but the award is not yet made.
The church was built in 1809; the chancel is repaired by the rector and is in good repair.
Plate: silver quart cup and half pint cup with cover and plate for bread. There is an iron chest for the registers in the rectory house.
Benefactions: Thomas Scriven Esq. gave £5 towards the rebuilding of the church; 8 small pieces enclosed from the waste are in the gift of the rector by leave of Godolphin Edwards.

14 Aug. 1845†. Thomas Gleadowe, R; Richard Wood, CW.

In the 1841 terrier certain lands were then specified as paying ½ tithe of cock and sheaf, but when they were commuted for a rent charge, the Tithe Commissioners decided that this exemption was not valid and a rent charge was determined equivalent to the whole tithe; in 1841 moduses of 1d per cow, ½d per calf, 4d per colt were said by the Tithe Commissioners to be 'not good', and the rector now has equivalent value; tithes were commuted in 1843.

Easter dues: 2d per communicant, 6d per tradesman or householder, smoke 1d, garden 1d, stall of bees 4d, 3 eggs per cock, 2 per hen to the rector and 2 eggs per cock and 1 per hen to the clerk.

Surplice fees: churching 6d, registering 6d, banns 1s, marriage with banns 2s 6d, with licence 6s, burial 1s.

Clerk's fees: churching 6d, marriage with banns 1s, with licence 2s 6d, burial 1s 2d; salary £4 4s.

The rector has 2 pews in the chancel and 1 in the church.

Benefactions: the CWs pay 5s p.a. to the rector at Easter for distribution to the poor.

24 July 1849*. Thomas Gleadowe, R; Edmund Meredith and Richard Hotchkiss, CWs.

Clerk's salary is now £4 4s.

The chancel was entirely refitted and beautified by wainscoting at the expense of the present rector in 1847; a new wall was built to enclose the churchyard at the expense of the parish in 1849.

1884. R. W. Gleadow, R.

House with 6 rooms and a brew house on the ground floor, 8 chambers and 4 attics, 2-stalled stable, 2 loose boxes, saddle room with straw loft above, coach house, barn, cow house, pigsty, all of brick and stone and tiled, yard and garden ½ a.

Land: pasture lawn with orchards and shrubberies 6 a., Town End Piece 5 a., Rail M. 2½ a., Cote M. 3 a., Honets Pit Piece 6 a.

Tithe rent charge £405; fees average 7s p.a.

Schedule of registers from 1547. The churchyard was consecrated for burials in 1781; the churchyard has recently been extended.

Plate: 2 silver chalices, silver paten and flagon and brass alms dish.

Benefactions: a slang of land adjoining the road from Frodesley to Longnor given by Godolphin Edwards, then lord of the manor, is now enclosed as allotments for the poor; there are 5 garden allotments, 4 rent free (they pay 1d at intervals as an acknowledgment) and 2 cottages and gardens at a rent of £5 p.a.

Glazeley *see* Deuxhill and Glazeley

Great Ness

22 Oct. 1612. Thomas Heylyn, V; William Wicherley and William Thomas, CWs.

Part 1 *(Abdon to Llanfair Waterdine)*

House of 2½ bays with small bake house, sheepcote 1 bay, garden and orchard with backside 4 a.

Land: 1 land or selion in the field towards Little Ness 1 strike sowing of the new measure, 1 land or selion in Bromehyll F. of the same quantity, 1 land in Wood F. the like measure, a little meadow with 2 little ridges 1½ a. [bounds].

Half the tithe of corn of Felton Butler from the holly of Broomehill and the hawthorn on the hill to Wilcott pool, Crannymoss, St Thomas's Well and Ness Marsh is due to the vicar; tithe corn of the home closes and tithes of hay, wool and lambs are due from the whole parish.

21 June 1635.[1] Thomas Wilkes, V; John Heylyn and John Prichard, CWs.

House and little bay of backhouse, backside with hemp butt and garden.

Land: little meadow and little enclosure, little land in Broomhill F. within an enclosure of John Broome, little land in Wood F., little land in Baymosse F. [bounds].

In Felton Butler half the tithe corn is due and all the tithe corn from the home closes, all hay, offerings and other tithes; in Ness Strange half of all the corn is due; hay, wool, lambs etc.are due in the whole parish, except the township of Atton where it is only 2 parts, but all offerings.

14 Sep. 1685. Henry Bradley, V; Richard Graffton and Thomas Cooke, CWs.

New house of 2 bays with old barn 3 bays, garden, hemp butt and backside.

Land: small pieces of arable in the field toward Little Ness called Baymosse, Broomhill F. and Woodfield, little meadow, 2 little ridges 1½ a.

20 July 1693. Henry Bradley, V; William Povey and Thomas Minton, CWs. [5 other signatories].

12 July 1698. Henry Bradley, V; William Baddeley and Edward Atkis, CWs. [5 other signatories].

House of 3 bays, 1 bay erected 1697, with paled garden to the S., garden to the N., new orchard and backside adjoining 4 a., old barn 3 bays with stable and sheep cote of 1 bay lately erected and small fold yard before the barn about 30 yd. square.

Tithes: half a lamb is due at 5, 1 at 7, the minister paying 9d, he pays 6d at 8, 3d at 9, the parishioner paying 3d per lamb at all other numbers; wool follows the same custom, also pigs and geese; communicants pay 2d, 1d for a cow, ½d for a calf, 4d for a horse colt, 3d for a man colt, 6d for bees killed for honey or taken out of the parish, 1d smoke, 1d garden; flax, hemp and eggs are due in kind. Surplice fees: burials 6d, churching 6d, marriage by banns not exceeding 3s, marriage by licence not exceeding 5s.

Clerk's wages £2 by old custom paid by the CWs out of the parish lewn.

The church and the churchyard fence are repaired by the parish.

The marriage offerings of Shotatton are due to the vicar and two-thirds of the tithes except corn.

---

[1] Great Ness terriers for 1635 and 1752 are included in the baptism and burial register 1720–90 (SRRC, P114/A/1/3).

107

21 Oct. 1701. Henry Bradley, V; Richard Thomas and John Plimley, CWs. [6 other signatories].
House with a bay at the W. end built in 1697, a garden to the N. of the house laid out in 1698, new orchard and backside 4 a.
10s p.a. has been paid beyond the memory of man in lieu of tithes for the estate of Shelbrook.

28 May 1705. Henry Bradley, V; William Thomas and Thomas Roberts, CWs. [5 other signatories].
House of 4 bays, the western bay added in 1697 and another added 1703.

23 July 1718. John Collier, V; Thomas Minton and James Canlin, CWs.
The chancel belongs to the vicar; the repair of the roof, walls and windows belongs to the impropriator and vicar.

5 July 1722. John Collier, V; Thomas Wingfield and John Edwards, CWs.

6 July 1726. John Collier, V; William Thomas and William Griffies, CWs. [6 other signatories].

22 Aug. 1730. John Collier, V; Godfrey Duckit and Richard Whittakers, CWs.

1734. William Parry, V; Andrew Phillips and William Thomas, CWs. [6 other signatories].
The former glebe was exchanged by the last incumbent with John Edwards for a small enclosure called Marlpit Croft [bounds].

16 July 1736. William Parry, V; Richard Vaughan and John Williams, CWs.

31 Aug. 1739. William Parry, V; William Somerfield and Samuel Thomas, CWs.

17 Sep. 1742. William Parry, V; Richard Wild and John Stafford, CWs.

11 Sep. 1745. William Parry, V; John Povey and William Bate, CWs.

13 Sep. 1748. William Parry, V; Roger Edwards and William . . . [blackened], CWs.

21 Sep. 1752. William Parry, V; William Somerfield, CW.

14 Sep. 1756. William Parry, V; Richard Sandford and Richard [?]Punnelay, CWs.

21 Sep. 1759. William Parry, V; Richard Bevan and Thomas Davies, CWs.

1763. William Parry, V; Thomas Grice and Richard Cooper, CWs.

13 Sep. 1767. Thomas Parry, V; Rt. Matthews and Rd. Nunnerley, CWs.

8 Sep. 1772. Thomas Parry, V; Benjamin Bather and Thomas Tomkins, CWs.

21 Aug. 1775. Thomas Parry, V; Edward Davies and John Canlin, CWs. [7 other signatories].

1779. Thomas Parry, V; Thomas Wildblood, CW.

5 Aug. 1783. Thomas Parry, V; Richard Minton and James Canlin, CWs.

5 Aug. 1787. Thomas Parry, V; John Canlin and Edward Davies, CWs.

Part 1 (Abdon to Llanfair Waterdine)

25 Oct. 1792. Thomas Parry, V; Thomas Wildblood and Robert Edwards, CWs.

20 July 1797. Thomas Parry, V; Thomas Tomkins and John Thomas, CWs.

10 Aug. 1824. H. Cotton, V; John Wildblood, CW.
House with barn, stables, carriage house, cow house, pigsties, granary, garden, orchard and meadow adjoining 3 a.
Marlpit Close 3½ a., arable field near Hopton Hill *c*. 4 a.

13 Aug. 1828. H. Cotton, V; J. Bather and Thomas Jeffreys, CWs.

10 Aug. 1832. Henry Calverley Cotton, V; J. Bather and Richard Mansell, CWs.

1 Sep. 1836. H. C. Cotton, V; J. Bather and William Payne, CWs.

7 Sep. 1841*. H. C. Cotton, V; Thomas Jeffreys and Richard Wildblood, CWs.
House of brick and slate with granary, barn, stables, carriage house, cart house, cow house, pigsties, mangle house, stable yard, stack yard, garden and grass field adjoining 3 a.
Meadow called Marlpit Croft 3½ a., Hill F. arable 4 a.
A loan was obtained from QAB in 1822 to extend the parsonage, balance outstanding £82 7s 1d.
The repair of the chancel belongs to the impropriators, being the vicar, prebend of Holdgate, John Bather Esq., R. Scott Waring Esq., Thomas Jeffreys Esq., John Povey, Mr Edward Bather, William Payne.
Plate: large cup, small cup and paten all of silver, flagon and 3 plates of pewter. There is an iron chest for the registers in the parsonage house.
Benefactions: rent charge of 5s p.a. on Mrs Marygold's estates near Wellington and near Wem distributed on Good Friday; 5s rent charge on the Plough Inn, Wellington also distributed on Good Friday 3 years out of 4 and the 4th at Kinnerley; the parish bought land at Melverley which is let at £1 15s p.a.; Mrs Hester Farmer left a house in Castle Foregate, Shrewsbury which is let at £20 p.a., the rent being for poor decayed housekeepers in St Chad's Shrewsbury, Guilsfield, Great Ness and Kinnerley in rotation; Revd William Parry, the former vicar, erected a school with a small grass field, yard and garden adjoining at Nesscliffe for poor children; the school is endowed by Sir Orlando Bridgeman who left £20, Sir John Langham £10, Mrs Pridie £20, Revd William Parry £25, Mrs Mary Parry £25: this £100 is at interest, J. Edwards and the minister of Great Ness being trustees.

14 Aug. 1845*. H. C. Cotton, V; Robert Suckley, CW.
House with entrance hall, 3 sitting rooms, kitchen, housekeeper's room, pantry, servants' hall, back kitchen, larder, 2 staircases, 6 main bedrooms, water closet, 5 servants' bedrooms, 2 cellars, 4 stables, coach house, saddle room, barn, granary, cow house, pigsties, cart house, mangle house, 2 necessaries, garden, shrubberies and garden 1½ a.
Tithes have been agreed to be commuted for £329 3s 9d.

24 July 1849*. H. C. Cotton, V; Samuel Smith and John Wildblood, CWs.

The tithes of Wilcott and Nesscliffe have been commuted for £29 2s, Felton Butler for £90 10s, Alderton £13 2s, Kinton £56 6s 7d, Great Ness and Hopton £109 5s 2d, Shotatton in Ruyton £30 18s; total £329 3s 9d.

27 July 1853. C. Kenyon, V; William Payne and Samuel Minton, CWs.

5 Aug. 1857*. C. Kenyon, V; William Payne and Samuel Minton, CWs.

1884*. Land: 2 fields *c.* ½ mile away of 4½ a. and 4 a.
Income: tithe rent charge £324; average fees £1 15s 6d p.a.
Schedule of registers from 1589.
Plate: 2 silver chalices, 1 plate and 1 silver paten, 1 plate and 1 pewter alms dish.
Benefactions: £100 and £1,200 yield £342 p.a. for the school; Mrs Hector Turner £25 p.a. 1 year in 4 from the rent of a farm near Shrewsbury, Mrs Margaret Dyos 30s 3 years in 4 from a small farm at Melverley and in 1851 the interest of £100 from Charlotte Edwards for the poor.

Greete

n.d. [?1589].[1] John Holland, parson; Roger Smyth and John Tyler, CWs.
Edward Fox is patron.
House with kitchen and 2 barns in good repair.
Land: *c.* 48 a., 22 a. arable, 6 a. meadow, 20 a. pasture, being Ledwich Fur. 5 a. arable, Mill Hill 4 a., Parsonage Croft 5½ a., Park Fur. 3 a., 1 a. in Stominacre F., Red Brynke, 1 a. in Ash F., 1 a. in White Cross F., Parsonage M., Mashford M. 2 a., Penkeshill 6 a., Harle 2 a., Stocking 1 a. Nether Close 2 a. [bounds]; there are no commons.
Tithes amount to *c.* £4 p.a.

Grinshill

1682. [Samuel Jones, C] George Killvertt and William Keye, CWs.
House of 2 bays with a garden 'as we supose of Right belonging to the church & Formerly The Ministers dwelling house' is now in the occupation of John Hillton who rents it and the tithe from Mr Cleaton.

16 Sep. 1685. [Samuel Jones, C] John Cureton, CW.
Tithes: the minister has anciently been paid 10½d for hay and 2d one year and 3d the next for grain; wool and lambs are due at 7 with odd ones accounted on to the next year; young pigs pay nothing the first litter, then 1 in 10 with no counting on; apples are paid at 'what the parish please'.
Offerings: 4d for a housekeeper and his wife, ½d for children, 2d for servants, 1d for a stall of bees put down, 2d for colts, 1½d for cow and calf'.

21 June 1693. [Samuel Jones, C] Richard Cureton, CW.

16 Aug. 1698. Francis Price, minister; Richard Cureton and Thomas Embrey, CWs.

---

[1] A Greete terrier with no date but probably 1589 is included in the printed parish register (Shropshire Parish Register Soc.), p. vii.

110

Part 1 (Abdon to Llanfair Waterdine)

The minister receives £6 p.a. from the patron; it was formerly £8.

1701. Robert Embrey, CW.
The patron, Richard Cleaton of Lea Esq. allows £6 for the service of the cure; William Key by will 10 Apr. 1669 left £50 to trustees for the use of the minister; Francis Price receives £2 10s p.a. from this; Richard Cleaton obtained £200 from the charity of Capt. Jones in London for the better maintenance of parish churches, and this has been spent on land at Withington and is leased.

1705. Francis Price, minister; Samuel Cureton, CW.

23 July 1718. Francis Price, minister; William Maddox, CW.
Surplice fees: burial 1s, registering a child and churching 1s, marriage 5s.
Clerk's fees: burial 6d, baptism and churching 6d, marriage 1s; wages: 1s per house.
The minister has a seat on the N. side of the chancel and a new seat has been lately erected in the chancel for the use of Mr Gardner of Sansaw by permission of the patron and parishioners.
The minister receives £6 from the parson, £10 from land in Withington and the interest of £50 left by William Key in the hands of the minister until it can be conveniently laid out.

5 July 1722. Francis Price, minister; John Embrey, CW.

7 July 1726. Samuel Betton, minister; William Heath, CW.
'This is a copie of the Terrier kept among the Inhabitants but what other may be in the hands of the Patron or any other Person who hath formerly rented the Tythes I know not'.

7 Aug. 1733. Samuel Betton, minister; John Kilvert, CW.

23 June 1736. Samuel Betton, minister; John Embrey, CW.

1 Sep. 1739. Samuel Betton, minister; William Heath, CW.

18 Sep. 1742. Samuel Betton, minister; . . . [worn] Cooke, CW.

11 Sep. 1745. Samuel Betton, minister; William Embrey, CW.

14 Sep. 1748. Samuel Betton, minister; Samuel Dulson, CW.

6 Oct. 1756. Samuel Betton, minister; John Kilvert, CW.
£50 from William King with money from other charitable legacies for the benefit of the poor has lately been laid out on a purchase of land near Wem.

2 Sep. 1752. Samuel Betton, minister; John Embrey, CW.

20 Sep. 1759. Samuel Betton, minister; William Groome, CW.

1805.
Copy of 1736.

8 Aug. 1828. Francis Salt, minister; Samuel Minton, CW.
Copy of 1752.
Addendum: annual value of the living 1828: the patron and lay rector, John Wood Esq. of Grinshill, pays £6 p.a., 25 a. of land in Withington is worth

£40 10s p.a., 10 a. in Clive £22 10s p.a., 4 a. in Clive £8 10s p.a., land at Coton, Wem £1 13s p.a., £4 0s p.a. interest on £110 from the sale of timber at Withington some years ago in the hands of the patron; surplice fees amount to a few shillings p.a.

Aug. 1832. Francis Salt, perpetual curate; John Leeke, CW.
Copy of 1736.
Value of the living in 1832 £80 12s. p.a.

14 Aug. 1845. Sebastian Gambier, perpetual curate; Richard Barklay and John Jessop, CWs.
Revd J. Wood, patron.
Land: Church F. in Clive 10 a., Grandary F. at Sansaw 4 a., Leaches 5 a., Near Leaches 5 a., 2 doles in Coppice M. 3 a., Lea Berries 3 a., Green Bank 3 a. and Shutyard in Withington 3½ a.; total 38 a. leased for £98.
The incumbent, the poor and the education of 6 children each take one-third of the rent of a house and land at Coton, Wem; the lands at Withington are charged with £1 p.a. to the poor of Berrington.
The living was augmented from the Parliamentary Grants Fund with a grant of £20 7s 4d yielding 12s 2d p.a.
Plate: silver cup and paten.
Clerk's salary £3 p.a.
The church is new with no chancel; the repair of the whole is chargeable to the parish.

1849*. John Wood, patron and soon to be incumbent; Richard Barkley, CW.

1857. John Wood, patron and incumbent; Charles Boore, CW.
Income: land at Withington is worth £57 10s p.a.; 11 a. of land at Clive bought in 1783 £18 p.a., a further 3 a. at Clive bought in 1819 £8 (the Clive title deeds are in the hands of the governors of QAB); one-third of the rent of land at Coton is worth £1 12s 8d (a much higher rent is expected next Lady Day when a 99 year lease expires), the Shrewsbury and Crewe Railway has lately paid £50 for passing through these lands; the £50 is at present in the Salop Savings Bank, the minister having one-third of the interest; it is contemplated to lay out the £50 in improving the land; the Parliamentary Grants Fund gives 12s 2d p.a.; an endowment fund yields £35, partly contributed by timber on the glebe *c.* 1817 and for a time in the hands of the patron who prevailed on the governors of QAB to receive it in 1852.

1884*. [John Wright, incumbent].
House built in 1878 with 4 a. of land.
Income: Church F. 10 a. and Grandary F. 4 a. at Clive, 8 fields 25 a. at Withington (charged with £1 p.a. for the poor of Berrington); one-third of the rent of land at Coton goes to the incumbent, one-third to the poor and one-third for education; half the rent of land at Park Farm, Guilsfield being £18 7s 6d is shared with Clive; the incumbent receives £6 from the Corbet Charity; Eccl. Com. pay £20; fees are small and usually returned.
Schedule of registers from 1592.

Part 1 (Abdon to Llanfair Waterdine)

Plate: chalice of 1776, paten of 1688 and flagon of 1880, all of silver, brass alms basin and pewter flagon of 1704.

Habberley

n.d. [?1589].[1] Thomas Hynckes, parson; Roger Davies and Richard Rider, CWs.
Richard Mytton of Shrewsbury is reputed patron.
Land: 13 strike seedness of arable in the fields of Habberley, pasturing for 4 beasts in Hart Beach L., dole of meadow, 1 a. of commons in Marsley [bounds].

10 May 1607*. Thomas Hynckes, parson; William Gwynne and William Phipps.
House with barn, cow house, kitchen, stable, backside, orchard and garden.
Land: pasture called Hartbach 16 a., pasture called Black Sitch enclosed with 5 a. of arable, 1½ a. meadow, New L. 8 a., 2 ridges arable in Cross F., 1 butt arable in Pittshill F. [bounds].

14 Sep. 1624. Richard Norgrave, parson; Edward Wyldbloud and Richard Gittins, CWs.
House with barn, kitchen, backside, garden and outhousing at the upper end of the town over against the church.
Land: pasture called New L., 2 little pastures in Bridgebrooke F. lying together adjoining the forest on one side, 2 ridges in the upper end of Cross F., short headland in Pitthill field [bounds].

Hadley[2]

1884*. James Barton, V.
The church was consecrated 24 Oct. 1856.
Income: tithe rent charge awarded 1874 £224 12s 6d; Eccl. Com. £500 granted in 1863; QAB in 1858 consented to accept £260 15s 2d; pew rents for 75 sittings £30; fees average p.a. £17 16s 9d.
Schedule of registers from 1856.
Plate: silver chalice.
Benefactions: John Millington of View House, Ketley gave £30 in 1876, the interest to be given at Christmas to 6 poor widows who attend the church regularly.

Hadnall[3]

7 Sep. 1841. William Oliver, C; Charles Hubbert and Edwin Groom, CWs.

---

[1] The Habberley terrier in SRRC (P118/F/1/1) is undated and listed as ?1627 but is probably 1589.
[2] Hadley was formed into an ecclesiastical parish from part of Wellington parish in 1858: *Victoria history of Shropshire*, xi. 263.
[3] Hadnall was an ancient chapelry of Myddle parish formed into an ecclesiastical parish in 1856: *P.O. directory of Shropshire* (1879), 327. See also Myddle terriers.

There is no parsonage house.

The incumbent has £60 p.a. from land at Criggion, Montgomeryshire and £12 p.a. from QAB.

Fees: burials 1s 6d, churching 1s, headstones 5s.

Clerk's fees: burials 1s, churching 6d; salary: £1 12s p.a.

The repair of the chancel belongs to the chapelry.

Plate: cup, paten and flagon of silver. There is an iron chest for the registers.

£15 p.a. is paid to the incumbent by the rector of Myddle for distribution to the poor, being part of a bequest left by a former rector of Myddle; there is no account of this in the church.

14 Aug. 1845. William Oliver, C; John Home and Edwin Groom, CWs.

There is no chancel, the whole chapel is repaired by the rates of the chapelry.

£15 p.a. is paid to the incumbent by the rector of Myddle being part of the interest on £2,000 left by a former rector of Myddle for the poor of the parish including Hadnall; there is an account of this in Hadnall church.

1884*. William Oliver, V.

There is no parsonage house.

Income: Old Mills Farm with house and 34 a. land at Criggion rented at £60 p.a.; QAB £13; fees average £3 0s 6d p.a.

Hadnall was formerly a chapelry of Myddle parish and was made a separate parish in 1856; the rector of Myddle has since then paid £100 from the tithe rent charge, but it is agreed that the next rector of Myddle will pay the full apportionment of Hadnall i.e. £287 11s 6d.

Schedule of registers from 1783.

Plate: silver chalice, paten and flagon and brass alms dish.

Benefactions: £300 7s 6d yielding £6 0s 2d from Dame Mary Hill for the schoolmistress and £342 6s 10d yielding £10 5s 4d for clothing poor children; £15 p.a. is paid by the rector of Myddle being part of the Earl of Bridgwater's charity.

Hanwood

1589. [John Hatton, R] Thomas Medlicott and Robert Downe, CWs.

The parsonage formerly belonged to Thomas Medleycote, Edward Phelippes and Thomas Kylvarte, but John Onslowe has bought it.

House with barn and backside.

Land: 14 a. of pasture, 5 a. arable and ½ a. meadow; no common pasture, only the fallow.

All tithes are due from 6 houses.

4 June 1607. Morgan Evans, parson; Thomas Medlicot and Robert Downe, CWs.

House of 3 bays with barn 3 bays and backside.

Land: enclosed pasture called Parsons Heath 9 a., Parsons Bank enclosed 3½ a., enclosed pasture called Mill Hill 2 a., 4½ a. arable in Middle F., the 8th cock of hay is due or one-eighth part of Hanwood M. 6 a.

Part 1 (Abdon to Llanfair Waterdine)
Harley[1]

18 Oct. 1612. Thomas Bent, R; John Doughty and Robert [?]Serpiche, CWs.
House and kitchen under 1 roof, barn and stable with a close and garden adjoining of *c*. ½ a.
Land: Sandibrook L. 10 a., pasture in West F. called Scuttersfurlong 3 a., pasture called Harp, 2 pastures lying together called Plashbrook Leasows 10 a., pasture called Heyfield, 3 butts in East F. [bounds].

8 Sep. 1679. Benjamin Jenks, R; Richard Detton and Francis Langley, CWs.
Land: Sandy Brook L. 12 a., Hay F. L. 8 a., arable in the parish field near Wigwig, Flashbrook L. *c*. 8 a., Harp M. 1 a., Scutters Fur. *c*. 3 a., a pike in the parish field next to Cressage, ¼ a. in fields near the parsonage house, *c*. 1 a. in gardens and orchards.
[3 copies, 2 of parchment and 1 of paper].

16 Aug. 1698. Benjamin Jenks, R; Thomas Carter and Thomas Checkleton, CWs.
House of 4 bays with outbuildings 9 bays.
Tithes are all due in kind; there are no calves in kind because the dairies are small, but 6d is due per calf and 1d for every cow giving milk; wool and lambs are due in kind, lambs being due not only at 10 but at 7, 8 and 9 without an allowance for odd numbers; likewise for geese.
Surplice fees: marriage with licence 5s 6d without making abatement for poverty, baptisms 6d, burials 6d, funeral sermon 10s.
Easter dues: each communicant 2d, tradesmen's hand and men servants 4d, maidservants 2d, corn mill profits 2s, garden and smoke 2d.
The clerk's wages are paid by the CWs.

25 Nov. 1701. Benjamin Jenks, R; John Symonds and Henry Tudor, CWs.

2 May 1705. Benjamin Jenks, R.

23 July 1718. Benjamin Jenks, R.
Tithes: wool and lambs are due not only at 10 but at 7, 8 and 9, allowing 3d per lamb up to 10.
'Beyond the particulars of this Terrier I must repeat here the noble Charity Lately bequeathed by the Right Honble. Earle of Bradford deceased'[2] to the poor of Harley Parish being £14 p.a. quarterly for 99 years, the distribution being managed by the rector with the advice of the parish officers where they apprehend most need.

1722. Benjamin Jenks, R; Robert Clinton and John Hunton, CWs.
The chancel and 3 seats there belong to the rector; the fence of the churchyard belongs to the parish.

5 July 1726. William Painter, R; Henry Powell and Richard Hanson, CWs.

---

[1] Harley was transferred from Lichfield diocese to Hereford in 1905: *Victoria history of Shropshire*, ii. 1.
[2] Francis Newport, created 1st Earl of Bradford in 1692, lord of the manor of Harley died in 1708; his main seat at this date was at Eyton on Severn.

Land: Sandybrook L. 12 a., arable in part of the field near Wigwig, Hayfield L. 8 a., Flashbrook L. 8 a., Harp M. 1 a., Scutters Fur. 3 a., pike of arable in the parish field next to Cressage.
The rector has no seats or burial places in the church, nor is he obliged to repair any part of it. There are 3 seats in the chancel which are the rector's, though he can sell them.

28 Aug. 1730. William Painter, R; Thomas Langley and William Hanson, CWs.

7 Aug. 1733. William Painter, R; Robert Clinton and William Cookson, CWs.

16 July 1736. William Painter, R; Thomas Reeves and William Roberts, CWs.

1 Sep. 1739. William Painter, R; John Dale and William Hanson, CWs.

18 Sep. 1742. William Painter, R; William Shutt and John Ruttley, CWs.

11 Sep. 1745. William Painter, R; William Corfield and William Hanson, CWs.

20 Sep. 1752. [John Greaves, R] James Dewhurst, C; John Cookham and John Buttler, CWs.

11 Aug. 1756. [John Greaves, R] James Dewhurst, C; Richard Woof and Thomas Taylor, CWs.

1763. [John Greaves, R] James Dewhurst, C; Francis Hall and George Edwards, CWs.
Land: Sandybrook L. 10 a., Scutters Fur. pasture in West F. 3 a. with the common field on the S., Harp pasture 1 a., Flashbrook L. being 2 pastures 10 a., Hayfield L. and ½ a. of land behind the barn.

11 Sep. 1767. [John Greaves, R] James Dewhurst, C; William Corfield and William Madley, CWs.

1772. [John Greaves, R] James Dewhurst, C; William Hall and Richard Peck, CWs.

Aug. 1775. James Dewhurst, R; Thomas Wainwright and George Edwards, CWs.

7 Sep. 1779. James Dewhurst, R; Richard Davies and William Bradley, CWs.

5 Aug. 1783. John Russell, C; Richard Woof and W. Cookson, CWs.

1792. James Cope, C; John Newton, CW.
Copy of 1730.

1801. George Adney and William Bradley, CWs.
Copy of 1698.

1805. John Gibbons, R; George Adney and Richard Woof, CWs.

1824. J. Gibbon, R; R. Woof and George Adney, CWs.
Glebe *c.* 48 a.; croft adjoining the house 2 a., Great and Little Fur. 7 a., L. 5 a., Rushy M. 4 a., Schutters M. 4 a., field of 5 a., Southern M. 6 a., Butchers M. 3 a., Cottage L. 1 a., 2 pieces near Plaish Brooks of 6½ a. and 4¾ a.; 2 cottages and a garden were included in the exchange with Lord Darlington by which the rector obtained 37 a. of land next to the house.

116

1832. John Gibbons, R; Richard Cartwright, CW.
Land: 36½ a. near the house and 2 other pieces at a distance.

7 Sep. 1841. John Gibbons, R; George Adney and John Crowther, CWs.
House with drawing room, dining room, study, kitchen, brew house, 10
bedrooms, garden and 9 bays of outbuildings.
Land: Home M. 2 a., Cottage Croft 1 a., Butchers M. 3 a., Southern M. 5 a.,
Rushy M. 4 a., Long M. 4 a., The F. 5 a., The L. 5 a., Gritty Fur. 5½ a., other
Gritty Fur. 1 a. in the occupation of the rector; West Plaishbrook Piece 7½ a.,
East Plaishbrook Piece 4 a., 2 cottages and gardens leased; total 48 a.
Surplice fees: marriage by banns 5s, by licence 10s 6d, burial 1s, churching
1s, headstone 2s 6d, tombstone £1 1s, vault £2 2s.
Clerk's fees: marriage by banns 2s 6d, by licence 5s, burial 3s including
making the grave and tolling the bell.
The tithes have been commuted for £260.
Plate: 2 silver salvers and 1 cup. There is an iron chest for the registers. The
interest on £20 is distributed to the poor; there are no other benefactions
for the poor.
c. 11 a. left to the parish for repairs to the church is worth *c*. £19 16s p.a.

14 Aug. 1845. John Gibbons, R; George Adney and John Crowther, CWs.
There is a good parsonage house.
[2 copies, 1 labelled 1853].

Hengoed[1]

1856. Albany Possendale Lloyd, minister.
[Included with the terrier are an engraving of the chapel with a caption
stating that the foundation stone was laid 16 Aug. 1849, the chapel opened
for divine service 11 June 1850 and consecrated by the bishop of St Asaph
15 Aug. 1853, and a map of the glebe land in 1856 4 a. with the
churchyard]. A district has been legally attached and £40 p.a. secured on
Selattyn rectory, £15 from Whittington and £6 from QAB.
Plate: paten and cup of silver, the gift of the incumbent. There is an iron
chest for the registers.
Inventory: barrel organ which plays 39 tunes, oak chest in the vestry with a
funeral pall, 2 iron stoves, oak communion table with crimson cloth, vestry
table, surplice cupboard, wash hand stand, chair and zinc cistern in the
vestry yard.

High Ercall
(*and see* Rowton)

21 Oct. 1612.[2] George Wood, V; Thomas Barker and George Bratten, CWs.

---

[1] Hengoed was formed into an ecclesiastical parish from parts of Selattyn and Whittington
parishes in 1854: *P.O. directory of Shropshire* (1879), 328.

[2] There is a transcription of the High Ercall terrier for 1612 (taken from a copy of 1720) in
Shropshire Notes & Queries, N.S. iii (1894), 17, and of the 1693 terrier ibid. 47–9.

'One fair ancient dwelling house of Timber covered with Slate Shingle and Tyle' of 5 bays with barn 4 bays with a shore adjoining, stable, cow house 2 bays with a shore adjoining, garden and little orchard yard of 3 a.

Land: 2 several closes or leasows enclosed by the vicar out of of the town field called Cunningtree F. 14 a., Gaston L., a close by Almon Hedge, 6 a. of arable in strips in Cunningtree F., 2 little enclosures in Little F. of High Ercall, 1 called the croft by the Parkside of 4 a. and 1 of 3 a. called the leasow by Bathwallfieldsyde, 6 butts in the same field, 3 other butts of 3 a. mainly sowed with Little F., 8 a. of arable in strips in Poole F., Little M. of 2 a. near Bradford Bridge.

Tithes: all lesser and vicarial tithes as wool, lambs, pigs, geese, hemp and flax, fruit, apples, pears, wardens, hops and garden stuffs are due to the vicar; the farm of Rodenhurst pays for greater and lesser tithes a composition of 7 strikes of rye of the old measure of Shrewsbury which is 12 gallons to the strike; the greater and lesser tithes of Houghton township and also Isombridge are due except for certain parcels which the farmers of the chapels claim; the vicar in the court of Lichfield recovered the right to corn, wool and lambs from John James's tenement which the farmer of the chapels is said to claim but has made no claim for 5 years; John Taylor of Longden anciently paid 3 strike of eels for the weir on the Tern, he told the court his tenant should pay, but of late they have been withheld; John Leighton acknowledges his land is part of High Ercall parish and owes duties, but he is to be tolerated to attend divine service at Rodington. Mortuaries are due.

Easter duties except for certain houses 'whereof some part goes to the chapels as the new farmers of his Maj. pretend'; these have lately been recovered in the ecclesiastical court by the present vicar and are now in suspense by prohibition from the common law. [This section is underlined].

n.d. [No signatories].

The vicarage house is not yet fininished but is likely to be of 4 bays.

Land: Mill M. adjoining the River Roden, a small parcel adjoining Ercall Park, pasture called Badwell Field Cornery, 10 strike seedness of rye in Clemstrey Park, Reethorn, parcel of arable of 5 strikes seedness in Wallton F., Moore L. of about 20 strikes of hard corn adjoining Osbaston Town F., 14 butts being *c.* 18–19 strikes in Cunningtree F., 4 butts being 3 strikes of hard corn in Poole F., 6 butts or 4 strikes in Little F.

1693. [Richard Blakeway, V].

16 Aug. 1698. Richard Blakeway, V; Richard Warmesley and Richard Simpole, CWs. [11 other signatories].

Vicarage house of brick of 3 bays with 3 floors, barn and beast house 4 bays, orchard, 2 gardens, fold yard and backside of 1½ a.

Land: Clemstree Park 5 a., Black Butts 11 a., Barnfield Corner 3½ a., Park Croft 1 a., Mill M. 1 a., 25 butts in Conary F.

The vicar has a seat in the church on the S. side near the pulpit; the N. gate of the churchyard is the only part which belongs to the vicar.

Part 1 (Abdon to Llanfair Waterdine)

Tithes: hay, corn, grain are due in Haughton except on 2 parcels and in Isombridge except 2 tenements and 40 butts belonging to the former chapel; tithes of lambs, wool, pigs, geese, hemp, flax, apples, pears and eggs are due in kind throughout the parish except the township of Roden, the farm of Sleap, 1 tenement in Poynton, 1 in Rowton and 1 in Cold Hatton which only pay 2d per communicant at Easter; lambs are tithable if they fall within the parish and wool if it is shorn within the parish, even if the sheep have only been there a short time; 2 eggs are due per hen and 3 per cock, the vicar starting to gather them on the Monday before Palm Sunday; 1½d is due for a cow and calf, 1d for a barren cow, 2d for a colt, 1d for a hive of bees put down and 1d for smoke and garden; communicants pay 2d, except young people of 16 and over who live with their parents who pay ½d.

Surplice fees: 8d for churching, 8d for burial, 2s for a marriage with banns and 2s 6d with a licence; inhabitants of Rodington and Upton Parva pay burial fees to the vicars of Ercall.

Clerk's wages: £3 6s 8d p.a. paid by the CWs and 1d or 1d worth of eggs from every house around Easter.

1701. Richard Blakeway, V; Samuel Roycroft and Robert Humphreys, CWs.
Tithes: Poynton Farm pays 5s in lieu of all tithes; Rodenhurst Farm pays 9 strikes and 1 peck of rye.

2 May 1705. Richard Blakeway, V; Thomas Barker and John Ward, CWs.
Land: Clemstree Park 5 a., Black Butts or Moore L. 12 a., Badwell F. Corner 3½ a., Further Badwell F. Corner 5 a., Conary L. 8 a.
Tithes of corn and hay in Haughton is due except for 2 leasows and in Isombridge except 2 leasows belonging to a former chapel there; parcels in Sugdon and Rodington pay small tithes to the vicar of High Ercall except Roden, Poynton, Rowton and 1 tenement in Cold Hatton pay no tithe; 2 other tenements in Cold Hatton only pay one-third tithe and Sleap only half; Poynton farm pays 5s in lieu and Rodenhurst farm 9 strikes and a peck of clean rye.

7 Aug. 1733*. L[awrence] Gardner, V; Thomas Spenlove and Robert Humphreys, CWs.
Tithes are due on certain butts in Lady F. and on part of Rodington farm.

1736. Law[rence] Gardner, V; William Rodenhurst and Thomas Croxton, CWs.

1739. Law[rence] Gardner, V; William Allen and Andrew Dawes, CWs.

19 Sep. 1742. Law[rence] Gardner, V; Robert Clarke and William Slater, CWs.

11 Sep. 1745. Law[rence] Gardner, V; Richard Humphreys and Samuel Allen, CWs.

26 Aug. 1748. Lawrence Gardner, V; Edward Thomas and Walter Morgan, CWs.

30 July 1752. John Douglas, V; Thomas Wood and John Riden, CWs.

119

Glebe terriers of Shropshire

14 Sep. 1756. Henry Wood, C; Thomas Spenlove and Thomas Juckes, CWs.

21 Sep. 1759. Henry Wood, C; Edward Rowlands and John Dickin, CWs.

1763. Henry Wood, C; Andrew Hitchin, CW.

1767. Henry Wood, V; William Randles and Thomas Slater, CWs.

12 Oct. 1772. Henry Wood, V; Allen Clark and Robert Page, CWs.
Copy of 1733 with an addendum dated 28 Apr. 1768—by award made by arbitrators chosen by the vicar of High Ercall and S. Allen of Isombridge to determine the customary manner of setting for the great tithe in that township the 11th cock or mow is due; this notice was displayed in church 24 May 1768.

12 Oct. 1775. Henry Wood, V; Edward Thomas and John Hollace, CWs.

17 Aug. 1779. Joseph Walcam, minister; Robert Page and Allen Clarke, CWs.

4 Aug. 1783. Edward Thomas and Benjamin Colley, CWs.
Copy of 1733.

1787. Samuel Steedman and Walter Taylor, CWs.

25 Oct. 1792. John Wood, V; John Rodenhurst and John Adney, CWs.

24 July 1797. James Marston, minister; Thomas Brookes, CW.

28 Sep. 1801. J. Marston, minister; Samuel Elsmore, CW.

28 June 1805. Richard Madeley, CW.

22 Sep. 1810. James Marston, minister; John Adney, CW.

1814. J. Marston, minister; Samuel Elsmore, CW.
Copy of 1733 and the arbitrators' judgement of 1768.

5 Aug. 1824. James Marston, minister; Richard Elsmore and Richard Bickerton, CWs.

1828.
Copy of 1733 and 1768 judgement.

1836. A. Alison, V; John Meredith, C.
Copy of 1733 with 1768 judgement.

7 Sep. 1841. R[obert] Forester, V; Edward Steedman and John Whitfield, CWs.
House with entrance hall, 2 sitting rooms, 3 bedrooms with attics over, kitchen with bedroom over, pantry and cellar, new 3-stalled stable, coach house, saddle room, hay loft, granary, cow house for 2 cows and pigsty, close and garden of 1½ a.
Land: Mill M. 2 a., pastures called Badafield Corner 3½ a., Far Badafield Corner 5 a., Clemstree Park 4½ a., Conery F. 4½ a., Conery F. 3 a., Lower Black Butts 5 a., Lower Black Butts also 5 a., all but the first 4 leased.
Surplice fees: marriages by licence 10s, by banns 5s, burials 8d, churching 2d, single vaults above ground £3 3s, flat stone over a grave 10s 6d, headstone 5s.

120

Clerk's fees: marriage by licence 5s, by banns 2s 6d, burials 4d, tolling the bell and making the grave 4s 10d, churching 4d; salary: 6s 8d p.a. and £2 p.a. from the Duke of Cleveland.

Tithes are partially commuted but not yet confirmed.

The repair of the chancel belongs to the Duke of Cleveland and is in good repair.

Plate: chalice and plate of silver. There is a good iron chest for the registers.

Benefactions [no details] are displayed on a board and total £199.

14 Aug. 1845*. R[obert] Forester, V; William Blakeway and Robert Icke, CWs.

Tithes have been commuted for £432.

Benefactions amounted to £199 but part has been lost through neglect and now amount to £160 less £13, being the cost of obtaining them; the interest on £147 is distributed on St Thomas's Day.

24 July 1849. [Robert Forester, V] William Blakeway, CW.

Mortuaries have never been known to be demanded or received.

15 Apr. 1861. George Bucknell, V; James Wilding, CW.

32 a. of glebe land has been exchanged for a farm at Nesscliffe worth £10 p.a.

Surplice fees amount to c. £8 p.a.

1884*. [Lionel de Heriz, V].

House of 12 gables built in 1855 with entrance hall, 3 sitting rooms, 5 bedrooms, WC, servants' room, 4 attics and a box room, school room, large kitchen, back kitchen, pantry, dairy, good cellars, boot house, coal house and WC in back yard, 3-stalled stable, saddle room, hay loft, granary, coach house, cow house, 2 pigsties, large open shed, fold yard, turnip house, cart house, tool house, fowl house, rick yard, pleasure ground and kitchen garden 1 a.

Land: formerly much scattered but exchanged by Revd R. J. Forester and Henry, Duke of Cleveland, the patron, in 1854.

Income: tithe rent charge £445 3s; fees average p.a. £15.

Schedule of registers from 1585.

Plate: 2 silver chalices and patens, silver flagon and brass alms dish.

A free grammar school was founded by Thomas Leeke, Baron of the Court of the Exchequer, 1 Feb. 1663 and endowed with 53 a. of land in Sarnau, Montgomeryshire. The schoolhouse became dilapidated and in 1877 was judged incapable of repair; the master, Revd C. H. Hogg was on his retirement in 1876 allowed a pension of £40 p.a. by the Charity Commissioners. At a meeting of the governors 12 Apr. 1878 it was agreed on the motion of Hon. R. C. Herbert to sell the site of the school and invest the money with the Charity Commissioners.

Highley

n.d. [?1589]. George Powntney, C; Nicholas Bradley, Thomas Charnock, Richard Palmer, Richard Holway.

John Littleton is patron of the vicarage.

House with close adjoining of 1½ a.

Land: 10 a. in 10 parcels in South F., land in Cockshutt F. and in Rea F. [details torn], 12 a. of pasture, 2 a. of meadow [bounds].

Tithes are due except on corn, 'he hath not one sheffe of any kynd of grayne'.

3 Feb. 1625/6. Robert Barrett, V; Francis Holloway, Richard Harries and William Monkton, CWs.

Vicarage house and close on which it is situated on the N. side of Rea F.

Land: Innage or Little Close enclosed out of Rea F. 2 a., 4 short butts in Rea F. ½ a. enclosed by Robert Barrett, pasture and meadow called Cliffe with the River Severn on the E. with a little close at one end where the Lady Chapel stood 6 a., leasow or pasture lately enclosed out of the common called Highley Wood in lieu of pasture 10 a., 4 ridges in South F. 2½ a., furlong enclosed out of Cockshutt F. 3½ a.

The parishioners of Highley being all freeholders exchanged and enclosed the common field lands 'for theyr more commodious use thereof, therefore the said Robert Barrett like wyse for the good of the Church' with the consent of the patron; the land had been dispersed in Rea F., South F. and Cockshutt F. [details and bounds given in each field before enclosure and of exchanges].

Hinstock

19 Oct. 1612. John Reynolds, R; Richard Wilkes and Peter Leland, CWs.

Parsonage house of 2 bays with barn 3 bays, little stable and other houses of office 3 bays, barn yard adjoining, 2 gardens, 1 adjoining the house, the other on the kitchen side and an orchard adjoining the churchyard.

Land: 12 butts in 5 parcels in Blakeley F., 6 butts in 3 parcels in Hincks F. and 12 butts in 4 parcels in Hie F. [bounds].

31 Aug. 1635. Nathaniel Pudyfatt, R; William Rostid and William Hughes, CWs.

Land: an enclosure at the lower end of Lower Lea F., 1 a., 3 lands and 2 pieces in Upper Lea F., enclosure of 2 lands in Marsh F., 2 lands in Blakeley F., 4 lands and 1 piece in Hole M., 6 lands and 1 piece in Link F., 4 lands in High F., 3 lands in Barrcroft F.

12 Sep. 1682. Amias Vaughan, R.

House of 2 bays with barn 5 bays and a small turf cote.

Land: 4 butts in High F., 3 butts in Barecroft F., Wheat Yield Croft of 3 butts, 4 butts in Lea F., 2 butts and a pike in Blacklow F., 1 butt in Green Reans, a small croft rented for 5s p.a., 2 butts and a pike in Link F., small pike of *c*. 1 peck seedness in a piece of Bedworth's called Long Rope in Link F., 1 butt near William Yate's new piece, 1 butt on Long Fur.

28 Sep. 1685. Amias Vaughan, R.

12 Sep. 1693. Amias Vaughan, R; John Holmes and Thomas Perkison, CWs.

House with a kitchen garden and flower garden.

Part 1 (Abdon to Llanfair Waterdine)

Land: 2 butts and a pike in Blakelow F., a small intake near Heathley's house let at 5s p.a., 4 butts in Lea F. *c.* 1 a., 3 butts and some small pikes called Wheat Yield, 1 butt in Blantern's Green Reans *c.* 3 pecks seedness of rye, 1 butt called Gig Hole of *c.* 3 pecks seeding of rye, 2 butts in Barecross, 1 butt near Link F. gate *c.* 3 pecks of rye, a small butt in Yeardley's called Long Rope, 1 butt and a small pike of 1 seeding of rye, 1 butt and 4 small pikes called Long Rope of 1½ pecks seeding, 1 butt in High F. called Elder Tree *c.* 3 pecks seeding, 1 butt in High F. called Bithome Butt *c.* 3 pecks, 1 marled butt in High F. *c.* 1 peck of barley, 2 butts and a pike in Blanter's Yields *c.* 1 a.

Tithes belong to the rectory from time out of mind; at present they are valued at £26 p.a.

30 June 1698. Amias Vaughan, R; Edward Bass and Thomas Bolis, CWs.

Parsonage house of 2 bays with a little house of easement, bake house, turf cote and coal house 1½ bays erected by the present rector, barn 5 bays with bays for rye, barley, hay and threshing, and 2 pigsties next to the barn.

Glebe land enrolled at the last court of Robert Corbet—small cottage on the glebe land with a smith's shop and a small place to put his coals, turf cote and a small sheepcote on forks, 2 small gardens with apple, plum and pear trees and a small butt belonging, let for 10s p.a., fold yard about the house, stable yard, hemp butt, flower garden, kitchen garden; 6 a. of glebe land being 4 butts in High F., fallow every 3rd year, 3 butts in Barecroft, small enclosure called Wheat Yield of 3 butts, 4 butts in Lea F., 2 butts in Blakelow F., 1 butt in Green Reans; small croft at the back of Heathley's house let for 5s p.a., 2 butts in an enclosure called Yields, 1 butt and a pike on Colon Fur., 1 butt on Long Rope, 1 butt at Link F. gate.

Tithes: Widow Barnfield of Pixley's house in Chetwynd has 2 enclosures on which tithe corn is paid equally to the rector of Hinstock and Chetwynd; Hinstock Grange has a modus; John Moreton of Ellerton Hall, Cheswardine has a meadow which pays 2s to the rector of Hinstock; Sir John Corbet has a birch wood called Lockley Wood bought from the Duke of Norfolk and has had 2 falls since; the bailiff, Thomas Howle said £10 was due in tithes per fall and he put it in his accounts, but has not paid it; the rector was terrified to sue Sir John as the vicar of Drayton met with failure in a similar case; the 2nd fall in 1693–4 was charcoaled and Thomas Moreton, attorney sued Sir John but he has since died; then the tenant asked 'honest' Mr Robert Moreton of Shifnal to sub pena John Moreton of Ellerton who bought the charcoal for £36 8s 8d and he agreed to pay the tithe to save costs; the custom of lambs is 1 at 7 allowing the parishioners 1½d to make up 10 and 2 at 17 allowing 1d.

Clerk's wages: 6d per ploughland, 3d per cottage and 2d per cote.

1701. Amias Vaughan, R; Andrew Bentley and Richard Stockdale, CWs.

4 May 1705. Griffith Vaughan, R; John Holmes and Roger Raye, CWs.

Land: Lea F. and Wheat Hills 2 a., New Piece 3 a., Way F. *c.* 1 a., Gig Hole Butts, 2 butts in High F., 1 butt in Richard Roster's, small enclosure of *c.* ½ a., small cottage with smith's shop and 2 small gardens of *c.* ½ a.

Tithes: all tithes are due in kind except for ½d per calf; pigs and geese are due at 7; colts pay 4d at Easter.

Surplice fees: burials 4d, churching 4d, registering 6d, marriages 2s 6d.

24 July 1718. Griffith Vaughan, R; James Bentley and John Deakin, CWs.

Land: 9–10 a., all enclosed being Parson's Piece 5½ a., Lea F. 3 a., New Intake 1 a., small butt enclosed in the croft of Joseph Roster and a little intake near the common [bounds].

All tithes are due in kind except hay [named compositions]; men and maid servants and children over 16 pay 2d; stall of bees ½d.

The minister has 1 seat in the church and 1 in the chancel anciently erected; the rector repairs the chancel but none of the churchyard fence.

6 July 1726. Griffith Vaughan, R; James Howle and Thomas Jones, CWs.

29 Aug. 1730. John Haines, R; William Chalinor and Thomas Bolas, CWs.

9 Aug. 1733. John Haynes, R; John Deakin and William Howle, CWs.

15 July 1736. John Haynes, R; James Poole and John Corfield, CWs.

31 Aug. 1739. John Haynes, R; Thomas Brazenell and George Howle, CWs.

27 Aug. 1742. John Haynes, R; Joseph Simson and Richard [?]Brune, CWs.

20 Aug. 1745. John Haynes, R; George Steventon and John Griffiths.

9 Aug. 1748. John Haynes, R; John Hassall and James Poole, CWs.

1 Aug. 1752. John Lea, C: John Deacon and Thomas Naginton, CWs.

14 Aug. 1756. John Power, C; Matthias Wilcox and Francis Ansill, CWs.

20 Sep. 1759. John Power, C; William Challenor and Robert Plant, CWs.

6 Sep. 1763. John Power, C; William Tilst and Josias Hassel, CWs.

15 Sep. 1767. John Power, C ('instead of Mr Roberts who is not come to reside'); William Poole and William Arkinstall, CWs.

7 Sep. 1772. Edward Watkins, minister; Josiah Hassall and Robert Plant, CWs.

21 Aug. 1775. Edward Hughes, C; Thomas Austin and John Bostock, CWs.

6 Sep. 1779. T. Lloyd, minister; Matthias Willcox and Ralph Cotton, CWs.

4 Aug. 1787. Charles Hodgkin, minister; George Grenney and Job Downing, CWs.

18 Oct. 1797. Richard Mason Peake, C; James Poole and William Challenor, CWs.

24 Aug. 1801. George Taylor, R; William Brittain and George Traynell, CWs.

1 July 1805. George Ravenscroft, C; George Traynell and John Challenor, CWs.

25 Sep. 1810. George Ravenscroft, C; William Davis and Samuel Wright, CWs.

9 Aug. 1824. H. Cotton, R; Samuel Beeston and Walter Meakin, CWs.

Part 1 (Abdon to Llanfair Waterdine)

Parsonage house with 2 small parlours, kitchen, back kitchen, pantry and 5 small rooms upstairs, tithe barn with a threshing floor and 2 bays for corn, drift house and stable of 3 stalls and a loft over, small garden and shrubbery and stack yard.

Land: arable and meadow of 13 a. being Lea F. 3½ a., Town F. with Little Rope 5 a., New Intake 1 a., small piece in the field of Mr Corbet Howard, allotment of common in Lockley Wood of c. 2½ a.

12 Aug. 1828. Samuel Beeston, CW.

Parsonage house with entrance hall, 3 parlours, storeroom, pantry, kitchen, brew house and 2 cellars under, 5 principal bedrooms and 3 dressing rooms.

16 Aug. 1832. Thomas Simkin and James Machin, CWs.

31 Aug. 1836. Walter Meakin and William Griffiths, CWs.

9 Sep. 1841. William Griffiths, CW.

Parsonage house with entrance hall, 3 sitting rooms, laundry, kitchen, 2 pantries, scullery, washhouse, cellars under the drawing room and hall, old timber-framed barn separated from the house by a narrow fold yard, stone wall and shrubbery, garden shrubberies, drying ground, fold and rick yard.

Land: 14 a. being Lea F., Lea F. Croft, Upper and Lower Town F., Little Rope, Links Croft, common piece in Lockley Wood, quillet in the field of William Howard, cottage and garden opposite the National school.

Tithes have been commuted for £530; there is no Easter roll.

Clerk's fees: marriage by banns 2s, marriage by licence 2s 6d, baptism 4d, burial including sexton's fee and tolling 5s 10d; salary: those with poultry pay eggs at Easter, those with a plough pay 8d, tradesmen 4d.

The chancel is in good repair except the ceiling; the whole church needs to be ceiled and the work is in progress.

Plate: 1 small silver chalice, a very small silver paten, pewter flagon and pewter plate.

There are no benefactions.

13 Aug. 1845*. H. Cotton, R; William Griffiths and William Davies, CWs.
The glebe land is leased for £22 17s p.a.

24 June 1849. H. Cotton, R; William Davies and John Reeves, CWs.

16 Apr. 1849. Document giving the consent of the patrons, R. Corbet, Reginald Corbet and H. Cotton, for the demolition of an old cottage of timber and thatch; the garden is to be added to the rectory garden.

26 July 1853*. Bertie Johnson, R; William Davies and Joseph Sutton, CWs.

17 Apr. 1861*. Bertie Johnson, R; William Davies and Henry Jones, CWs.
Clerk's salary £5.

20 Apr. 1869. Bertie Johnson, R; William Davies and Henry Jones, CWs.

Parsonage house with entrance hall, 4 sitting rooms, laundry, kitchen, 2 pantries, scullery, larder, dairy, wash house, front and back staircase, 6 bedrooms, 2 dressing rooms, bathroom, closet and 2 cellars.

The clerk is paid £6 by the parish.

1884*. Herbert Harvey, R.

House built 1866 with a loan of £1,600 from QAB, with stables, piggeries and garden; part of the garden was given to build the schoolmaster's house.

Land: 3 arable fields, 3 pasture fields and 2 others totalling 11 a. leased for £16 p.a. except for 2 pastures which the rector has.

Surplice fees: burial 8d, marriage by licence 5s, by banns 2s 6d; average for 3 years £1 p.a.

Schedule of registers from 1695.

Plate: chalice and paten of silver, chalice, paten and flagon of plated gilt and brass alms basin.

Benefactions: a cottage now in 2 dwellings used to be almshouses left for the poor, the donor and date unknown; the rents were received by the church, but now by the managers of the schools.

Hodnet
(*and see* Moreton Say; Weston under Redcastle)

14 Oct. 1612. William Deacon, parson; John Podmore and Thomas Dickens, CWs; William Cadman curate of Moreton Say and Roger Hill, CW of Moreton Say.

Dwelling house with outbuildings 12 bays, orchard and garden and 3 little garden crofts 4 a. with Hodnet park to the W. and S.

Land: 12 lands or little butts lying together in Lea F. 3 a., 9 lands lying together in Wollerton F., 2 a., a butt and 2 headlands also in Wollerton F., 16 small lands and 2 headlands together in Sandy F., 3 a. called Parsonage Flatt, another 6 lands 1½ a. also in Parsonage Flatt, croft called Kyneland 1 a. [bounds].

Moreton Say chapel belongs to the parsonage; there is a dwelling house of 4 bays with outbuildings, garden and orchard adjoining and a barn.

Moreton Say land: a close above the town 3 a., enclosed pasture 4 a., little meadow lying along the common lane, little croft and meadow 2 a. at the end of the closes, little meadow on the backside of the house with an orchard of ½ a. lying alongside the chapel yard, 2 little crofts of *c*. 1 a. bounding on Bostock's land.

31 Oct. 1682. Da. Atkins, C; John Bolas and John Morris, CWs.

Dwelling house of 3 bays with barn, stable, cow house etc. 11 bays, orchard, garden and little meadow below the moat 3 a. in all.

Land: piece of land leading down to Hodnet Hall 2 a., Church Croft 1 a., Lea F. 1 a., Kineland 1 a., Wollerton Flatt 1½ a., 2 parcels of 1 a. and ½ a. in Sandy F., churchyard 1 a.

17 Sep. 1685. Da. Atkins, C; William Lochard, Andrew Morrall and Samuel Cartwright, CWs.

Dwelling house of 3 bays with outbuildings 12 bays, garden, hemp yard and orchard.

Hodnet land: little meadow called the M. below the Moat, Kineland, Woollerton Flatt, 2 pieces in Sand F. called Sandfield Flatt, Church Croft, Lea F. [bounds]; commons on Hodnet Heath.

Part 1 (Abdon to Llanfair Waterdine)

12 Sep. 1693. Nathaniel Cureton, C.

House with barn, stable, brew house, fuel house, backside and 2 gardens.

Tithes of corn, hay and all the small tithes and all ecclesiastical rights and duties are due in the several hamlets of Hodnet, Wollerton, Peplow, Bolas Parva, Espley, Hopton, Hopley, Kenston, Weston, Wixhill, Hawkstone, Marchamley, Lostford, Moreton Say, Bletchley, Woodlands and Longford.

Moreton Say: house with barn, garden and backside; also 8 pieces of meadow, pasture and arable land.

27 Nov. 1701†. [Edward Jones, R] William Lewis, Thomas Harris, CWs. [9 other signatories]. House of 4 bays with bake house and brew house 3 bays, pigeon house 1 bay, stable and cow house 2 bays, tithe barn 7 bays (1 bay taken down), garden, orchard, backside and fold yard 2 a.

Land: ½ a. in Sandy F. and Parsonage Croft 2 a. exchanged for 6 a. in Sandy F.; Church Croft and Hemp Butt 1½ a., Lea Croft 2½ a., Wollerton Flat 2½ a., 3 a. in Sandy F. [bounds].

Tithes are due in kind, though there is a modus for hay, hemp and flax throughout the parish; barren cow 1d, cow and calf 1½d, 4 cows and calves 6d, 5 cows and calves 2s 6d, 7 cows and calves 5s, 10 cows and calves 5s and so on, 5 paying half and 7 or 10 whole; wool is paid in kind at 1lb at 7 or 10, ½lb at 5, under 5 ½d per lb; lambs in kind ½ at 5, whole at 7 or 10, 1, 2, 3, 4, 6 at ½d each; pigs at 7 or 10, under 7 nothing; 7 young geese pay 1, 10 the same; colts 4d, bees 2d for every stall put down and killed.

Offerings: married couple 4d, single person over 16 2d, garden 1d, smoke 1d, herbage 1s 8d per £. Mortuaries are due.

Surplice fees: publishing banns 1s, marriage 2s 6d, burial 6d, churching 4d.

The curate's salary is ad libitum at present; the rector allows him the glebe land, surplice fees and £30; the rector allows the curate at Weston (though he is not bound to do so) £12 p.a.

The clerk's wage is paid by the CWs.

4 May 1705. Richard Price, R; Isaac Martin and John Bolas, CWs.

Parsonage house with hall, parlour, kitchen, 2 little chambers, little buttery and adjoining kitchen, backhouse, brew house, all 5 bays, old pigeon house 1 bay now used to lay coals and other fuel, stable, cow house 2 bays, tithe barn 7 bays, garden, orchard, backside and fold yard.

Land: 2 closes with the street from Hodnet to Wem to S., Church Croft and a hemp yard adjoining 2 a., Leafield Croft 3 a., Revelands Croft 3 a., Wollerton Flatt Croft 3 a., 8 a. enclosed in Sand F.

16 Apr. 1719. Richard Price, R; John Cartwright and George Harris, CWs. [12 other signatories].

Land: Parsonage Croft 2 a. and little piece c. ½ a. in Sandy F. exchanged for c. 6 a. in Sandy Common F., Church Croft and hemp but 1½ a., Lea Croft 2½ a., Revelands 2 a. formerly exchanged for part of Parsonage Croft, Wollerton Flatt 2½ a., 3 a. in Sandy F.

For collecting and paying of the great and small tithes and surplice fees and other dues ancient custom is referred to. [Not stated what this is].

Glebe terriers of Shropshire

1722. Richard Price, R; Samuel Phillips and Samuel Jennings, CWs.
The curate's salary is ad libitum of the rector.
The clerk's wages are paid by the CWs.

6 July 1726. Richard Price, R; Joseph Turner and Thomas Churton, CWs.
Thomas Griffiths, the present curate, has £30 p.a. and the surplice fees.

1730. Thomas Griffiths, C; William Dicken and William Hampton, CWs.

12 Nov. 1733. James Beauclerck, R; R. Hill and Robert Pigot, CWs.

1736. Thomas Griffiths, C; Walter Milner and John Astley, CWs.
The curate's salary at present is £50 and the surplice fees.

1739. Thomas Griffiths, C; John Massey and Thomas Powell, CWs.

16 Sep. 1742. Benjamin Wase, minister; George Harris and John Cartwright, CWs.
Tithes: payment is variable and they are let, leased or gathered according to the will of the rector except where there is a fixed modus which relates to hay only in certain places.

17 Sep. 1742. Robert Peplow, curate of Moreton Say; Henry Bucknal and William Cooper, wardens.
Small tithes and ecclesiastical duties are due from the townships of Moreton, Bletchley, Woodlands and Longford.

29 Aug. 1745. Benjamin Wase, C; James Jones and Thomas Burrows, CWs.

10 Sep. 1745. John Snelson, C [of Weston]; Thomas Massey and John Cooper, CWs.

9 Aug. 1748. W[illiam] Dicken, C; William Teese and George Harris, CWs.
The curate's salary is £40 and surplice fees.

18 Sep. 1752. W[illiam] Dicken, C; Thomas Walmsley and John Chidlow, CWs.

16 Sep. 1756. W[illiam] Dicken, C; George Harris and Peter Light, CWs.

20 Sep. 1759. W[illiam] Dicken, C; Joseph . . . and Thomas . . . CWs [worn].

6 Aug. 1763. W[illiam] Dicken, C; John Massey and Thomas Barlow, CWs.

1767*. James Pratchet, C; William Adam and Rowland Morris, CWs.

1812.
Map and particulars of land proposed to be exchanged between Richard Heber Esq. and Revd Reginald Heber.[1] Commission of enquiry of the Bishop of Lichfield and local parsons as to the parsonage house; Reginald Heber M.A. rector of Hodnet, has requested consent for taking down the parsonage house and the buildings belonging to it and to rebuild on land

---

[1] Reginald Heber was born at Malpas, Cheshire. His father inherited the estate and living of Hodnet from his mother and became rector. In 1807 Reginald Heber was ordained and became rector of Hodnet which had been reserved for him since his father's death in 1804. In 1822 he became Bishop of Calcutta and died at Trichinopoly in 1826. He wrote many well-known hymns: *Dictionary of national biography*.

called Lea Piece which is intended to be given in exchange for the purpose by Richard Heber Esq. patron under the act of 17 Geo. III for promoting the residence of the parochial clergy. The commission are to find out when the incumbent entered the living, what money he has received for dilapidations and how it has been used, whether there has been wilful damage or neglect and what damage has been caused by such neglect. On the dorse Oswald Laycester, rector of Stoke on Tern, and William Judgson, rector of Adderley, state that the parsonage house was very ancient when Reginald Heber entered it, he has been there since 5 July 1807, has received nothing for dilapidations and there has been no wilful negligence; the house should be taken down and replaced with new buildings.

Specification for building a new rectory house in brick to be completed by March 1814 for £5,380 exclusive of the reuse of old materials.

Bond of Thomas Heber of Moreton Say to James, Bishop of Lichfield re a mortgage to raise £5,000 from Revd Hugh Cholmondley of Chester and William Shipley Esq. to build a new rectory.

1814.

Statement of account: £5,000 has been received and paid to J. Hiram Haycock architect. Signed by the Bishop of Lichfield, Richard Heber patron and Reginald Heber rector.

1828. [Charles Cholmondley, R] William Lewis and Thomas Harris, CWs. [9 other signatories]. Copy of 1701.

1832. Oswald Leycester, R; John Powell and John Hughes, CWs. Copy of 1701.

When Reginald Heber was rector a new house and offices were built and there were many exchanges of land between him and Richard Heber Esq., his brother.

9 Sep. 1841. S[amuel] H. Macaulay, R; Robert Graham and Samuel Morris, CWs.

Rectory house with dining room, drawing room, study, housekeeper's room, butler's pantry, kitchen, scullery, larder, servants' hall, laundry, dairy, brew house on the ground floor, 5 good bedrooms, 3 dressing rooms, a sitting room, 4 servants' rooms and a WC on the upper floor, bake house, hen house, 5-stalled stable, 3-stalled stable, coach house, saddle room, gig house, barn 2 large bays, pigsty and shed and greenhouse in the garden; another house with garden and orchard of c. 2 a.

Land: lawn 6 a., Big Holloway M. 2 a., Little Holloway M. 1½ a., School F. 2 a., plantation in the lawn; none of the glebe land is let.

Tithes: tithes on corn and hay are payable but there is a modus in Marchamley, Hodnet, Kenstone, Weston and Wixhall; the small tithes are let at composition; the tithes of the whole parish including the great tithes of Moreton Say are agreed to be commuted for a rent charge of £2,290 p.a.

Rector's fees: burials 10d, marriage by banns 4s, churching 6d.

Clerk's fees: burials including grave digging 5s 2d.

Inventory: 2 chalices with covers, 1 paten, 2 plates, all of silver, 3 surplices, 3 Common Prayer books, 1 bible and office book.

Benefactions: 12 a. of land in Wem, parcels of 4 a. and 3 a. of land adjoining the turnpike from Hodnet to Drayton, 4 pieces of land in Drayton 3 a., 6 cottages with gardens on Hodnet Heath 2 a. and 2 cottages near the Pinfold in Hodnet are rented for £101 1s; a bequest from the Hill family of Hawkstone paid by Rowland Hill yields £21 interest p.a.
There are 2 chancels, 1 belonging to the rector and 1 to the patron, both in good repair.

23 July 1849. S[amuel] H. Macaulay, R; Walter Minor and John Beacall, CWs.
Rectory house with 5-stalled stable, carter's 2-stalled stable, cow house, barn, coach house, saddle rooms, granary, pigsties, cart shed, bake house, poultry house 1½ a., flower garden, shrubberies and kitchen garden 1½ a.
Land: Lawn 12 a., Holloway M. 4½ a., Church Croft 2 a.
Fees: marriage by banns 5s, by licence 10s, burials 10d.
The tithes including the great tithes of Moreton Say have been commuted for a rent charge of £2,285.

1884*. Richard Cholmondley, R.
House, garden and shrubbery 4 a.
Land: 19 a. is occupied by the rector 19 a.
Income: £836 3s 7d from the sale of land on Hodnet Heath was invested in consols; tithe rent charge from the chapelry of Weston and Wixhill £1,735.
Schedule of registers from 1657.
Plate: silver and 2 silver gilt chalices, 2 silver gilt paten, silver gilt flagon, silver gilt, 2 brass and 1 pewter alms dish.
Benefactions: £200 5s from Sarah Price; £9 p.a. from the rent of land in Drayton parish; £1 10s p.a. rent charge on Drayton Common; 6s rent charge on Little Drayton heath; interest on £76 8s 8d, part for the school and part for bread for the poor; £31 11s 6d for 7 cottages and gardens in Hodnet; £6 for 2 a. in Hodnet; £12 for 4 a. in Hodnet; £24 for 6 a. in Wem; £17 10s for 7 a. in Wem; £21 interest on bequests by various members of the Hill of Hawkstone family paid by Viscount Hill.

Holdgate

n.d. [?1589]. [Notes on partial transcript; original illegible]. William Legg and John Howells, CWs.
The Bishop of Hereford is patron.
House . . .
Land: 44 a. of arable, common on Brown Clee, 16 a. in a field towards Shipton, 5 parcels in Little F. [bounds].

Hope Bagot

n.d. [?1589].
George Hill is the reputed patron.
House with kitchen, barn and other houses of office.
Land: 24 a. of arable in parcels of 3–4 a. pasture [extent illegible]; pasture on the Clee for sheep and cattle.

Hope Bowdler

8 May 1616. Peter Steaven, R; Philip Phillips, Thomas Wilkes and John Myntton, CWs.

House of 4 bays with garden, barn 4 bays, hemp butt and close called Parsonage Yard.

Land in Hope Bowdler: pasture 6 a., enclosed meadow and arable called Parsons L. 7 a., enclosed arable called The L. 7 a., parcel of enclosed arable and pasture called Bradebridge Yate, Pykes enclosed 2 a., close called Stannetwall 1½ a., enclosed leasow called Heslow 4 a.

Land in Chelmick: close 3 a., parcel of arable 2 a., ridges in Fogg F., Ditchcroft F. and Cross F. [bounds].

[2 copies].

Hopesay
(and see Aston on Clun)

1589.

The queen is patron.

Land: ridges in Nether F. and Mill F.

[There is more detail, but the document is faded and damaged].

6 June 1607. Roger Grene, R; Thomas Ricas. Thomas Hewes, Gryffith Whittall.

House and barn with orchard, garden and close adjoining.

Land: land in Middle F., leasow 7 a., Upper Samford L. 7 a., Lower Samford L. 8 a., Crooked Fur. L. 8 a., Bridge yard meadow 1 a., Pytt M. 8 a., meadow adjoining 4 a., 2 other meadows 2 a. and 1 a., 2 meadows called Bradley 2 a., 14 a. arable in Grenewaies F., leasow 8 a., Syche Close adjoining ½ a., Roding L. 17 a. [bounds].

23 Apr. 1636. Richard Awnsham, R; Griffith Maddox and Francis Eyton, CWs.

Land in Hopesay: Ranley Close 13 a., Upper Samford 4 a., New Close 5 a., Crooked Fur. 14 a., Pytt M. 8 a., enclosures called Backside and Sych adjoining the parsonage 10 a., Lower Samford 4 a.

Land in Little Brampton: 2 meadows 3 a., meadow in Brome 1 a., Longlangett and Marsh in Hopesay 3 a., meadow called Honny Hill 2 a. [bounds].

Hopton Castle

n.d. [?1589]. [Thomas Tilston, C. Names of other signatories damaged].

The daughters and 2 heirs general of Robert Corbet of Moreton Corbet have the rights of patrons.

House with sheepcote, stable and ox house.

Land: arable being 11 a. in East F. called Whatfyld, 12 a. in South F. called Knowell F., 5 a. in closes in West F. and 4 a. meadow [bounds].

Tithes of corn, wool, hay, hemp, flax, geese and lambs are due.

10 Dec. 1604. Thurston Tilston, C; William Wynon, Thomas Wright and John Spendar, CWs.

House with kitchen adjoining, 2 barns, cote, orchard, 2 gardens and backside adjoining.

Land: 2 little leasows in Radwood F., 1 a. in Clay Pits, little meadow called Claypits L., Twytchin L., 3 several parcels in Bulwall, 2 gobbets arable and 2 short edges in Bulwall, 1 a. between these and the wood, 4 a. in 5 parcels in Great Hope, 4 a. in 4 parcels in Upper Knowle F., 2 little leasows in Upper Radwood F., 2 leasows near Welshman's Wood, hemp yard and 3 parcels of hay ground [bounds].

Hopton Wafers

n.d. [?1589]. [Edward Churcham, R] Humphrey Norgrave and John Harper, CWs.

Mr Hyde is reputed patron.

House with hall, kitchen, barn and other necessary housing.

Land: 10 a. meadow, 12 a. arable, 20 a. pasture, 4 a. wood, common pasture on the Clee.

Tithes of the whole parish are due.

11 Dec. 1604. Edward Churchman, R; Thomas Hey, John Heycocks.

House with kitchen, barn, stable and other edifices, orchard, and garden; also another house with barn, orchard and garden adjoining the churchyard.

Land: arable in the common fields being 8 ridges and 1 headland in Mearbage F. lately enclosed, 2 a. in Shote F., pasture called Ryddinge or Heathy L. butting on a pasture belonging to the Guild of Ludlow.

15 Jan. 1682/3. John Wheeler, R; George Mantle, John . . ., Richard Hyde, CWs.

Richard Hyde is patron.

House with stables, barn and other housing.

Land: *c*. 40 a. after exchange [bounds given]; common of pasture on Titterstone Clee.

The rector has the tithes of the whole parish except of the manor house of Mr Hyde for which he has White F. in lieu.

Hordley[1]

24 Oct. 1612. Hugh Roden, R; Humphrey Bromfield and John Phillips, CWs.

House with barn, beast house and yard.

Land: Pike M., Pike Moore M.; there have been 16 strikes seedness in each of the 3 fields of Hordley but the meares and bounds are now not known and no incumbent has possessed them since the time of William Powys *c*. 40 years past.

The great tithes of Higher and Lower Hordley are due, but only one-third of the tithes of Bagley township.

---

[1] Hordley is also included in the Baschurch terrier for 1698.

Part 1 (Abdon to Llanfair Waterdine)

1679. Philip Vaughan, R; William Whattall and Thomas Barret, CWs.

n.d. [c. 1670–80]. [No signatories].

1682. [Philip Vaughan, R] Thomas Barret and John Bagley, CWs.
Land: Pike Mores 1 a., meadow adjoining the backside.

1693. Richard Andrewes, R; William Rogers and Richard Bagley, CWs.
House of 14 yd. × 5½ yd. with barn 16 yd. × 6 yd., cow house and stable 7 yd. × 16 ft, 2 small gardens and a meadow adjoining bounded on the N. by the land of Edward Kynaston, patron.
Land: moorish piece of 2–3 a. to the S. of Tetchill Moor, 2 moorish pieces and a meadow in Lower Hordley [bounds].
Tithes are due in kind from Upper and also from Lower Hordley except the water mill which pays 6d p.a.; Bagley township pays only one-third of the general tithe.

1698. Richard Smalman, R; John Bagley and Henry Davies, CWs.
Parsonage house adjoining the road to Ellesmere of 3 bays with barn of 3 bays S. of the house, beast house of 1 bay N. of the house, garden to the E. 10 yd. square, backside 2 a. and fold yard before the door 12 yd. square.
Land: Moor Piece 1½ a., Little M. 1 a., Pick Moor 4 a.
Easter dues: 4d for a man and wife, 2d for a servant, 1½d for cow and calf, 1d for a barren cow.
Tithes: half a lamb is due at 5 with 3d at 7, 8 or 9; pigs and geese likewise.
Surplice fees: burials 1d, churching 4d, registering 4d.
Clerk's wages: £1 p.a. paid by the CWs.

1 May 1701. [Richard Smalman, R. No signatories].

21 Oct. 1701.[1] Richard Smalman, R; John Hanson and Arthur Groome, CWs.

2 May 1705. Richard Smalman, R; Robert Jackson and John Reynolds, CWs.

23 July 1718. William Janns, C; Robert Jackson and Edward Davies, CWs.

5 July 1722. William Janns, C; John Cureton and Joseph Clark, CWs.

7 Aug. 1733. John Huntbach, R; John Cureton and Thomas Owen, CWs.

23 June 1736. John Huntbach, R; Thomas Owen and Edward Rogers, CWs.

14 Aug. 1739. John Huntbach, R; Thomas Buckley and John Bruckfield, CWs.

1742. John Huntbach, R; Edward Rogers and John Reynolds, CWs.
[Register 14 Sep. 1739–25 Aug. 1742].

1748. John Huntbach, R; Edward Rogers and Thomas Owen, CWs.

12 Oct. 1752. John Huntbach, R; J. Lacon and Thomas Price, CWs.

1756. John Huntbach, R; John Cureton and John Bruckfield, CWs.

1759. John Huntbach, R; John Reynolds and Thomas Price, CWs.
Copy of 1701.

---

[1] A copy of the Hordley terrier for 1701 is included in the parish register of 1754–1812 (SRRC, P141/A/1/2).

1763. Thomas Barrett, R; John Cureton and Samuel Jebb, CWs.
Copy of 1701.

12 Aug. 1767. Daniel Griffiths, R; Edward Davies and Thomas Whattall,
CWs.
Copy of 1701.

12 July 1775. [Daniel Griffiths, R; CWs' names faded].

1793. Daniel Griffiths, R; Thomas Cureton and [?]Margrett Lee, CWs.
Copy of 1701.

1801. [Daniel Griffiths, R] Francis Bickley and Robert Wambrey, CWs.
Copy of 1701.

1805. [Edward Kynaston, R] William Brookfield and Joseph Hignett, CWs.
Copy of 1701.

1810. [Edward Kynaston, R] Joseph Hignett and John Dodds, CWs.
Copy of 1701.

1824. [Edward Kynaston, R].

14 Aug. 1845. John Moore, R; Edward Lewis and Edward Martin, CWs.
Old parsonage 15 yd. × 5½ yd. with dairy and cellar and bedrooms above
projecting at the back towards the road 3 yd. × 6¾ yd. and a cart house at
the angle, brick buildings with slate roofs a barn 2 bays 19 yd. × 6½ yd.,
stable for 4 horses 5 yd. × 6½ yd., beast house and bing for 9 cows 10 yd.
× 6½ yd., pigsties and outlet for 4 pigs 5 yd. × 5 yd., fold 18 yd. × 14 yd.,
garden at the back 15½ yd. × 13½ yd. and garden in the front 28 yd. ×
23½ yd., all now leased.
New rectory house built in 1841, partly with money from QAB and partly by
an annual charge on the living with 17 yd. × 11½ yd. with a projecting
dining room 2½ yd. × 6 yd., back kitchen and coal house 10¼ yd. × 3¾ yd.
attached but under a separate roof, adjoining garden house, saddle room,
privy, stable for 2 horses, coach house with hay loft over 10 yd. × 7½ yd.,
milk house 3 yd. × 3 yd., shoe house and wood house; the kitchen yard
11 yd. × 8 yd. is divided by a brick wall from the stable yard and both are
surrounded by a brick wall, kitchen garden, pleasure garden and shrubberies.
Land: Higher and Middle Ox Pasture 6 a., Upper Ox Pasture 4 a., Pike M.
7 a., Yew Tree Croft 1½ a., Stable Croft 1 a., Parson L. 4 a., Woodcote M.
2 a., meadow in Bagley adjoining the River Perry 17½ a.
Surplice fees: grave 1s, 2s 6d to the sexton for digging grave and tolling the
bell, walled grave 2s 6d to the minister and sexton, vault £1 1s, headstone
or cross 2s 6d, flat stone 5s (all double for people from out of the parish),
marriage by banns 3s 6d, by licence 10s, churching 1s.
The church is ancient 57 ft × 27 ft with a vestry of brick on the N. built *c*. 18
years ago 10 ft × 10½ ft, churchyard 23 yd. × 46 yd.; the new E. window
and wall was put up by John Moore in 1844 and the new S. window by the
parish in 1845; at the same time a large portion of the S. wall was rebuilt.
Inventory: communion table with a red cloth the gift of Elizabeth Moore,
other linen, 2 chalices and a silver plate the gift of John Moore, rector,

pewter paten, silver plate, 2 pewter plates, pulpit cushion, bible printed in 1714, 2 prayer books, prayer book with the Old and New Testament (the books were repaired at the cost of Viscount Dungannon in 1842), 2 bells, marble font restored by John Moore, bier, hearse cloth, 2 oak chests, 1 for vestments and the other for maps and plate, deal chest for the bier, oak table, chair and form for the vestry and iron chest for the registers which date from 1686.

1884. T. Edward Meredyth, R.

House with the 'usual' number of sitting rooms, bedrooms and servants' rooms, back kitchen and coach house with bedrooms above in a separate bay attached, attached dairy, larder, coach house, saddle room with room over, garden house, 2-stalled stable with hay loft over, detached cow and cart house, loose box, piggeries, ornamental garden, plantation, kitchen garden and orchard 1½ a.

Land adjoining the rectory house 7½ a., meadow in the township of Bagley 17 a. let in allotments to 8 tenants.

Tithe rent charge £272; £1,173 19s 10d invested with the Eccl. Com.; average fees *c.* £2 18s 8d p.a.

Schedule of registers from 1686.

Plate: silver chalice, paten, flagon and alms dish.

Hughley[1]

n.d. [?1589].

Francis Gatteger is patron.

House with kitchen, barn, orchard and another little house.

Land: pasture adjoining house 2½ a., ½ a. pasture enclosed with North F. of Hughley on one side, 1 a. of pasture above West F., ½ a. of meadow enclosed in West F., ½ a. enclosed in North F., 5 a. arable in West F., 1 a. arable in East F. and . . . [faded] [bounds]; common of pasture in the fields and common lands for 6 beasts, horses, sheep, swine and other cattle.

Tithes are due on corn, hay, milk, calves, wool, lambs, pigs, geese, hemp, flax and fruit.

19 Nov. 1639. Gil[bert] Cole, R.

House of 4 bays with barn 3 bays, orchard and garden.

Land: leasow called Christen 5 a., another leasow 16 a., leasow called New Enclosure under Hotchkis Hill 4 a., Bridgeway Acre, meadow at end of Lower Town M. 1 a., Colley M. ¾ a., Garnetts M. ¼ a. [bounds].

17 June 1802. M[ichael] Stephens, R; Thomas Madely, CW.

House with brew house, barn, stable, tying for cattle and garden.

Land: 30 a. of glebe in Hughley [details given but very faded]; 3 a. lately enclosed in Preen.

All tithes are due in kind except a modus of £1 18s paid by Orlando, Lord Bradford.

---

[1] Hughley is also included in the Stanton Long terrier for 1607.

Surplice fees: burials 6d and registering 4d, churching 4d, registering baptism 2d, publishing banns 1s, marriage and registering 2s 6d, marriage by licence 5s.

Tithes: cow and calf 6d, barren cow 1d, colt 3d, lamb 3d, 1 pig in 10 or 2d, 10th lb of wool, 1 goose in 10.

Offerings: 6d each house.

12 July 1810. Morgan Jones, R; Richard Corfield, Moses Heath, CWs.

Tithes: wheat is due at 11th sheaf, barley, oats and peas 10th cock; tithe hay, clover and fodder is subject to a modus of £1 18s p.a. but clover mowed for seed is tithable as grass; sheep are tithed at 10th, odd lambs 3d, sheep taken to winter 20d per score and 1½d per lamb, wool is due at the 10th lb; pigs at the 10th and 2d per odd one, geese at the 10th and 2d per odd one; cow and calf 6d, barren cow 1d, colt 3d, stall of bees when put down 4d, 10th peck of apples and pears, 10th bushel of potatoes; 8d for running the mill; 2d offering, 1d smoke, 1d garden, 3 eggs per cock, 2 per hen, ducks the same; 10th heap of hemp or flax; tithe underwood; herbage 20d in the £.

Hyssington[1]

n.d. [early 17th century]. Thomas Brooke, Ludovic Gwynne.

The chapel of Hyssington was parcel of the priory of Chirbury. Thomas Burrell patron of Chirbury has built a new house on part of the priory lands adjoining the chapel and appointed a chamber in it for the curate.

There is no glebe.

26 May 1607. Rowland Parkes, C; Thomas Brooke and Ludovic Gwyn.

Hyssington is an impropriation which belonged to the dissolved priory of Chirbury; it has been bought by John Niccols of Salop, draper.

House of 4–5 bays with barn, kitchen, hemp yard and garden.

There is no glebe.

Ightfield

1612. George Tatnall, R; Richard Whittingham and George Sempole, CWs.

Mansion house of 3 bays with barn and other houses of office 6 bays, garden, orchard and backside.

Land: Dovehouse Yard, Calvescroft, Windmill F., Heath L., 2 pastures called Cow L. and Dunkesmore Croft, St Johns Hill, Wood L., Lees near the demesne lands of Sir George Mainwaring, Clay End, all pasture closes [bounds]; 2 cottages and 2 orchards adjoining the churchyard; total *c.* 32 a.

Tithes: there are only 7 ploughlands in Ightfield and only 25 houses and cottages in the whole parish.

20 Nov. 1635. John Arnwey, R; Richard Whittingham and Randle Wiggin, CWs.

House with barn, cow house, stable and kilnhouse.

---

[1] Hyssington is partly in Montgomeryshire and partly in Shropshire.

Part 1 (Abdon to Llanfair Waterdine)

Lands: churchyard of 1 a., St Johns Hill 10 a., Cow L. 8 a., Dunkesmore Croft 8½ a., Heath L. 4 a., Windmill F. 6 a., Dovehouse Yard and Calves Croft 8 a. Clea End 7 a., Wood L. 5 a., Lees 7 a., yard and garden 1½ a. [bounds]; Wollomes house 2 bays and yard ¾ a., cottage and garden ½ a.

25 Sep. 1682. George Hand and Thomas Parker, CWs.

Parsonage house with barns and yards at the end of the town next to Calverhall; 2 houses and gardens near the church leased.

1 Oct. 1685. [No signatories].

1693. [No signatories].

Tithes of corn of every kind are paid in kind; tithes of hay are due in kind except from Mr Mainwaring who pleads custom to have his demesne exempt from all sorts of tithes and pays £4 p.a.; all over 16 pay 2d, house and garden 1d, barren cow 1d, cow and calf 1½d, 2 eggs for a cock and 1 for a hen, 4d for a colt, every handicraft 4d Easter dues; wool is due at 1 at the 7th and 2 at the 17th fleece; lambs, pigs, geese ducks likewise at Midsummer; hemp and flax are due when pulled.

30 June 1698. Francis Hudson, R; Richard Savage, CW.

Parsonage house of 3 bays with cow house 2 bays, hay barn 2 bays, barn 3 bays, fold yard, backside and garden; another house 2 bays, cow house 1 bay, barn 1 bay and backside near the churchyard and the street; cottage 1 bay and a garden.

Tithes: all sorts of grain are due at the 11th sheaf or mow; hay is due at the 12th cock ready for carriage; Mr Mainwaring pays £4 at Michaelmas as a modus for all his demesne except Beards Yard and Marld Stocking which pay in kind; 2s per pound is due for herbage.

Surplice fees: marriage by licence 2s 6d, by banns 1s, burials 1s, churching 4d.

Clerk's wages: paid by the CWs and on their order by church collection.

23 Oct. 1701. Francis Hudson, R; Ralph Churton and John Harper, CWs.

4 May 1705. Francis Hudson, R; Richard Williams, CW.

Tithes are due on corn at the 11th 'hattock'.

24 July 1718. Thomas Adams, R; John Walmsley and Richard Williams, CWs.

Two little houses near the churchyard are inhabited by poor people.

Land: Cow L. 8 a., Dunxmore 5 a., Wood Piece 4 a., St John's Hill 6 a., Leas 4 a., Clay-ends 5 a., Windmill F. 4 a., Heathpiece 3 a., Duff Yard 7 a., Simpole's Yard ½ a., Williams's garden ½ a., fold and garden ½ a., churchyard 1 a. [bounds].

Surplice fees: marriage by licence 5s, by banns 2s 6d, burials 6d and entry in the register 6d, churching 6d, copying the register 5s.

The minister has no seat or burial place in the church; a seat was erected in the chancel about 30 years ago by James Haynes and another by the present incumbent about 4 years ago; Mr Binney the late rector built one, but the owner of the house he lived in instead of the decayed parsonage claimed it.

The repair of the chancel belongs to the rector and 10 roods of the churchyard fence.

6 July 1722. John Justice, R; J. Swanweeck and Jonathan Blantorn, CWs.

29 Aug. 1726. John Justice, R; J. Madeley and Richard Williams, CWs.
The clerk's wages are part paid by the CWs and part customary.

29 Aug. 1730. John Justice, R; John Turner and John Weever, CWs.

9 Aug. 1733. John Justice, R; George Harper and John Madeley, CWs.

15 July 1736. John Justice, R; George Harper and Cornelius Pye, CWs.

31 Aug. 1739. John Justice, R; George Harper and John Turner, CWs.

17 Sep. 1742. John Justice, R; George Harper and John Turner, CWs.

29 Aug. 1745. John Justice, R; George Harper and Thomas Smith, CWs.

9 Aug. 1748. John Justice, R; George Harper and Thomas Smith, CWs.

31 July 1752. John Justice, R; Thomas Swanwick and . . . [blackened], CWs.

16 Sep. 1756. John Justice, R; John Harper and John Madeley, CWs.

19 Sep. 1759. John Justice, R; Thomas Smith and John Bishop, CWs.

27 Aug. 1763. John Justice, R; John Madeley and John Turner, CWs.

1767. John Justice, R; John Harper and Thomas Smith, CWs.

17 Sep. 1772. Thomas Edwards, C; John Madeley, CW.

29 July 1775. Thomas Edwards, C; John Turner and George Walmsley, CWs.

1779. [No signatories].

22 Oct. 1792. T. Lloyd, minister; Richard Cliff and John Dimelow, CWs.

25 May 1797. T. Lloyd, minister; Robert Blantern, CW.

24 Aug. 1801. T. Lloyd, C; John Holland, CW.

1805. William Madeley, CW.

9 Aug. 1824. Kenrick Pick, R; John Turner, CW.

12 Aug. 1828. John Justice, R; John Turner, CW.
Land: Cow L. 9 a., Dunsmoor 9 a., Wood Piece 6 a., St Johns Hill 5 a., Near St Johns Hill 4 a., Heath F. with allotment 5 a.
Lands exchanged by act of parliament by the rector of Ightfield and Sir Rowland Hill of Hawkstone in 1828: Near Dove Yard M. 4 a., Far Dove Yard 5 a., Windmill F. 5 a., Clay End 7 a. and part of Dunsmoor in exchange for Church M. 8 a., Hill F. 5 a., Lower Stoney F. 6 a., Higher Stoney F. 3 a.
Additional fees: breaking the churchyard for a stranger 10s 6d.

16 Aug. 1832. John Justice, R; John Turner, CW.
Rectory house with 5 rooms below stairs and 8 bedrooms, 4-stalled stable; also 2 other houses.

Part 1 (Abdon to Llanfair Waterdine)

7 Sep. 1836. John Justice, R; John Turner, CW.

9 Sep. 1841. John Justice, R; John Turner, CW.
Rectory house with stables, barn and cow house but no garden; also 7 cottages with gardens inhabited by poor people.

13 Aug. 1845. John Justice, R; John Turner and Samuel Walmsley, CWs.
Parsonage house with stables, coach house, garden, barn and cow house.
Tithes have been commuted for £175.
Benefactions amount to £112 [no details].
Communion plate of silver and pewter [no details]. There is an iron chest for the registers.

1849. John Justice, R; Samuel Walmsley and John Turner, CWs.
Cottages: blacksmith's house, shop and garden, Old Rectory House Cottage, 2 stable cottages, 2 cottages in the churchyard and 1 other cottage.

1884*. T. Edward Meredyth, R.
House with stables, coach house, cow house, piggery, shed and garden.
Land: Far St John's Hill 5 a., Near St John's Hill 3½ a., Church M. and Hill 13½ a.
Income: a modus of £4 2s 6d is payable from the demesne lands; tithe rent charge £174; £102 12s 2d from the Eccl. Com. being interest on £3,500 arising from the sale of glebe land in 1882; fees average c. £1 p.a. .
Schedule of registers from 1558.
Plate: silver chalice, paten and flagon and brass alms dish.
Benefactions: John Gregory gave £400 in 1849, the interest of £12 for the poor of Whitchurch and Ightfield being spent on 1,000 yd. of calico given in lengths of 10 yd. to 100 poor people, 39 being of Ightfield.

Kemberton

1612. John Corbet, parson; William Harris and Richard Pixley, CWs.
Rectory house and outbuildings of 12 bays, orchard and garden.
Land: 30 butts in 16 parcels in Havenell F. 20 strikes seeding, 23 butts in 10 parcels 14 strikes seeding in Nedge F., 17 butts in 7 parcels 9 strikes seeding in Brookfield, 4 small pastures containing 20 strikes seeding, 2 doles in Grimes M. which will bear 1 small load of hay [bounds].

25 Aug. 1682. Andrew Cox, R.
Rectory house of 4 bays with a barn 4 bays, 1 bay for hay, a cowhouse and stable.
Land: Blakefallows 3½ a., Broomy Close 6½ a. and Broad Close 9 a. all enclosures in the NE. of the parish towards Evelith; Parsons Croft 3½ a., Colts Fur. 6½ a. and Lineway 6 a. all enclosures in the S. of the parish.

18 Sep. 1685. Andrew Cox, R; Andrew Linell, CW.

12 Sep. 1693*. Edward Aston, R; William Bucknall and Edward Williams, CWs.
Rectory house of 3 bays with barn and cowhouse adjoining 5 bays, stable ½ bay, orchard and garden ½ a.

Glebe terriers of Shropshire

Land: pasture called Linway L. 6 a. to W. of the road from Kemberton to
Bridgnorth, Betts Headland close 6 a., 2 closes 3 a. called Parsons Croft,
Blakefallows 2½ a., a close on the road from Kemberton to Evelith mill,
Evelith L. 6 a., 2 pastures called Evelith Broom Leasows, meadow ¼ a.
adjoining Evelith L., 2 doles of ½ a. in a common meadow called
Grimsmeadow; all except these 2 doles are enclosed [bounds].
All tithes are payable in kind.

17 Aug. 1698. Edward Aston, R; Richard Fowler, CW.

Land: in addition to the closes and doles of meadow the rector has the right
to pasture 40–50 sheep on Upton Heath common in Shifnal parish, they are
usually turned on to Brimstree Hill, the rector paying Shifnal parish 5s p.a.
for this privilege.

Tithes: corn and hay are tithed at the 10th sheaf; lambs, pigs and geese at the
10th, or if there are not 10 at the 7th, the owner taking 2, the rector the 3rd,
every lamb under 7 1½d; wool is tithed at the 10th fleece, or if there are
not 10 at the 7th; 1½d is due per calf, 4d per colt, every communicant 2d,
smoke and garden 1d, barren cows 1d, stall of bees killed 4d.

Surplice fees: burials 6d, marriages 2s 6d, churching 4d.

Clerk's fees: burials 1s, christenings 1d, marriages 1s; wages: every plough
land 4d and 1d worth of eggs at Easter, every cottage 2d.

23 Oct. 1701. Edward Aston, R; Robert Slaney and William Bucknall, CWs.

4 May 1705. Edward Aston, R; Mathew Roden and John Wedgwood, CWs.
The yearly value of the rectory is £55–60 p.a.

4 July 1718*. James Devey, R; William Roden and William Bucknall, CWs.
Tithes now include clover.

Clerk's wages *c.* 7s p.a.

c. 1711 the rector had 2 seats erected in the chancel; the rector repairs the
chancel and the fence on the N. of the churchyard as far as his fold; the
chapel belongs to the patron, John Foster.

7 July 1722. James Devey, R; Thomas Wykes and John Harbridge, CWs.

Land: pastures called Park 20 perches, Lynnway 6 a., Betts Headland 6 a.,
Parsons Croft 3 a. and Blakefallows 3 a., 3 enclosures lying together now
called Brickkiln L., Paddock and Tongue Dale 9 a., pasture called Evelith
Brook L. 6 a., 2 doles in a common meadow called Grims M. [bounds].

6 July 1726. James Devey, R; William Roden and Samuel Whistons, CWs.

29 Aug. 1730. James Devey, R; William Roden and John Garmson, CWs.
The chapel in the church now belongs to Humphrey Pitt, patron.

9 Aug. 1733. James Devey, R; John Harbidge and Richard Wright, CWs.
Clerk's wages: £1 p.a. paid quarterly.

15 July 1736. James Devey, R; William Lynell and Richard Harper, CWs.

1739. James Devey, R; John Roden and John Harbidge, CWs.
2 doles in the dole meadow belong to the rector in lieu of tithe hay.

Clerk's fees: churching 1d, ringing or tolling at funeral 1s, making graves
6d, amen at the grave 2d.

Part 1 (Abdon to Llanfair Waterdine)

17 Sep. 1742. Thomas Hooper and Richard Wright, CWs.

16 Oct. 1745*. William Banks, C; John Roden and William Whistons, CWs.

13 Sep. 1748. William Banks, C; John Roden and William Bucknall, CWs.

19 Sep. 1752. William Banks, C: William Whistons and Richard Clowes, CWs.

14 Aug. 1756. Robert Binnell, R; Robert Hurd and Jonathan Clark, CWs.

16 Sep. 1756. George Baker, C.

20 Sep. 1759. Robert Binnell, R; Richard Harper and William Bucknall, CWs.

1763. Robert Brown, C; Robert Glover and John Reynolds, CWs.

15 Sep. 1767. George Baker, R; Robert Glover and John Hammond, CWs.

21 Oct. 1772. George Baker, R; Robert Glover and John Hammond, CWs.

21 Aug. 1775. George Baker, R; Robert Glover and John Hammond, CWs.

6 Sep. 1779. George Baker, R; Robert Glover and John Hammond, CWs.

4 Aug. 1783. Robert Dean, C; Robert Glover and John Ward, CWs.

23 Oct. 1792. Richard Mountford, R; George Willdey Hurd, CW.
John Foster is patron.

24 July 1797. William Leake, C; George Willdey Hurd, CW.

26 Aug. 1801. William Leake, C; Edward Cartwright, CW.

1 July 1805*. John Williams, C; John Cherrington, CW.

9 Sep. 1841*. George Whitmore, R; Henry Thomason, CW.
Rectory house with 6 rooms on the ground floor and 8 above, an attached coach house, stable for 5 horses, saddle room and garden.
Land: Grims M. ½ a., Paddock ¼ a., churchyard ½ a., garden patch ½ a., Broomy Close 7 a., Blake Fallows or Apple Tree L. 3 a., Paddock 2 a., Evelith L. 5 a., the M. 2 a., Parsons Croft 3 a., Bets Headland 6½ a., Near Lyn Way L. 3 a., Far Lyn Way L. 3 a.; total 37½ a.
Tithes have been commuted for £320 and £9 for the glebe land.
The vicarage of Sutton Maddock is annexed but a separate terrier has been returned.
Surplice fees: marriage 5s, burial 1s, churching 1s, vault £5, headstone £1 1s.
Easter dues were included in the tithe commutation; no mortuaries are due.
Clerk's fees: marriages 2s 6d, burials (the clerk also being sexton) 5s 6d, churching 6d; the present salary paid by the church rate is £3 3s p.a.
Land tax is £4 3s.
The chancel is now in a bad state but will be repaired immediately.
Communion plate: 1 silver cup, 1 pewter plate and 1 pewter cup. There is an iron chest for the registers.

1884*.
Income: tithe rent charge £329; fees average p.a. £2.

Schedule of registers from 1659.
Plate: 2 silver chalices, 1 silver paten, glass and silver flagon and brass alms dish.
Benefactions: Oct. 1857 William Henry Slaney of Hatton Hall [Shifnal parish] gave land for a school.
[Sketch plan of the glebe land within the village, also land held by the Slaney trustees and Lord Sudeley].

Kenley[1]

29 Nov. 1693. Benjamin Jenks, C; Francis Blackway and John Evason, CWs.
Kenley is a donative with no lands or buildings. The tithes are farmed by Wid. Newport for £30.

16 Aug. 1698. Benjamin Jenks, C; Thomas Baker and Richard Hall, CWs.
All tithes are due in kind and either gathered or set by the incumbent with the leave and permission of the Earl of Bradford.
Surplice fees and offerings are the same as Harley except that nothing is due for tradesmen's or servants' hands.
The clerk's wages are paid by custom from the various houses.

25 Nov. 1701.[2] Benjamin Jenks, C; John Hatton and Thomas Hudson, CWs.

2 May 1705. Benjamin Jenks, C.

23 July 1718. Benjamin Jenks, minister.
A 'noble charity' of £14 p.a. has been lately bequeathed by the late Earl of Bradford to be distributed quarterly to the poor of Kenley for 99 years; the present distribution is decided by the minister with the advice of the parish officers who know where there is most need.
The chapel is good order and the yard is well fenced.
There is no house or land.
Tithes are due in kind or compounded.

5 July 1722. Benjamin Jenks, minister; John Jonstons and Richard Hughs, CWs.
The chancel and pews belong to the incumbent, but the churchyard fence belongs to the parish.

7 July 1726. George Carver, minister; Richard Russell and Richard Hughes, chapelwardens.
Tithes: no calves are due because the dairies are small, but 6d is due per calf and 1d per cow which gives milk; 6d per colt is due; wool and lambs are due in kind, the lambs at 7, 8 or 9, not only at 10, allowing 3d per lamb to make up to 10; pigs and geese are tithed likewise.

---

[1] Kenley was transferred from Lichfield diocese to Hereford in 1905: *Victoria history of Shropshire*, ii. 1.
[2] There is a copy of the Kenley terrier of 1701 in the parish register of 1682–1771 (SRRC, P148/A/1/1).

Part 1 (Abdon to Llanfair Waterdine)

Surplice fees: marriage by banns or licence 5s, churching 6d, burial 6d, funeral sermon 10s.

Offerings: 2d is due per communicant at Easter.

The minister has no seat or burial place in the chapel, nor is he obliged to repair any part; the chancel is the curate's.

28 Aug. 1730. Thomas Walter, C; William Evason and Richard Hulett, CWs.

7 Aug. 1733. Thomas Walter, C; John Carter and William Underwood, CWs.

16 July 1736. Thomas Walter, C; William Hall and William Bryan, CWs.

1 Sep. 1739. Henry Bowdler, C; William Evason and Richard Roberts, CWs.

18 Sep. 1742. D. Hemas, C; William Evason and William Hall, CWs.

27 Aug. 1745. Thomas Walter, minister; James [?]Whaild and Joseph Dyles, CWs.

11 Aug. 1748. G. Podmoor, C; W. Bryan and Hugh Low, CWs.

21 Sep. 1752. George Podmore, C; William Hall and Edward Crowther, CWs.

11 Aug. 1756. James Dewhurst, C; William Evason, CW.

20 Sep. 1759. James Dewhurst, C; Richard Wyers, CW.
Copy of 1701.

7 Sep. 1779. James Dewhurst, C; William Farmer and John Bishop, CWs.

7 Aug. 1787. James Cope, minister; John Jones and Robert Hamnett, CWs.

25 Oct. 1792. Archibald Alison, minister; John Jones and James Daniel, CWs.

28 June 1805. William Prosser, C; Richard Crowther, CW.

1824. John Gibbons, C; John Bayley, CW.
29 a. was given for glebe in lieu of tithes when Kenley Common was enclosed.[1]

7 Sep. 1841. Henry Clarke, C; Richard Crowther, CW.
There is no parsonage house.
Glebe: 9 fields, 2 cottages, 29 a. in total, all leased.
Surplice fees: marriage by banns 5s, by licence 10s, burial 1s, churching 1s, headstones 10s.
Clerk's fees: marriage by banns 2s 6d, by licence 5s, burials 3s, baptisms 6d; salary: £1 12s p.a. and the use of the churchyard.
Taxes and rates usually amount to c. £12 8s p.a.
The chancel is in tolerable repair.
Communion plate: flagon and 2 plates of pewter and a silver cup. There is an iron chest for the registers.

14 Aug. 1845. Henry Claydon, C; George Hamon, CW.
Tithes have been commuted for £143.

---

[1] The commons of Kenley were enclosed by Act of Parliament in 1793; 30 acres allotted to the rector as glebe was divided by him into ten lots to accommodate poor people of the common who had the largest families: *Victoria history of Shropshire*, viii. 95.

Glebe terriers of Shropshire

3 Aug. 1849. Henry Slade, minister, chaplain to the Earl of Clarendon; Richard Roberts, CW.

27 July 1853. Henry Slade, incumbent; Richard Roberts, CW.

1857. Henry Slade, incumbent.
The whole of the church and chancel were in 1855 put in complete repair by Revd H. Slade and the patron, the Duke of Cleveland, assisted by the parishioners.

Ketley[1]

1884*.
House built in 1880 of Donnington brick and Grinshill stone window sills with entrance hall, drawing room, dining room, study, kitchen, scullery, larder, pantry, cellars, 5 bedrooms, dressing room, housemaid's closet, WC, attic for lumber, detached outbuildings of 2-stalled stable, harness room with lofts over, coach house, laundry, coal house and gardens *c.* 1 a.
Income: small cottage let for £4; 2 arable fields of 4½ a. and 6 a. let for £21; tithe rent charge of £62 4s 6d awarded in 1880; £17 p.a. awarded by the Eccl. Com. in 1880 and £68 and £40 in 1881; £61 1s 4d from QAB; pew rents *c.* £7 13s 4d p.a. paid to the vicar and £3 15s to the CWs; fees average *c.* £16 13s 4d p.a.
Registers from 1838.
Plate: silver chalice and paten and 2 pewter alms dishes.

Kinlet

31 May 1589. Humphrey Southall, Allyn Browne alias Smyth, CWs. [Also 6 sidesmen].
The queen is patron of the vicarage.
House with little kitchen and barn.
Land: 3 a. arable, ½ a. meadow [bounds]; there is no common pasture.
All privy tithes and offerings are due on calves, wool, lambs, sheaf of home closes; there are certain known money payments for hay for every inhabitant.

1607. Thomas Bent, V.
House with little kitchen, barn, garden and orchard.
Land: 4 closes adjoining the house, 3 of arable 5 a., 1 of meadow ½ a.

4 Apr. 16[?21, torn].[2] Thomas Kent, clerk; Edward Wheeler and Henry Hill, CWs.
Privy tithes are due on calves, wool, lambs and sheaf of home closes; £1 17s 6d p.a. is paid for tithe hay made up by individual payments

---

[1] Ketley was formed into an ecclesiastical parish from part of Wellington parish in 1880: *Victoria history of Shropshire*, xi. 274.

[2] There is a copy of the Kinlet terrier for ?1621 in the parish register of 1657–1705 (SRRC, P150/A/1/1).

Part 1 (Abdon to Llanfair Waterdine)

'accustomedly payed before the memory of man'. [List of 49 names with their holdings and payments varying from 3d to 2s].

Kinnerley[1]

30 Sep. 1630† [Copy]. Ralph Kynaston vicar; Roger Thornes, Edward Lloyd, CWs. [6 other signatories].

House with barn, garden and hemp butt ½ a.

Land: Kaymore 4 a., ½ a. and 4 short butts of arable in the common field called Maes y Rhudnearne, parcel of arable to N. of the church 1½ a., 2 parcels in Maes y Bella in Dovaston township 1 a. [bounds].

Tithes are due on 2 parcels of land in Kinnerley township; tithes are due on wool, lamb, geese, pigs, flax, honey, kine and mares; some years past Anthony Cowley, vicar of Kinnerley, demanded predial tithes not before paid, and the parishioners agreed to give him 1d from every house at Easter in exchange for tithe hemp only, and it was then agreed that vicar Cowley and his successors should have half an enclosure called Golthey in lieu of predial tithes which were never paid; vicar Morris and then Ralph Kynaston continued to have Golthey in Edgerley township [bounds].

1636. [Document too worn and faded to read].

22 Feb. 1685/6. Thomas Clapham, V; Humphrey Clarke, CW. [5 other signatories].

House of 2 bays with little garden and hemp butt adjoining, and barn 3 bays.

Land: 1 enclosure of arable of 7 strike sowing of Winchester measure, another of 3 measures called Little Llannach, both in Kinnerley, furlong of 2 Winchester measures in the common fields of Kinnerley and Argoed, 3 a. enclosed pasture in Edgerley, furlong in the common field of Edgerley called Maesybryn of 2½ Winchester measures, another furlong in the same field off 1½ measures, 2 further pieces, 1 in Kinnerley and 1 in Edgerley and 2 butts in Bellan F., Dovaston [bounds]; 1 piece of turbary in Kinnerley and 1 in Edgerley.

Tithes are due on wool, lambs, flax, honey, pigs and geese. Easter dues and mortuaries are due in the whole parish.

6 Aug. 1710. Thomas Clapham, V; Richard Lloyd, CW.

Tithes: ½ lamb is due at 4 the vicar paying 1d, at 6 lambs ½ is due and 1d, at 7 lambs ½ is due and 2d, at 8 a whole is due the vicar paying 2d, 1d at 9d and the parishioner paying 1d at all other numbers; wool shorn in the parish is due likewise with 3d for odd parcels; also due on flax, honey, pigs and geese; herbage is due from foreigners at 1s 8d per £ and 4d per month per score of sheep on the common.

Easter dues: widows and widowers 4d, all over 16 (unless they live with their parents) 2d, cows 1d, calves 1d, colts 2d and smoke and garden 1d.

---

[1] Kinnerley was transferred from St Asaph diocese to Lichfield in 1920: *Victoria history of Shropshire*, ii. 1.

Surplice fees: baptism and churching 1s, burial 6d, marriage by banns 1s 4d, publishing banns if 1 of the parish 1s, if 2 of the parish 2s, marriage by licence 5s, burial in the chancel 6d 8d.

Clerk's wages: 1 sheaf of winter corn—wheat, muncorn or rye—and 1 sheaf of barley or oats p.a. from every person that sows in the parish is paid by the impropriator out of the corn tithe.

15 Nov. 1710. Thomas Truston and Richard Lloyd, CWs; Richard Payne, overseer; Edward Payne, titheman. [Many other signatories].

Vicarage house of 3 bays with barn 3 bays, stable, 2 shores, 2 gardens and a hemp butt ½ a.

Land: churchyard 1 a., Cae Maior in Kinnerley 4 a., 4 short butts of arable in the same field called Rhuddwerne 1 a., another parcel of ½ a. in the same, 1½ a. of meadow near the church, 2 parcels in Maes y Belan in Dovaston 1 a., parcel called Galthly in Edgerley, 2 ridges in Maes y Bryn in Edgerley of 6 hoops seedness of Oswestry old measure and 1 other butt or selion in the same, parcel of arable adjoining of 5 hoops of Oswestry called Pwll Lloyd.

Tithes: *c.* 103 years past Anthony Cowly, vicar, demanded all predial tithes due by law and not paid and agreed to accept 1d p.a. per house at Easter in discharge of the tithe of hemp and also half an enclosure of land called Gethly, Edgerley; this holds to this day.

30 Aug. 1749. E[van] Lloyd, V; J. Thomas, C.

House of brick, timber and thatch with cellar, buttery adjacent not ceiled or plastered, brewing kitchen with earthen floor not ceiled or plastered, passage from kitchen to parlour with pantry not ceiled, kitchen partly of brick not ceiled, parlour with mortar floor not ceiled but whitewashed and study with boarded floor adjoining the parlour on the ground floor and on the first floor a ceiled room over the kitchen, ceiled room at the stair head, large ceiled room over the parlour part plastered, 2 small rooms over the parlour part plastered and 3 garrets plastered, 2 little courts, 2 gardens and yard.

Land: Cae Maior 4 a., 4 butts in Haddwern 1 a. to the N. of the church, 2 parcels of arable in Maes y Bella in Dovaston, Gethly and 2 ridges in Edgerley, 2 other small pieces of arable; the vicar has right of common in every township where there is glebe land; there are a few ash and sycamore trees in the churchyard.

The parish clerk has £3 p.a. from the impropriator's tithes.

Inventory: silver flagon given 1733, silver cup and cover 1607, another silver cup and cover, book of Common Prayer, Book of Homilies, register book, CWs' account book and English bible.

10s is due to the vicar charged on the Dyffryd estate for a sermon on Good Friday.

The N. chancel belongs to the Dyffryd estate and is repaired by Mrs Hanmer; the S. chancel belongs to the impropriator and the church to the parishioners; the churchyard wall on the N. is repaired by Knockin and the rest by the various townships of Kinnerley.

12 July 1791. David Pritchard, V; Samuel Ward and Edward Rogers, CWs. [17 other signatories]. House with parlour and lodging above in brick and

Part 1 (Abdon to Llanfair Waterdine)

slate, the other end with the kitchen and passage and rooms above, 2 small rooms part timber and part brick and stone, thatched, study adjoining thatched, bake house slated with a cellar under, thatched barn, stable and cow house with hay bay over, part timber, part stone, yard, garden and small fold yard.

Land: churchyard with elms, firs and beech planted by the present vicar, small close called Vicarage L. planted with elms, beech and poplar by the vicar, pasture close of 1 a. called Llanerch Uschan, pasture called Gongall lately enclosed, close enclosed out of Edgerley Wood 3 a., close called Gelthy or Vicarage M., close of arable [name torn], close of arable in Tyn y Coed lately enclosed from the common 1 a., 2 parcels of turbary [very fully described].

7 Aug. 1856*. E[dward] Bridgeman, V; Thomas Bather and T. Payne, CWs.

House of brick with 2 sitting rooms, kitchen, scullery, larder, 4 bedrooms, 2 garrets, 2-stalled stable, carriage house, pigsty, coal house, saddle room and harness cleaning shed, all of brick with slated roofs.

Land: 2 parcels of meadow of 2½ a. and 2 a. in Argoed and Kinnerley, 2 parcels of arable 1½ a. and 1 a. in Kinnerley F., Allotment M. 1 a., arable croft 1½ a., Vage, garden and croft 1 a., churchyard 1 a., 7 a. of arable in Dovaston in 5 parcels, 2 a. of meadow in Edgerley 11 a. of arable in 5 parcels in Edgerley; total 31 a.

Tithes: Kinnerley and Argoed tithes have been commuted for £13 12s 2d, Dovaston for £6 17s 8d, Edgerley for £44 9s 9d, Maesbrook Uchan for £37 15s 5d, Maesbrook for £25, Osbaston for £17 5s, Tyn y Coed for £9 and Kynaston for £11; total £170.

Surplice fees: vault in the churchyard 2s 6d per foot, headstones 10s 6d, tombstone £1 1s.

Inventory: flagon, 2 silver chalices, 2 pewter patens, red velvet pulpit cushion, cloth for communion table, 2 surplices, book of prayer and an old one for the clerk, Book of Homilies, vestry book from 1849, turret clock and 3 bells.

Schedule of registers from 1677.

The NE. half of the chancel is repaired by Dyffryd farm, Maesbrook Ucha, the SE. half by the impropriator of the great tithe, the church and the churchyard fence by the parish.

Knockin[1]

10 Apr. 1687. Joseph Webster, R; William Jones and James Thomas, CWs.

2 'slender and low' bays of barn with each bay 15 ft wide, 6½' high from the ground sill to the wall plate and 1 bay 18 ft long and the other 16 ft.

Land: ½ hoop sowing near the W. end of the church.

---

[1] Knockin was transferred from St Asaph diocese to Lichfield in 1920: *Victoria history of Shropshire*, ii. 1. The terriers for 1763, 1774 and 1791 survive only in the printed parish register (Shropshire Parish Register Soc.), 36–42. The 1856 terrier is at LRO and also in the printed parish register.

Tithes are due on all grains—wheat, rye, barley, oats, peas and french wheat—hay, hemp and flax; tithes of wool and lambs, pigs, geese, eggs and honey are due from all the parish except the Farm on the Heath which pays half; all holding pasture who are not inhabitants pay herbage; all pay Easter dues.

Inventory: large bible, Common Prayer book, Book of Homilies, book of singing psalms, register, book of accounts, Book of Canons Ecclesiastical, surplice, 2 cloths, 1 of wool and 1 linen for covering the communion table, pulpit cushion, chalice, pewter can and small silver plate for 'decent bearing of the bread'.

The chancel is repaired at the minister's charge.

[2 copies].

9 July 1701. John Jones, R; Nicholas Hilton and Samuel Whitfield, CWs.

The tenant of Heath Farm has not paid the half tithe he should; the dispute has been referred to counsel, but there has been no decision.

30 July 1710. Joseph Webster, R; Rowland Hilton and Richard Morris, CWs.

Glebe: very small hemp yard near the rectory house with well-known boundaries and barn of 2 bays.

30 Aug. 1719. Richard Lloyd, minister; William Challener and James Whittakers, CWs.

Tithes: lambs are due half at 5, at 6 half lamb and 1d, at 7 a whole lamb, the rector paying 3d at 8, 2d at 9, if there are under 5 then 1d per lamb; 1s 8d per £ is due on pasture and 4d per month per score of sheep.

17 July 1763. John Jones, R; Thomas Issard, Richard Jones and Timothy Sides, CWs and overseers. [5 other signatories].

Land: little piece at the W. end of the church, not enclosed, with a building of 2 low and slender bays.

Easter offerings: widows and widowers pay 2d, all over 16 not living with their parents pay 2d; cow 1½d, barren cow 1d, colt 2d, smoke and garden 1d.

Fees: churching 1s, publishing banns if one party is of the parish 1s and if both 2s, marriage 1s 6d, marriage by licence 5s.

Inventory: quarto bible, folio Book of Common Prayer, 2 register books, book of accounts, linen surplice, woollen cloth for the communion table, napkin, pulpit cushion, pewter can, silver chalice and small silver salver.

The chancel is repaired at the expense of the rector and the rest of the church at the expense of the parish.

11 June 1774. John Jones, R.

9 July 1791. John Jones, R; Samuel Whitford and Richard Hilton, CWs.

'A Terrier taken, made and renewed according to the old Evidences and the knowledge of the Ancient Inhabitants'.

Tithes of all sorts are due to the rector in their several kinds except from Heath Farm from which half of all tithes are usually payable, but of late years the whole has been demanded by the lessee of the tithes, but refused;

the dispute has been referred to counsel, but is not yet determined and no tithe is meanwhile paid.

Inventory: cup inscribed 1663, silver cup 1780 and small silver salver 1732.

Clerk's wages: 10s p.a. paid by the rector and £2 by the CWs.

1 Aug. 1856. Thomas Finches, minister; Richard Hilton and Richard Lloyd, CWs.

Tithes were commuted 5 Sep. 1846 at £328, at which time there were 900 a. arable in the parish, 635 a. pasture and meadow and 27 a. woodland.

Glebe: a small building, partly barn and partly dwelling.

Fees: churching 1s (double if non-resident), marriage by licence 5s, by banns 2s 6d, burial 1s (double if non-resident), new vault £4 4s, iron railing £4 4s, tombstone £2 2s, flat stone £1 12s, headstone 10s 6d.

Kynnersley

1612. William Bailye, R; John Gravenor and Robert Whittingham, CWs.

Rectory house of 2 bays thatched with straw with 2 fireplaces, kitchen 2 bays with kiln, barn 3 bays with stable at the end, cart house, 3 bays for cattle, garden and orchard.

Land: 2 little closes 1 a. and 4 beasts grass in a pasture called The Gale enclosed. 'There is noe other severall pasture or meadowe ground belonginge to the parsonage but such as lately was inclosed and taken out of the common moore for which there is rent payd by the parson to the lord of the mannour. All which grounde the lord of the mannor or the freehoulders may at there pleasure cast open or make common as it was before'. *c.* 2 a. and a gravel pit in Rodway F., 24 butts in 8 parcels in Sydnay F., 14 butts in Hill F. [no bounds].

There are only 12 tenements or plough lands in Kynnersley and there are no gentlemen yeomen or freeholders in the parish; the parson has 2 oxen and 2 mares to sow his land and carry corn and hay.

Tenths of 12s 2d are due to the king for the rectory.

9 Nov. 1635. Thomas Wright, R; William Cowper and John Symons, CWs. [7 other signatories].

Rectory house with orchard adjoining, little house of 1 bay leased and tenement with barn of 2 bays leased.

Land: little croft at the town's end near Sidnall F., land in Sydenhall F., Rodeway F. and Hill F., 2 beasts' grass in New Piece, 2 in Cowmoore and 4 in Gale [bounds]; 7 pieces in Hawe Moor are in controversy between Thomas Wright, rector and Andrew Bayley, clerk of Wolverhampton.

Corn, hay and 'all other things' are tithable in kind.

4 Sep. 1682. George Plaxton, R;[1] Thomas Whittingham, William Cherrington.

---

[1] George Plaxton became vicar of Sheriffhales and rector of Kynnersley in 1673 to give him an income; his main occupation was agent to William Leveson-Gower of Lilleshall and Trentham. He is said to have revitalised the management of the Leveson-Gower estates and to have been years ahead of his time: R. Wordie, *Estate management in eighteenth-century England* (1982), 24–7.

Land: 7 pieces in Haw Moor *c*. 29 a. called Parsons Pieces divided by large ditches by Buttery way, Gale Edge 2 a., Gale 3 a., 2 beasts' grass in Cow Moor, 2 beasts' grass in Newpiece Fur. 2 a., little meadow 1 a., little croft next to Sidenhall F. 1 a., 14 butts in Sidenhall F., 14 butts in Rodeway F., 18 butts in Hill F.; commoning on all the moors belonging to the manor of Kynnersley, also on Tibberton Moor, Wall Moor and Gale Moor for all cattle.
Tithes are due on corn, hay, hemp and flax etc.

Nov. 1686. George Plaxton, R; Richard Price, C; Thomas Baker and John Gravenor, CWs.
No compositions are due in this parish.

29 Sep. 1693. George Plaxton, R; Richard Price, C; Thomas Baker and William Cherrington, CWs.
Rectory house of 2½ bays with large barn 3 bays, malt kiln or kitchen 2 small bays, stable 1 bay adjoining the barn, beast houses 3 bays, little cart house, yard, fold, orchard and garden; also a cottage and a small piece of building.

21 July 1714.
[A large part of this terrier is missing. Field land is given with full bounds but is incomplete].

13 July 1730. Jeffrey Williams, R; Thomas Masterson and John Harper, CWs.
House of 4 bays of substantial new brick building with barn 3 bays with a threshing floor and cart house at the end, stable and beast house 4 bays, cottage and garden.
Land: hemp yard, backside and garden 1 a., Nether Fur. 1 a., Over Fur. 2 a., New Close 7 a., Orchard Plat 8 a., Gale Edge 3½ a., Gale 5 a., Lambut End 3 a., Croft 1 a., Buttery Croft 2 a., Near Piece 4 a., Over Piece 3½ a., Gale L. 4 a., Cratch Piece 3 a., 3 Day Math M. 4½ a., 4 Day Math M. 5 a., 5 Day Math M. 6 a., 2 cow gates on Cow Moor 3½ a., Roadway Flat 2 a., Dole ½ a., Parsons Piece 3 a.
'... the Rector of Kynnersley has and immemorially had & enjoyed ... commoning in Adeney Common ... and when it was some time agoe divided they acknowledged that ... [gap] acres was the share of the Rector and they promised to allow for the same 10s per acre proportionably to be divided among and paid by the severall persons who had their share in the same but This has not been yet performed'.
Tithes are due to the rector in kind if demanded. 'All the Uplands in the whole parish were formerly one open Town field and was every year in Tillage, and consequently there could be no Milch-cows kept by any one parishioner in such a Number as that any Calves could be gathered in kind and then the usual method was and still continues to be for every Living to pay 2s 6d yearly and every half living to pay 1s 3d for their Calves and one penny for each cow. But now all the Lands being lately enclosed, there may be such Dairyes kept hereafter as may afford calves to be gathered in kind'. The 7th lamb is taken the rector receiving 3d per lamb for all when the number is under 7; wool is taken at the 10th fleece; pigs at the 7th, but nothing is paid or received under 7; fruit is due in kind.

150

Part 1 (Abdon to Llanfair Waterdine)

Easter roll: cottagers pay 1d for a cow and 2d for each calf; all the parishioners pay 2d for each colt, 1d for each stall of bees, 1d per house, 1d per garden and every communicant 2d.

Surplice fees: churching 1d, marriage with licence 5s, with banns 2s 6d, burials 1s, funeral sermon 10s (on a specified text £1).

9 Aug. 1733. Jeffrey Williams, R; Joseph Palin, CW.
Land: the whole glebe is 76¾ acres.

15 July 1736. Arthur Spender, C; John Hooper, CW.

31 Aug. 1739. Joseph Dickenson, C; William Bill, CW.

17 Sep. 1742. Joseph Dickenson, C; John . . ., CW.

29 Aug. 1745. Richard Hopley, C; Edward Bill, CW.
N.B. the Butt next to the gate in Parsons Croft at the Town End belongs to Richard Hooper's living for which 2s 6d tithe hay is allowed him.

13 Sep. 1748. John Hargreaves, R; John Harper and Thomas Whittingham, CWs.

19 Sep. 1752. Richard Ogle, C; William Weston, CW.

16 Sep. 1756. Richard Ogle, C; Thomas Weston, CW.

20 Sep. 1759. Richard Ogle, C; Richard Hooper, CW.

6 Sep. 1763. Richard Ogle, C; Richard Roe, CW.

15 Sep. 1767. Richard Ogle, C; Thomas Latham, CW.

7 Sep. 1772. Richard Ogle, C; James Tibbits, CW.

6 Sep. 1779. Richard Ogle, C; John Podmore, CW.

4 Aug. 1783. Richard Ogle, C; Thomas Latham, CW.

23 June 1787. Thomas Spencer, minister; John Hooper, CW.

26 Aug. 1801. Richard Spearman, minister; William Hooper, CW.

1805. Richard Spearman, minister; William Hooper, CW.

20 Mar. 1817.
George Granville Leveson Gower Marquess of Stafford, patron of Kynnersley, the Bishop of Lichfield and Revd Thomas Butt, rector, assent that after the act for dividing and allotting and enclosing, draining and improving the common moors called Sydney Moor, Small Moor, Rodway Moor, Waters Upton Moor and other commons in Wrockwardine, Eyton, Kynnersley, Waters Upton, Crudgington and Sleap in High Ercall in 1801, Over New Piece 3 a., Cows Fur. and Over Fur. 4 a., Rodway Fur. 2½ a., Gale Edge 4 a. Gale 6 a., Cow Moor 3½ a., Johnsons New Close 8 a., Orchard Plat 8½ a. have been exchanged for *c.* 36 a. of the Marquess of Stafford's land.

1824. William Hooper.
Land: the glebe was formerly interspersed throughout the parish but is now more commodious: church and churchyard ½ a., house, building and gar-

den 6½ a., Lambut End 7½ a., Great Hill L. 8 a., Far Hill L. 7 a., Near Hill L. 7 a., Ten Days Math 11 a., Three Days Math 4½ a., Galey Piece 4 a., Cratch Piece 3 a., Upper Piece 3½ a., Near Piece 4 a., Near Rough Piece 9 a., Far Rough Piece 5 a.; total 83 a.

1828. Thomas Butt, R; William Hooper, CW.

The house is made of brick and tiled with a barn and cart house at the end and a stable and beast house of 5 bays thatched and in good repair.

9 Sep. 1841. Andrew Burn, R; John Adams, CW.

Parsonage house with 2 parlours, kitchen, pantry and another small room on the ground floor, cellar under the northern parlour, 6 rooms on the 1st floor, 4 attics, coach house, stable with 3 stalls, saddle room, waggon stable, feeding barn for 6 beasts, calf pen and turnip house, all with lofts over, barn with threshing floor.

Land: Lamb But Ends 7½ a., 2 parts of Boulds 2 a. and 3 a., Hill L. 7 a., Far Hill L. 6 a., Buttery Croft 8½ a., Three Days Math 4½ a., Ten Days Math 11 a., Near Piece and Far Piece 7 a., another piece 8 a., Near Rough Piece, part of Long Rough Piece 5 a.; total 83 a. leased.

Surplice fees: marriage 3s 6d, marriage with licence 10s, churching 1s, burial 1s, brick grave £3 3s, in proportion for vaults with £1 1s every time a vault is opened, 7s for headstones.

Clerk's fees: marriages 2s, churching 6d, burials 2s; wages: £6 p.a. was voted in the parish vestry.

Tithes were commuted for £360 p.a.

The repairs of the chancel belong to the rector and it is now in good repair.

Communion plate: 2 silver chalices, 1 silver plate, a small paten and a large silver flagon. There is an iron chest for the registers kept in the parsonage house.

13 Aug. 1845. Andrew Burn, R; John Adams, CW.

16 Apr. 1861. Andrew Burn, R; Richard Ogle, CW.

1884*. Andrew Burn, R.

Brick house of 4 substantial bays built by Geoffrey Williams, rector, in 1722 with barn, turnip house, cart house, shed, cow house, coach house and saddle room added in the time of Revd Thomas Butt.

Land: 83 a., 76 a. leased, the rest round the rectory and in the rector's occupation.

Tithe rent charge £340.

Schedule of registers from 1691.

Plate: 2 silver chalices and patens and a pewter alms dish.

Lawley[1]

1884*.

House with fair-sized dining room, small drawing room, very small study, kitchen, pantry, larger, small back kitchen, 6 bedrooms, 1 dressing room,

---

[1] Lawley was formed into an ecclesiastical parish from parts of Wellington and Little Wenlock parishes in 1867: *Victoria history of Shropshire*, xi. 281.

small entrance hall, 1 WC in porch and 1 in yard, kitchen garden and flower garden but no outbuildings.

Income: tithe rent charge £186 8s 9d; Eccl. Com. £111 13s 4d; QAB £2 9s 8d; fees average p.a. £1 15s 8d.

Registers from 1865.

Plate: silver chalice, paten and flagon.

Leaton[1]

15 Apr. 1861. Stratford Leigh, minister; William Hickman and Thomas Bates, CWs.

Church and churchyard 1 a., garden and pleasure ground 1 a., F. 3 a.

The minister has a rent charge on Leaton estate of £40 and £65 from the Eccl. Com. £400 from the Diocesan Society is awaiting investment.

20 Apr. 1869. Richard Cholmondley, minister; William Hickman and John Molyneux, CWs.

1884*.

Parsonage with outbuildings, garden 2 a. and 3 a. of land adjoining.

Income: £40 rent charge on the Leaton estate; Eccl. Com. £65 in 1860; £13 6s 8d p.a. yield on a £400 grant by the Lichfield Church Extension Society in 1865; fees average £3–5 p.a.

Registers from 1859.

Plate: silver chalice, silver and silver gilt patens, silver flagon, silver and brass alms dishes.

£150 is invested for church repairs.

Lee Brockhurst

24 Oct. 1612. Thomas Groome and Richard Holbrooke, CWs.

House with garden, little backside, barn and yard; another barn and yard is leased.

Land: Pool Meadow L., Wiggensley, Pearle, New L., Little Croft, Holloway Croft, all pastures and enclosed butt called Marl Butt.

31 Oct. 1682. Peter Gibbons, R; William Walford and William Newans, CWs.

House of 2½ bays with barn 3 bays and shore and hemp yard of *c.* 1 strike sowing.

Land: Lane Croft 2½ a., Barn Yard 1 a., Pool M. 3 a., Wiggensley 2 a., Pearle L. 3 a., Goose L. 2 a., Holloway L. 2½ a., little piece called Hill Door *c.* ½ a.

Tithe is due in kind on everything; there are no customs.

1685. Peter Gibbons, R; William Newans and William Walford, CWs.

House of 2 bays with a shore called a buttery, barn 3 bays with threshing floor and shore at the end to tie up beasts.

---

[1] Leaton was formed into an ecclesiastical parish from parts of the parishes of Fitz, Preston Gubbals and St Mary, Shrewsbury in 1860: *Kelly's directory of Shropshire* (1891), 339.

Tithes of corn, hay, wool, lambs, hemp, apples, pigs and geese are due in kind, but 1d per cow, ½d per calf, 1d smoke, 1d garden, 1d colt and 1d stall of bees.

6 Sep. 1693. Peter Gibbons, R; William Newans and Robert Phillips, CWs.

1699. Peter Gibbons, R; John Wolfe and William Walford, CWs.
House of 2½ bays with shore or buttery at the E. side and hemp yard of *c*. ½ a. behind, at the bottom of which is a barn of 2 bays with a hay bay at the E. end and a shore at the W.

21 Oct. 1701. Peter Gibbons, R; Robert Phillips, William Walford and William Newans, CWs.

2 May 1705. Peter Gibbons, R; William Walford, CW.
[Baptism register 16 Nov. 1701–29 Oct. 1704].

n.d. Richard Hughes, C; Arthur Prescott, CW.
The repair of the chancel belongs to the rector and the fence on the W. side of the churchyard.

1733. Samuel Ray, CW.
The rectory is impropriate by a lay rector; the curate has for his salary but what the owner is pleased to give him; the lay owner receives all the surplice fees.

1736. John Peat, CW.

1742. Thomas Brooks, CW.

1745. William Holmes, CW.
Tithes: cows 1d, cow and calf 1½d, 4 cows and calves 6d, 5 cows 7½d, 7 cows and calves 5s; wool is collected in kind, 1lb at 7 or 10, ½lb at 5, ½d per lb under 5; half a lamb at 5, a whole at 7 or 10, ½d each under 7; nothing is due for odd pigs under 7; 2d is due per stall of bees put down and killed; married couples pay 4d, single persons over 16 2d, gardens 1d, smoke 1d, herbage 5 groats in the £. Mortuaries are due.
Surplice fees: marriage by banns 1s, by licence 2s 6d.
Curate's salary £8.
Clerk's wages 13s.

21 Sep. 1752. John Snelson and Thomas Nicklin, CWs.

18 Aug. 1775. John Snelson and Rowland Heath, CWs.

22 Oct. 1779.[1] Robert Pugh, C; Richard Wood, CW.
The rectory is impropriated and belongs to George Walford Esq.; the curate had formerly no salary only what the lay rector pleased which was usually £8 p.a. and lately £10, but the curacy has lately been augmented with £200 by the governors of QAB and the present rector has charged the rectory, glebe and tithe with the yearly rent charge of £10 p.a. for ever.
Until recently there was formerly no house and barn on the glebe land.

---

[1] There is a copy of the Lee Brockhurst terrier for 1779 in the parish register for 1715–1812 (SRRC, P158/A/1/2).

Part 1 (Abdon to Llanfair Waterdine)

3 Aug. 1783. Robert Pugh, C; William Bickerton, CW.

7 Aug. 1787. Robert Pugh, C; William Bickerton, CW.
The present clear value of the curacy is £18 p.a., £4 being the interest on £200 granted 29 Sep. 1776 and £4 on the interest of £200 granted 29 Sep. 1786 by QAB and £10 charged on the rectory and tithes.

25 Oct. 1792. Robert Pugh, C; William Bickerton, CW.
The curate has a further £4 p.a. interest on a grant of 1790.

24 Aug. 1801. Robert Pugh, minister; William Buttrey, CW.
The church is oblong being c. 37 ft from E. to W. and 14 ft 6 in. from N. to S.; the chancel was formerly separated from the church by a screen which has now been removed for the convenience of the inhabitants; the chancel amounts to about one-third of the building and is repaired by the impropriator, William Walford of Wem.

29 June 1805*. Robert Pugh, minister; James Heatley, CW.

26 Oct. 1810*. Robert Pugh, minister; James Heatley, CW.
A yearly rent of £16 is due on a piece of land called Big Aston F. near Rye Bank, Wem c. 10 a. bought 27 July 1805 from Revd Richard Hill of Prees; £8 rent is due on Trench L. in Tilley and Trench, Wem 3½ a. bought from Lloyd Bayley of Preston Brockhurst; the minister also has £4 interest on £200 granted by QAB 25 Mar. 1809; the improved yearly value of the living is £38.

12 Aug. 1828. Francis Salt, minister; James Heatley, CW.
John Walford Esq. of Wem pays £10, land near Wem is leased for £40, land at Rye Bank, Wem for £16 and 4 a. of land near Wem for £8.

Aug. 1832. Francis Salt, C; James Heatley, CW.

6 Sep. 1836. Francis Salt, C; James Heatley, CW.
The glebe land was sold many years past to the late Sir Richard Hill by the patron, George Walford Esq.

14 Aug. 1845. Sebastian Gambier, perpetual curate; Samuel Heatley and William Staples, CWs.
27 a. in Wem are valued at £86 p.a. [named tenants].
The tithes are received by the lay impropriator and have not yet been commuted.
Fees: marriage by banns 2s 6d, publishing banns 1s, registering a marriage 1s, marriage by licence 5s, burial 1s 6d, churching 1s 6d, vault £3, opening a vault £3, flat tombstone 10s, brick grave 7s 6d, headstone 2s 6d, tablet in the church £10.
Clerk's fees: marriage by banns or licence 2s 6d, burial 2s, churching 1s; salary: £2 10s.
The whole church has been lately repaired.
Plate: silver cup and paten. There is an iron chest for the registers.
There are no benefactions or land left for the repair of the church.

1884*. F[rederick] Burder, V.
There is no parsonage house.

Income: 8 fields at Tilley, Wem 27 a. rented at £64; QAB £387; fees average
£1 4s 6d p.a.
Schedule of registers from 1566.
Plate: silver chalice and paten and pewter alms dish.

Leebotwood[1]

1698. John Robins, C; Richard Jordan and Thomas Cartwright, CWs.
There is no house or glebe, only a churchyard which is let for 2s 6d p.a.
The curate has £8 10s from the impropriator, Mrs Anne Corbett of
Shrewsbury.
Tithes: communicants pay 2d p.a. to the curate and 1d per cow, 1d for bees,
4d per colt; the impropriator has the tithe of lambs, pigs and geese in kind
and 6d for odd calves and lambs; grass and hay is paid in kind except
Broad M. which pays 6s 8d p.a.; if any land is let to strangers, they pay
1s 8d per £; if parishioners take in sheep for the winter, they pay 1d per
sheep and 1d for any lambs which fall.
Surplice fees: marriages 1s 2d, publishing banns 1s, churching 4d, burial 6d.
The clerk receives 3d per house.
'Our Curate is very well satisfyd with what he hath and Wee with Him'.

25 Nov. 1701. John Robins, C; John Brown and Richard Langford, CWs.
Tithes: the curate has Easter duties which amount to *c*. £1 10s being 2d per
communicant, 1d house, 1d garden, 1d bees, 1d cows, 4d colts.
Surplice fees: marriage by licence 5s, marriage by banns 2s 6d, churching
6d, registering baptism 6d, burial 10d for parishioners, 1s 8d for strangers,
registering burials 6d, funeral sermon 6s 8d.
Clerk's wages are customary, some tenements pay 6d, other houses 3d.

24 Apr. 1706. John Robins, C; William Colebarne and John Sankey, CWs in 1704.
The churchyard is let for 2s 6d p.a.
The fees and Easter book do not amount to more than £2 10s p.a.
There is no terrier for Longnor, it being a chapel of ease to Condover; the
curate receives only £5 p.a. for serving it.

23 July 1718. John Robins, C; Richard Kendrick and John Dickins, CWs.
The tithes belong to Sir Richard Corbet of Longnor and are leased for
£20 p.a.; there are no moduses except Broad M. pays 6s 8d p.a.

4 July 1722. John Robins, C; Richard Kendrick and Richard Langford, CWs.

7 July 1726. John Robins, C; John Dickins and Edward Rogers, CWs.

28 Aug. 1730. David Rice, C; Thomas Langford and Samuel Wood, CWs.
There is no seat in the church or chancel belonging to the minister nor is he
obliged to maintain any part; the church is upheld by the parish and the
chancel by Sir Richard Corbet who has one seat and the freehold of the
soil.

---

[1] Leebotwood was transferred from Lichfield diocese to Hereford in 1905: *Victoria history
of Shropshire*, ii. 1.

Part 1 (Abdon to Llanfair Waterdine)

Tithes are paid in kind except 1d per cow in lieu of 'lactuals';[1] Sir Richard Corbet or his farmer receives all other tithes in kind—11th cock of hay, 11th sheaf of grain, 10th lamb, 10th fleece, 10th pig, 10th goose—if there are less than 10, he either counts on until the next year or agrees as he can for the odd ones.

Clerk's fees: baptisms and churching 1s, digging a grave 1s, 4d for ringing the passing bell (fees are double if the deceased is a stranger), 2s from the CWs for ringing 5 Nov.; wages: 15s paid by the CWs and 2 eggs per cock and 1 per hen in Lent.

The township of Betchcott lies in the parish and has seats in the church and mends 17½ yd. of the hayment of the churchyard.

1733. David Rice, C.

16 July 1736. David Rice, C; Thomas Langford and Thomas Langford, jun., CWs.

18 Oct. 1739. David Rice, minister; Joseph Davies and William Rogers, CWs.

17 Sep. 1742. David Rice, C; Thomas Hanley and Richard Everall, CWs.
The curate has £8 10s from Sir Richard Corbett being the ancient stipend and whatever else he as impropriator pleases.

10 Sep. 1745. David Rice, C; Thomas Dickin and Joseph Davies, CWs.

14 Sep. 1748. David Rice, C; Thomas Hanley and Richard Everall, CWs.
The governors of QAB Michaelmas 1745 gave £200 to augment the curate's salary and he receives the interest until a purchase of land can be made.

1752. David Rice, C; Richard Harrison and John Everall, CWs.
The interest on the grant from QAB amounts to £2 10s p.a.

1756. David Rice, C; John Everall and Edward Rogers, CWs.
A second augmentation of £200 was granted Michaelmas 1753.

20 Sep. 1759. David Rice, C; John Bishop and Richard Everall, CWs.

6 Sep. 1763. David Rice, C; Thomas Dickins and Thomas Pris, CWs.

14 Sep. 1767. David Rice, C; John Everall and Edward Rogers, CWs.

8 Sep. 1772. David Rice, C; John Bishop and John Everall, CWs.
The purchase of land with the grant from the Bounty Board is proving difficult.

4 Oct. 1783. William Cross Curtis, C; Samuel Heighway and John Everall, CWs.
The curate receives the ancient stipend of £8 10s which was formerly half the value of the tithes (though this would now be worth £50) plus whatever the impropriator pleases of his benevolence.
The township of Betchcott has 2 benches near the pulpit and the church door.

26 June 1787. Lewis Williams, C; William Harris and Richard Tomlins, CWs.

---

[1] 'Lactuals' was the term sometimes given to tithe milk.

Lady Day 1783 Robert Corbett Esq. paid Sir Richard Corbett's legacy of £200 in to the governors of QAB and the governors have added the like sum; the curate receives the interest until land can be purchased.

24 Sep. 1810. Richard Wilding, C; John Hoggins and John Dickins, CWs.
The curate now has *c.* 31 a. at Plas Bach, Oswestry let for *c.* £50 p.a.
Archdeacon Corbet of Longnor Hall is patron.

1824. Waties Corbett, perpetual curate; George [?]Stammell, CW.
Part of the farm at Plas Bach, Middleton township, Oswestry being a house, outbuildings and 31 a. with right of pasture on Middleton Common (since enclosed and an allotment added) is let for £52 16s; the other part of the farm was bought at the same time for the chapel of Longnor, since united to the church of Leebotwood.

1828. Waties Corbett, C; John Hoggins, CW.

Leighton

24 Oct. 1612. Richard Wolley, V.
House of 2½ bays of old building with barn 3 bays, old sheep cote, small orchard, garden and backside ½ a.
Land: 7s p.a. is paid to the CWs from a house and land near Wrekehill, rough pasture called Wigmorehurst, pasturing of 1 cow for the first quarter with Mrs Leighton's kine; 18 butts, 1 headland, 2 pikes and an enclosed furlong in 13 parcels in Lower F., 22 butts in 9 parcels and a furlong lately enclosed in Upper F., 19 butts and 2 furlongs in 10 parcels in the field towards Buildwas; 1 dole of meadow called Churchacre in Adeley [bounds].
Vicarial tithes of Leighton and Garmston townships are due, also one-third of the corn and hay of Eaton [Constantine] and half its Easter offerings, 2 parts of the corn tithes of the farm of Belswardine and all the small tithes.

1682. Samuel Willis, C; William Leighton and John Smith, CWs.
Land: 1 dole in Leighton meadow of 6 days' math SE. of the church, Wigmorehurst being part woodland *c.* 13 a., a piece of tillage called Old Heath *c.* 2 a., Burnt Croft 1 a., 3 a. lately enclosed, piece of pasture part lately enclosed called Four Leasows 11 a., pasture called Emstree L. 4 a.
[2 copies].

1685. [Samuel Willis, C] Richard Dycher and John Hall, CWs.
House of 3 bays with barns, ox house and stable 6 bays under one roof all in good repair, back house 1 bay, poultry house ½ bay, orchard and garden well fenced *c.* ½ a., yard and hemp butt ½ a.
Land: Hurst 16 a., Old Heath and a piece adjoining 2½ a., Cow L. 3 a., Whitebank 2 a., Four Leasows and Grainling Glatt 3 a., Yewtree L. 4 a., dole in Leighton M., small piece in Springays Fur.

29 Nov. 1693. Henry Binnell, V; Richard Vicars and James Hicken, CWs.
Tithes of wool, lambs, hemp, flax, geese and hay throughout the parish are due in kind; Eye Farm pays a modus of £2 p.a. and Belswardine £2; the demesne of Richard Leighton pays a modus on a cow's grass on his land from 1 May to 1 August; Rhees belonging to Lord Newport is tithe free; 10

individuals [named] pay moduses of 4d to 2s 6d for hay; one-third of the tithe corn of Eaton Constantine is due to the vicar.

16 Aug. 1698. Henry Binnell, V; John Worrall and David Davies, CWs.
Tithes: communicants pay 2d, 1d smoke, 1d garden, 1½d for cow and calf, 1d for barren cows, 2d for colts; 1 pig or goose is due at 7 without allowances; 1 lamb is due at 7 at the discretion of the vicar, allowing 3d each for odd lambs; 1 great pound of wool is due at 7, 8 or 9 allowing 3d per lb up to 10, under 7 the vicar reckons on or takes 3d per lb.
Surplice fees: burial 6d, registering burial 4d, churching 4d, registering baptism 6d, publishing banns 1s, marriage and registration 1s 6d, marriage by licence 5s.
Clerk's fees: payments of 4d or 2d from the parishioners [28 names] totalling 8s 2d.

21 Oct. 1701. Henry Binnell, V; Sylvanus Viggars and James Hicken, CWs.

2 May 1705. Henry Binnell, V; Richard Vickers and James Hicken, CWs.

23 July 1718. Thomas Cooke, V; Edward Beddoe and Peter Measham, CWs.
2 eggs are due per duck, 3 per drake, 2 per hen and 3 per cock.
The vicar repairs 1 wicket and c. 10 ft of rail.

28 Aug. 1730. William Dicken, C; Dositheus Grice and Richard Evans, CWs.

7 Aug. 1733. Thomas Cooke, V; Edward Jones and William Vickars, CWs.

16 July 1736. William Dicken, C; Francis Grice and Thomas Vickars, CWs.

1 Sep. 1739. Humphrey Parry, V; Jonathan Reynolds and Thomas Stringer, CWs.

18 Sep. 1742. Humphrey Parry, V; William Tart and John . . ., CWs.

11 Sep. 1745. Humphrey Parry, V; George Dixon and Thomas Plimmer, CWs.

14 Aug. 1748. Humphrey Parry, V; John Davis, CW.

28 Aug. 1752. Humphrey Parry, V; John Davies, CW.

1759. Stephen Prytherch, V; Thomas Smith and Richard Davis, CWs.
Vicarage house new built with 2 parlours in front, study and kitchen at the back, 3 upper rooms, 3 garrets and a brew house adjoining the best parlour.
A tenement worth £17 p.a. has been lately bought by QAB in Castle Caereinion, Montgomeryshire.

1763. Stephen Prytherch, V; . . . [blackened], CWs.

1767. Stephen Prytherch, V; E. Williams and Richard Davies, CWs.

7 Sep. 1772. Stephen Prytherch, V; Thomas Evans and Thomas Freeman, CWs.

22 Aug. 1775. Stephen Prytherch, V; Francis Nickols and Thomas Smith, CWs.

1783. Stephen Prytherch, V; Richard Praynolds and Thomas Tart, CWs.

Glebe terriers of Shropshire

7 Aug. 1787. John Holme, V.
Vicarage house built of brick, coped with stone and covered with tile, barn and outhouses thatched but in sufficient repair.
The church and chancel are 21 yd. × 9 yd.; the churchyard is nearly circular, 45 yd. in diameter.

1792. John Holme, V; Elizabeth Freeman and Richard Shelton, CWs.

24 Aug. 1801. [Henry Crump, V] Thomas Kinnersley and Thomas Cotterill, CWs.

29 June 1805. Henry Domvile, minister; Thomas Kinnersley and Richard Beacalls, CWs.
A copy of the endowment of Leighton vicarage can be found in the old register book at Lichfield.

24 Sep. 1810. William Corser, V; John Tart and Richard Worrall, CWs.

10 Aug. 1824*. Thomas Kynnersley and William Machin, CWs.
The vicar, Robert Maddocks, refuses to sign.
Barn, cow house, pigsty, granary and cart house 7 bays all tiled.

13 Aug. 1828*. [Robert Maddocks, V] Thomas Kynnersley and William Machin, CWs.

17 Aug. 1832*. [Robert Maddocks, V] Thomas Kynnersley and William Machin, CWs.

1836*. [Robert Maddocks, V] William Machin and William Pethan, CWs.
Land: the dole in Leighton M. 5½ a. has been lately enclosed.

7 Sep. 1841*. William Lewis, CW. John Humphreys the other CW is dead.
The vicar, Robert Maddocks, refuses to sign because he does not admit the validity of the various moduses and exemptions as he does not know the situation and acreages of the tenements for which these claims are made.

25 Sep. 1849*. Robert Maddocks, V; Harry Jeffreys and John Evans, CWs.
House with 2 cellars, entrance, 2 parlours, kitchen, scullery, pantry, closet, brew house, 3 bedrooms, 1 small dressing room, 3 bedrooms and a closet in the attic, shoe hole, coach house with granary over in the court, hen house, 2 3-stalled stables with hay loft over, barn 2 bays, cow house, 2 pigsties and cart house in the fold, garden and fold 1 a.
Land: Yew Tree L. 4 a., Hurst in 4 fields 17 a., Hurst Plantation 14 a., Old Heath F. 1½ a., Old Heath F. 2 a., Far Croft 1 a., Near Croft 3½ a., Middle Croft and Pit 2½ a., Upper Croft 3½ a., Upper F. 2 a., White Banks 2 a., New L. 3 a., Leighton M. 5 a.; total 64½ a.; the whole of the glebe is intermixed with the land of Robert Gardner [of Leighton Hall]; a small farm of 35 a. with a house at Castle Caereinion also belongs to the vicarage.
The grain tithes of Eaton have been commuted for £48 6s, the small tithes and hay tithes due to the vicar of Leighton for £93 19s.
Fees: registering baptism and churching 1s, publishing banns 1s, marriage by banns 2s 6d, by licence 5s, burial and registering 1s.
Clerk's fees: 4d, 3d or 2d Easter dues, 6d for churching, publishing banns 6d, marriage by banns 1s 6d, by licence 2s 6d, funeral and digging grave

2s 6d (double for strangers), 3s for ringing the bell 5 Nov.; wages: £3 for service through the year.

25 July 1853*. Henry Oswell, V; Richard Basnett, CW. Thomas Jervis the other CW has left the parish and is residing at a distance.

The repair of the chancel belongs to the impropriator of the great tithe, Robert Gardner, and is in good repair.

Plate: flagon and cup of silver, pewter plate and wooden alms dish. There is an iron chest for the registers.

There is a list of benefactors in the church.

28 July 1857. Thomas Prater, V; Richard Basnett, CW.

15 Apr. 1869. William Wingfield, V; Thomas Richards and John Beaman, CWs.

The house now has a conservatory.

1884*. [William Wingfield, V].

House of red brick with 2 cellars, entrance hall, 3 sitting rooms, kitchen, pantry, larder, scullery, 5 bedrooms, 2 dressing rooms, WC, 3 bedrooms in the attic, coal house, shoe house, brew house, garden house, coach house, saddle room, 2 stables with hay lofts, greenhouse, cow house, cart house, piggeries, garden and close c. 4 a.

Land: 41 a., cottage and garden and plantation called the Hurst 15 a. at Leighton; 62 a. and common rights in Castle Caereinion at a farm called Glyn purchased with the aid of QAB.

Income: tithe rent charge for one-third of the grain tithe of Eaton Constantine £48 6s, £93 19s for the small tithes of Leighton; fees average c. 19s.p.a.

Schedule of registers from 1662.

Plate: silver chalice, paten and flagon and pewter alms dish.

Benefactions: Richard Leighton by will gave £100 to the poor (this was invested in a turnpike trust now abolished and is now in the savings bank); Ann Lacon £5 p.a. to the poor; Mr Wareham gave £100, the interest for 4 poor women; Cornelius Reynolds gave £50 for the care of his monument and for poor widows.

Lilleshall
(*and see* Donnington Wood; St Georges)

22 Oct. 1612. Thomas Millington, V; Ryce Williams and Roger Key, CWs.

Vicarage house of 3 bays with barn 2 bays with cote adjoining, 1 little bay for necessary uses, 2 gardens adjoining the house and yard of 1½ strikes seedness of barley.

Land: 1 leasow of 15 strikes seedness rye and 1 meadow of 2 days' math [bounds].

1682. Henry Haughton, V; William Worrall and William Rustones, CWs.

'One Faire vicaridge House' with barn, stable, beast house, another little piece of outbuilding, garden, orchard and yard.

Land: Rudding M., Rudding L.

1685. Henry Haughton, V; Godfry Williams and William Shelton, CWs.

161

Glebe terriers of Shropshire

1693. Henry Haughton, V; Richard Hatchet and William Dawe, CWs.

1698.[1] Henry Haughton, V; Robert Adderley and Edward Renalls, CWs.
The vicar has the right to £21 10s in money from the inhabitants according to long used custom.

'In dei nomine Amen. Quia nos Rogerus permissione divina Covent' et Lich' Episcopus invenimus vicariam Eccl' parochialis de Lilleshall non est in certis portionibus ordinata quod inter Religiosos vicos Abbatem et conventum de Lilleshall rectores eiusdem et viccariam ipsius Eccl'e discordiam frequentius parere consuevit viccariam eiusdem taliter duximus ordinandum pro a'imis presentia utriusque viz. quod viccarius qui pro tempore fuerit habeat Mansum illum cum Gardino et partem adiacentem et unum Croftum quod vocatur Le Rudding cum prato ad finem illius Crofti adiacente que Willelmus de Preston quondam vicarius eiusdem habere consuevit Decimam omnium Hortorum et Croftorum pede Cultorum cum Communa pasture et aliis Asiamentis que dictus Willelmus et alii Viccarii habere consueverunt precipiat etiam omnes oblationes obventiones alteragium qualitercumque spectantes Dccimam Agnorum vitulorum pullanorum porcellorum Aucarum ovorum Lactis Lane Lini Canabi pomorum et omnia principalia mortuorum qua nomine mortuaria appellantur suis in animalibus sive in vestibus sive in quibusque rebus aliis consistunt Decimam feni villarum de Lilleshall Dunington et Hunington et Decimam panagii et ut hec nostra ordinatio perpetue memorie commendetur sigillum nostrum presentibus est appensum. Dat' apud Canewell iiii. non' Martii Anno Dom'i 1285 et consecrationis nostre viii.'.[2]

All receiving manservants pay 4d, maidservants 3d and sons and daughters 2d.

Surplice fees: marriage 2s 6d, burial 6d, churching 4d and registering 4d.

1701. Henry Haughton, V; William Light and William Raystans, CWs.

7 July 1722. Benjamin Clemson, V; James Spender and Robert Dawes, CWs.

6 July 1726. Benjamin Clemson, V; Thomas Woolley and Robert Brookes, CWs.

29 Aug. 1730. Benjamin Clemson, V; Richard Shelton and Edward Reynolds, CWs.

9 Aug. 1733. Benjamin Clemson, V; Thomas Turner and William Dawes, CWs.

15 July 1736. Benjamin Clemson, V; John Spearman and John Wood, CWs.

31 Aug. 1739. Benjamin Clemson, V; James Spender and William Picken, CWs.

---

[1] The Lilleshall terriers from 1698 to 1782 inclusive are stated on the dorse to have been used as evidence in a tithe dispute heard in the Exchequer.

[2] The misreadings of this transcript have not been corrected. For details of versions nearer to the original see *The Cartulary of Lilleshall abbey*, ed. U. Rees (Shropshire Archaeological and Historical Soc. 1997), p. 178.

Part 1 (Abdon to Llanfair Waterdine)

27 Aug. 1742. Benjamin Clemson, V; Edward Rylands and Robert Hawkins, CWs.

9 Sep. 1745. Benjamin Clemson, V; William Blockley and Thomas Moulton, CWs.

n.d. Benjamin Clemson, V; George Steventon and Robert Hawkins, CWs.
The clerk's wages are customary and paid by the inhabitants.

9 Aug. 1748. Thomas Hawkins and Robert Dawes, CWs.

31 July 1752. Joshua Brownlow and William Blockley, CWs.

13 Aug. 1756. C. Du Gard, V; Joseph Hughes and William Boycott, CWs.

14 Aug. 1759. C. Du Gard, V; . . . [worn], CWs.

6 Aug. 1763. C. Du Gard, V; William Spearman and . . . Light, CWs.

15 Aug. 1767. C. Du Gard, V; James Barber and Robert Hawkins, CWs.

20 Aug. 1775.[1] John Stanier, C; John Hall and Joseph Boycott, CWs.
A 'fair vicarage house' of 3 bays with barn, stable, beast houses adjoining the barn 2 bays, little piece of building adjoining the court on the S. of the house, garden, orchard and yard adjoining the orchard on the N.
Land: 2 leasows or pastures and 1 meadow adjoining called Rudding Leasows and Meadow 10 a.

6 Sep. 1779. Thomas Spencer, C; Joseph Taylor and Joseph Boycott, CWs.

4 Aug. 1783. Richard Ogle, V; Edmund Hector and Richard Dawes, CWs.
Land: Rudding M. 3½ a., Preston Way 3 a., Goose Nook 2 a., Heath 24 a.; total c. 41 a.; also a cottage and small garden.
Tithe corn is due on Shelton's Old Farm, Lilleshall; the custom formerly prevailed of paying the vicar £21 10s p.a. which custom by decree passed this year in the Exchequer was set aside and abolished; in lieu the vicar and the inhabitants agreed that 5d per acre was to be paid to the vicar for all lands and demesnes for all vicarial tithes; each cottage is to pay 6d p.a.; hemp and flax are to be paid in kind and 2s per acre for turnips.

6 Aug. 1787. H. Cotton, C; Thomas Spearman and Richard Dawes, CWs.

1792. J. C. Woodhouse, V; James Williams and Robert Dawes, CWs.
The vicarage house is old built.
Land: piece in Edgmond parish near Chetwynd called Chetwynd Yate, rood of land in Edgmond lately allotted from Chetwynd Common in lieu of common for Chetwynd Yate which was lately purchased by QAB, small piece of land N. of the churchyard called Hemp Butt.

17 Oct. 1797. S. Hartley, C; John Hammond and John Jones, CWs.

1805*. J. C. Woodhouse, V; Joseph Boycott and Benjamin Dawes, CWs.

1810. S. Hartley, minister; Joseph Boycott and John Duncalfe, CWs.

---

[1] The Lilleshall 1775 terrier is filed with the bishop's transcripts (LRO, B/V/7/1).

22 Oct. 1824*. John Blunt, V; Joseph Boycott and William Henney, CWs.
The vicarage house is a partly old and partly new building extended by the present vicar in 1816 with a passage and 2 parlours in front, study, large kitchen, back kitchen, pantry, brew house, dairy, small cellar (the last 3 being shorings at the back), 3-stalled stable and barn under one roof, cow house adjoining, small building used in part for a granary, garden, orchard, fold yard 1 a., pleasure ground, gardens and paddock of 2 a. on land received from the Marquess of Stafford by exchange in 1818 and hemp butt 1 rood; there is a cottage W. of the churchyard and a cottage and garden near Preston Lane, both cottages being part of the same exchange.
Land: Crimes part exchange and part old glebe 8 a., piece adjoining also called Crimes 3 a. by exchange, Rudding L. 7 a., Mill L. by exchange 3 a., Parsons M. 3 a., New Hays L. 12 a. by exchange; these 7 pieces of land form a rough triangle lying together [bounds]; Chetwynd Gate 7 a. in Edgmond with a small piece in lieu of common.

9 Aug. 1828. John Blunt, V; William Penson and Robert Dawes, CWs.
The measurements of land are taken from a map in Lord Gower's office.

6 Aug. 1832. John Blunt, V; Robert Dawes and Edward Wilde, CWs.

8 Aug. 1836. John Blunt, V; Robert Dawes and Benjamin Kite, CWs.

9 Sep. 1841*. J. Blunt, V; John Phillips and William Boycott, CWs.
Land: the land in Edgmond is leased at £13 10s p.a., the Hemp Butt for £1 1s, the cottage on Preston Lane for £1, another cottage is in the vicar's hands; the rest of the glebe and tithes are let to the Duke of Sutherland for 300 guineas p.a.
Donnington Wood chapel, patron the Duke of Sutherland, is licensed for marriages, the vicar receiving 5s and the clerk 1s.
Ckerk's fees: marriage 1s, churching 6d, burial with grave 6s, Easter dues *c*. £1 5s, cleaning the churchyard and walks £1, curfew bell £1 1s; salary £3 8s.
Communion plate: 2 cups, large paten and 2 small patens.
Benefactions: Mrs Rebecca Walthall left £10, the interest to be distributed to the poor of Muxton on St Thomas's Day; £5 from the Duke of Sutherland, the interest to be distributed on St Thomas's Day; Lady Katherine Leveson left a charge of £50 on the manor of Foxley, Northamptonshire.
The chancel belongs to the Duke of Sutherland and is in good repair.

13 Aug. 1845*. George Livingston Pointon, V; John Phillips and William Boycott, CWs.
Ancient glebe: Rudding L. and Parson's M. 10 a., Hemp Butt 1 rood leased for 12s 6d p.a.; a close called Grime 1 a.; Trevitt's tenement and 1 rood and a cottage known as Preston Way with 3 a. seem to have been conveyed by Earl Gower to the governors of QAB in 1748; 4 closes called Heaths 23 a. were exchanged with the Duke of Sutherland in 1818 for a cottage and garden occupied by the vicar's servant, a close of 2 a. in the vicar's possession as a pleasure ground, 2 gardens and paddock, a cottage and garden let at £1 p.a., several closes 22 a. known as Grimes Close and 2

closes 3 a.; the last 2 are let to the Duke of Sutherland for £51 p.a.; lands in Edgmond purchased by QAB in 1789 are let for £13 p.a.

The tithes of Shelton's Old Farm 110 a. were compounded for £25 p.a.; the vicarial tithes are rented to the Duke of Sutherland for £239; commutation has been agreed but the amount not confirmed.

Benefactions: £30 p.a. for the maintenance of 3 poor widows and £20 p.a. for apprenticing 2 poor boys.

23 July 1849*. . . . Bunsen, V; J. Phillips and John Higgins, CWs.

1884*. W. Price, V.

House with drawing room, dining room, study, large class room, kitchen, back kitchen, pantries, cellar, 7 bedrooms and closets, coach house, stables, wash house, pigsties and 2 gardens and field adjoining.

Land: 5 fields 37 a. W. of Kynnersley Drive farmed by R. Ralph of Honnington Grange, Lilleshall, cottage and garden rented for £3, another cottage and garden for £4, garden E. of the churchyard 12s.

Income: tithe rent charge of £297 (the vicar of Donnington Wood has £9 p.a. from this after the value of the whole rent charge for the year is ascertained, not £9 of the commuted amount);

£25 6s 6d from QAB; fees have averaged £10 p.a. over the last 3 years.

Schedule of registers from 1656.

Plate: 2 chalices, 1 large and 2 small patens and flagon, all of silver.

Benefactions: Lady K. Leveson/Foxley Charity of 1876 of £60 p.a. for pensioners and £10 p.a. for apprenticeships or scholarships for poor children (N.B. 1 Dec. 1882 the payment was reduced to £52 10s due to remission of rents); Temple Balsall Charity of £81 4s p.a. for 4 poor widows in the old parish of Lilleshall at present 3 in Lilleshall and 1 in Donnington Wood receive 8s per week; the interest of 5s 6d on Dame Walthall's bequest of £10 in Lilleshall Savings Bank is distributed to poor widows of Muxton.

Little Berwick[1]

1884*.

One of the almshouses is allotted to the curate.

Income: £5 13s 3d being one-third of the rent of ground at Ditherington, £8 5s 9d being dividend on stock in the London and N.W. Railway Co.

Note by the Bishop of Lichfield [in the SRRC copy only]: at the death of the Hon. Mrs Feilding, widow of Hon. Everard Feilding, a certain sum of money was secured for the augmentation of the benefice which since Mr Watson came to reside here he said he would make up to £200 and allow the curate to occupy either Upper Berwick or Rosehill Cottage rent free; in view of this liberality Bishop Selwyn advised that Mr Watson's contention that the chapel was a donative should pass undisputed. Justice Charles had told him that it was a donative, but this is undoubtedly wrong,

---

[1] Little Berwick was a private chapel in the parish of St Mary, Shrewsbury: Blakeway, 'History of Shrewsbury Hundred', *Trans. Shropshire Archaeol. Soc.* 2nd ser. i (1889), 479.

the curate has always been admitted and licensed by the ordinary of St Mary's.

[On the Lichfield copy only] The rural dean, Revd Thomas B. Lloyd, says that Berwick is claimed (wrongly) by Mr Watson as a donative and the curate therefore objects to give any information.

Little Drayton[1]

1884*. Newdigate Poyntz, V.
House with laundry, stable, carriage house, yard and small field 3½ a.
Income: £150 p.a. from the Eccl. Com. in 1847 and 1859, £40 7s 10d p.a. from QAB, £1 p.a. from 40 sittings by old custom.
Registers from 1848.
Plate: silver and plate chalices and patens, 2 plate flagons and brass alms dish.
Benefactions: £118 16s 3d p.a. for insurance and repairs of the church bequeathed by the will of H. B. Clive; in 1870 £200 was donated, the interest being for the poor in the workhouse.

Little Ness[2]

30 Sep. 1685. [No signatories].
House of 2 bays with a garden.
Land: Colling Headland, croft, Waltons L., 2 butts in Yarsmore, 2 butts in Long Fur., 2 butts in Cross M., 4 crofts together to the N. of the chapel, 2 butts in Tonghill, small parcel in Flowers M.; total 16 a.

15 Aug. 1698. George Hudson, vicar of Baschurch; He. Manwaringe, chapelwarden.
House of 2 bays with barn 2 bays, garden and backside *c.* 1 a.
Land: Lees 4 a., F. 3 a., croft 1½ a., 2 butts in Tonghill, 1 a. in Flowers M., ¾ a. in Leasow F., Colles Headland 2 a., furlong in Town F. 1 a., butt in Cross M. 1 a.; the land of Mr Bromley, lord of the manor of Shrawardine lies all round these lands.
Easter duties and tithes are paid to Baschurch; man and wife pay 4d, 2d for children of 21, 4d for a servant with 40s wages, 3d for 30s, 2d under that, 4d for a colt, 1d for bees put down, 1d for a garden; 1s 8d per £ is due for grazing land if held by non-parishioners. The incumbent receives one-third of the tithe of wool, lambs and pigs from 3 tenements in Ness Parva and Lord Craven two-thirds; Millford Mill and Adcote Mill pay 3s 4d at Easter.
Fees: burials 1s, marriages 5s, funeral sermon 6s 8d.

2 May 1705. George Hudson, V; Roger Griffies, CW.
All tithes and duties are paid to the vicar of Baschurch to whom the glebe land also belongs.

[1] Little Drayton was formed into an ecclesiastical parish from part of Market Drayton parish in 1848: *P.O. directory of Shropshire* (1879), 356.
[2] Little Ness was a chapelry of Baschurch parish. See also Baschurch terriers for 1612, 1693, 1722, 1845 and 1884 and Ruyton XI Towns terrier for 1612.

Part 1 (Abdon to Llanfair Waterdine)

House of 2 bays with sheepcote and cow house adjoining, barn on forks nearby.
The yearly profit from the chapelry to the vicar of Baschurch is *c.* £10 p.a.

5 July 1722. George Hudson, V; William Broughall, CW.
House of 2 bays with cow house, sheep fold, barn 2 bays, garden, orchard and yard.
Land: Chapel F. 3½ a., Lees 4 a., Higher Croft 1½ a., ¾ a. in Lord Bromley's Flowers M., 2 butts in Tongue Hill F., Field 4½ a., 4 butts, 2½ a., in a town field called Yarsmore F., Collis Headland 2 a., butt 1 a. in Lord Bromley's Cross M., privileges in Knib Heath and in Cliffe.
Fees are as in Baschurch.

7 July 1726. Stephen Parker, V; John Jones, CW.
1 bay of the barn is on forks, the other now on sills.
Land: 3 closes 10 a., 2 furlongs 1 a. in Tongue Hill, ½ a. in Flowers M., New Piece 4 a., 4 furlongs in Yarsmore 2 a., Collys headland 2 a., 1 butt in Cross M., all bounded by Lord Bromley's land.

28 Aug. 1730. Stephen Parker, C; John Farthing, CW.

7 Aug. 1733. Stephen Parker, C; Richard Wolfe, CW.

10 Nov. 1736. Stephen Parker, minister; William Gittins, CW.

14 Aug. 1739. Stephen Parker, V; Cornelius Rogers, CW.
[Baptisms 30 Aug. 1736–3 July 1739].

1756. Robert Jeffreys, V; James Edwards, CW.
The cow house, shore and cart house are on forks.

21 Sep. 1759. Robert Jeffreys, V; John Broughall, CW.

Little Wenlock
(and see Lawley)

24 Sep. 1589. John Wheelwright, William Alice, Edward Carver, John Podmore.
Sir Walter Leveson is patron.
Land: [faded].

n.d. [late 16th/early 17th century]. Edward Downton, parson.
House with barn, stable, necessary house to tie cattle and hay house.
Land: 1 close, land in the fields of Little Wenlock, no commons.

11 Dec. 1604. Edmund Downton, parson.
Land: 3 parcels in Timberwood F., 1 parcel in Cross F., 2 parcels in Wrekin F., 3 parcels in Quarry F. [bounds].

May 1607. Edmund Downton, parson; John Carter and William Grene, CWs.
Land: Timberwood F., arable in . . . [details illegible] piece of meadow enclosed out of it called Coal M., land in Cross F., Wrekin F. and Quarry F. [bounds].
Tithes are due in kind throughout the parish except hay in Huntington which yields a plot in lieu.

1632. George Baxter, R; Andrew Blackway and James Boorder, CWs.

Land: Whichwall M., 3 a., Colepit L., 1 a., Shaw, 4 a., parcels of 1 a. and 2 a. in Wrekin F.

Tithes are due in kind except 4d per calf, 1d per cow and ½d per lamb under 7.

17 June 1802. . . ., R [faded]; Richard Dorrall, CW.

House with barn, fold yard and garden.

Land: Whichwalls M. 3 a., little meadow called Harp, Colepit L. 1 a., Shawes 4 a. parcels of 1 a. and 2 a. in Wrekin F.

Tithes are due in kind except on hay in Huntington F. for which the inhabitants say they yield a certain plot of meadow which bears a small load of hay; 4d is due per calf, 1d per dry cow, 1d per lamb under 7 or they may be counted on.

Several small donations are distributed to the poor.

Llanfair Waterdine

n.d. [?1589]. John Best, Howell ap Rees, CWs.

Thomas Harley is patron.

Land: 20 a. of arable and pasture being 7 a. arable called Selley, Trebart 2 a., Llanbarn 3 a., Mynytrevthy 4 a. and a house, Ffynn vawr 3 a. [bounds].

Tithe of the 10th lamb, 10th sheaf, 10th fleece, 9 cheeses from those that make cheese, also tithes of pigs, geese, kids and one-tenth of honey.